MW01614813

THE GREEK AMERICAN
COMMUNITY
IN TRANSITION

THE GREEK AMERICAN COMMUNITY IN TRANSITION

Edited by

HARRY J. PSOMIADES
Queens College of the City University of New York

ALICE SCOURBY
C.W. Post Center, Long Island University

With a Bibliographic Guide by
JOHN G. ZENELIS

PELLA
PELLA PUBLISHING COMPANY, INC.
NEW YORK, NY 10001
1982

This book was published for The Center for Byzantine and Modern Greek Studies, Queens College of the City University of New York, and The Center for Mediterranean Studies, The American University, which bear full editorial responsibility for its contents.

Views expressed in this publication are those of the authors and do not necessarily reflect the views of the sponsoring institutions.

MODERN GREEK RESEARCH SERIES, IV, APRIL 1982

THE GREEK AMERICAN COMMUNITY IN TRANSITION

© 1982 by The Center for Byzantine and Modern Greek Studies, Queens College of the City University of New York, Flushing, New York 11367, and The Greek Seminar of the Center for Mediterranean Studies, The American University, Washington, D. C. 20016.

Library of Congress Catalog Card Number 82-81628

ISBN 0-918618-22-3

PRINTED IN THE UNITED STATES OF AMERICA
BY
ATHENS PRINTING COMPANY
NEW YORK, NY 10001

To
the memory of
THEODORE SALOUTOS

MODERN GREEK RESEARCH SERIES

The purpose of this monograph series is to promote and disseminate scholarly work on the history, institutions, and culture of the Greek people. It is jointly sponsored and edited by the Center for Byzantine and Modern Greek Studies, Queens College of the City University of New York, and the Greek Seminar of the Center for Mediterranean Studies, The American University. This is the fourth publication within the framework of the Modern Greek Research Project—Harry J. Psomiades, Professor of Political Science, Queens College of the City University of New York, and Theodore A. Couloumbis, Professor of International Relations, The American University, co-directors.

BOOKS OF THIS SERIES

TABLE OF CONTENTS

PREFACE

The papers contained in this volume were presented at a conference sponsored by the Center for Byzantine and Modern Greek Studies, Queens College of the City University of New York, on May 9-10, 1980. Both the conference at Queens College and the publication of this volume were made possible by grants from the Jewish and Ethnic Studies Project of Queens College, which is funded by the New York State Education Department in Albany, by the "IKAROS" Greek Club of Queens College, and by numerous Greek American community organizations. We are grateful to them.

We also wish to thank the *International Migration Review* (Center for Migration Studies of New York, Inc.) for permission to reprint Alice Scourby's article—"Three Generations of Greek Americans: A Study in Ethnicity" (Spring 1980) 43-52.

For their contributions to the conference and to this volume, we must thank in particular our colleagues whose names are listed in the table of contents; their punctual delivery of manuscripts and their cooperative acceptance of the brutalities of editing have been especially appreciated. The views expressed in each chapter are those of the individual authors and do not necessarily reflect the views of the remaining authors, the editors, or the Center for Byzantine and Modern Greek Studies.

We owe a special note of thanks to Dr. Ernest Schwarcz, Dean of the School of General Studies and Chairman of the Queens College Ethnic Studies Council, for his constant encouragement and support in planning the conference and in the publication of this volume. We are grateful to John G. Zenelis for compiling the Bibliographic Guide and acknowledge with gratitude the administrative and secretarial support of Anastasia Alexiades in the preparation of this volume. We are also indebted to John Marcopoulos, who served as

Assistant Director of the Center during the planning phase of the conference.

We recognize that no anthology can presume to cover every facet of its subject matter; nevertheless, it is our hope that this volume will provide a useful frame of reference and a guide for the systematic study of the evolving Greek American community. The paucity of data in ethnic literature with regard to Greek Americans gives the publication of this book a special urgency.

H.J.P.

Flushing, New York   A.S.

CHAPTER 1

THE NEW ETHNICITY: PRO AND CON

BY

ALICE SCOURBY

At the present time there is a plethora of literature dealing with the "new ethnicity," its components and its consequences for American ethnic relations and for international relations as well. Cyprus, Israel, Ireland, and Africa are but a few salient examples.

Historically, ethnic awareness and ethnic enclaves in the United States were an acknowledged part of a group's distinct history and were viewed by the host culture as stepping-stones in the process of acculturation and ultimate assimilation.

For more than a decade, the goal of assimilation has been challenged by that of cultural pluralism. This ideological shift can be traced to the Second World War, when reduced immigration and the accommodation of ethnic groups to the melting-pot ideal reduced appreciably the proportion of foreigners to natives, making the former less threatening both socially and economically. In addition, the international picture of that period thrust the United States into the role of leadership of the free world—a role incompatible with ethnic intolerance. At the same time, the social sciences highlighted our ethnocentric attitudes through cross-cultural studies and demonstrated empirically that ethnocentrism was inconsistent with the democratic ethos.

By the 1950s, the phenomenon of a religious revival was surfacing in social scientific research. The underlying premise of that revival was that religious pluralism was an established fact of American life; it provided an alternative way of being American. While ethnic customs and language were expected to attenuate over time, one's religion was to remain the focal point of identity and community.

The decade of the 1960s culminated in collective protest against discriminatory public policy toward minority groups. It acted as a catalyst in bringing into question the substance of that shared identity called "American." The protest movement of the sixties raised to a level of acute awareness the fact that in order to right inequities it was necessary to do so collectively. The problem of the primacy of focus became a critical one for effecting social change. Black Americans recognized that without retaining ethnic differences political input would be a moot question. The "roots" phenomenon symbolized the move from the melding of all ethnic groups to a reshaping of ethnic groups.

The reshaping of ethnic groups during the 1970s was reflected in the development of ethnic studies and bilingual programs that gained support from academic and nonacademic sources. The statement of policy by the "Ethnic Heritage Program" of the Department of Health, Education and Welfare (HEW) clearly described that trend: "In recognition of the heterogeneous composition of the nation and of the fact that in a multi-ethnic society a greater understanding of the contributions of one's own heritage and those of one's fellow citizens can contribute to a more harmonious, patriotic, and committed populace . . ."[1] Thus public policy and cultural pluralism were regarded as mutually reinforcing.

Moving into the 1980s, interest in ethnicity continues unabated. Brandeis University plans to open the first research center in the nation for the study of Jewish life in America. With a grant from the Charles H. Revson Foundation, the center will become the focus for a new look at the history and sociology of the American Jew.[2] The center will undertake a comprehensive study of American Jews and focus upon the character of Jewish family life and ethnic identity.

More recently Yale University has begun a campaign to

[1]US Department of Health, Education and Welfare, Bureau of Higher and Continuing Education, *Part E—Ethnic Heritage Program*, Public Law 95-561, November 1, 1978 (Washington, D.C.: US Government Printing Office, 1978) D-1.

[2]Kenneth A. Briggs, "Brandeis Plans the First Center for Study of Jewish Life in U.S.," *New York Times* (June 26, 1980) A16.

raise more than 6 million dollars to centralize and enlarge its Judaic studies program. One spokesperson for the university said, "The unique role of Judaism in the development of western culture and the contribution of Jews and their tradition to American life and letters have important consequences for a university. The Jewish experience constitutes a unique record of the interaction of an identifiable group with a vast spectrum of cultures."[3]

The university has already received 1.6 million dollars. It came mainly from three contributors, including an anonymous donor who gave one million dollars to endow a chair in the history of Judaism.

The program's aim is "to establish a distinguished humanities program accessible to all students and distinctively interdepartmental in nature. The program should appeal not only to specialists but to all who wish to inform themselves about the history and cultural contributions of a major religion."[4]

But what does this continuing interest in ethnicity mean? What new sentiments does it actually express? What individual and social needs are being met? From the point of view of its critics, ethnic pluralism is seen as fundamentally divisive to American society. Its opponents maintain that the new ethnicity has a built-in syndrome of the "we" and the "they" which sustains a pecking system that liberals throughout this century have been anxious to eradicate. To make ethnicity destiny, they argue, is to foster a policy of "separate but equal"—a policy fraught with xenophobia and localism.[5]

From the other side of the spectrum advocates of the new ethnicity see its revitalization of cohesiveness and enhanced self-image as positive, beneficial attributes.[6] This positive stance has caused ethnic groups to see themselves as promoters of their own welfare, but that is all to the good, it is argued; past inequities need redressing. The "old ethnicity" was too compliant, too insecure. It is precisely this tendency toward an aggressive ethnicity, their opponents claim, that

[3]"Yale Opens $6 Million Campaign for its Judaic-Studies Program," *New York Times* (February 15, 1981) 50.

[4]Ibid.

[5]Orlando Patterson, "The Ethnic Revival: What Hidden Dangers?" *Current* (April 1978) 35-7; Howard F. Stein and Robert F. Hill, "The Limits of Ethnicity," *American Scholar* (Spring 1977) 181-9.

[6]Michael Novak, *The Unmeltable Ethnics* (New York: Macmillan, 1972).

places local interests above national interests and obscures the ties that bind all Americans.

Exponents of the new ethnicity see the quest for community as a basic concern and one that is inextricably bound to ethnicity.[7] The thesis that they support is a familiar one: modernity with its megastructures cannot provide meaningful identification with a group that has formed the nucleus of social life throughout history. The pluralists readily admit the potential divisiveness of ethnicity, but they tend to emphasize its positive aspects, i.e., a sharing of common concerns, the warding off of anomie, and more equitable treatment by having all levels of society involved in a collective conscience. The proponents of this position maintain that if the assimilationists were to carry their argument against ethnicity to its logical conclusion, they would have to argue for the elimination of social class, religious denominations, education, and all those social phenomena that carry negative as well as positive attributes.[8]

While the assimilationists would agree that the quest for community is paramount in a rationalized, bureaucratized society, their contention is that subcommunities, while very important, must remain within the private domain; the same applies to religious institutions, the family, the foreign press, and ethnic voluntary associations. To permit personal ethnic interest to invade the public domain is to transform an ethnic group into somewhat of a pressure group.[9] It should be noted, however, that an operational definition of what all Americans hold in common is still forthcoming. Isaacs reminds us that ". . . what being American means is a matter still being worked out in the process, and it will probably continue that way indefinitely. . . ."[10] According to Glazer and Moynihan,[11] ethnicity has now become the effective focus for group mobilization for political ends that challenge the primacy of class and of nation. The core of the assimilation-

[7]Andrew Greeley, *Why Can't They be Like Us?* (New York: E. P. Dutton, 1971).

[8]Israel Rubin, "Ethnicity and Cultural Pluralism," *Phylon* 36:2 (June 1975) 140-8.

[9]Harold Isaacs, "The One and the Many: What Are the Social and Political Implications of the New Ethnic Revival?" *American Educator* (Spring 1978) 4-13.

[10]Ibid., 9-10.

[11]Nathan Glazer and Daniel P. Moynihan, *Ethnicity: Theory and Experience* (Cambridge, Mass.: Harvard University Press, 1975).

ist's position is that this ethnic resurgence is reminiscent of the schisms that have always bred intergroup animosities, a revival that can only lead to tribalism.

If we accept the sociological premise that a society composed of individuals is a monstrosity and that the basic concern we share is a quest for community, then the concept of tribalism may be viewed from another vantage point. Since alienation and anomie are endemic to modernity, one's private life is continuously threatened by these forces. It is the mediating structures of family, church, voluntary association, neighborhood, and subcultures which function to stabilize the private sphere. Beyond that, the megastructures themselves depend upon the "moral sustenance" of the mediating structures. The larger structures, according to this analysis, are too remote to provide the collective moral consciousness without which society could not survive. Instead of discouraging subcommunities, therefore, public policy should protect them and recognize the invaluable role that ethnic diversity plays, not only in providing meaning and identity in people's lives, but in preserving social stability.[12] Tribalism, divested of its pejorative meaning, becomes a partial panacea for the problem of alienation.

The controversy over the pros and cons of the "new ethnicity" is an ongoing one: no consensus exists. But the commanding fact is that ethnic groups do exist and persist. They may change, but it is believed that ethnicity continues to have an impact upon the lives of individuals and groups in overt and covert ways. It is the dynamics of this change that concerns us about the Greek ethnic experience.

---

[12]Peter L. Berger, "In Praise of Particularity: The Concept of Mediating Structures," *Review of Politics* 3 (July 1976) 339-410.

CHAPTER 2

GREEK AMERICAN STUDIES

BY

CHARLES C. MOSKOS, JR.

All told, more than 700,000 Greeks have crossed to these shores at one time or another. About two out of three of these Greek arrivals made America their permanent home. The initial mass influx of Greeks during the first two decades of this century coincided with the full force of American industrialization. Besides the majority working in manual jobs, a significant portion of the early immigrants catered to the needs of a swelling urban population by becoming proprietors of their own businesses. Since the reopening of the immigration doors in 1966, new concentrations of Greeks have arrived, mainly settling in our large northern cities. Most of the newcomers make up a service labor force, but many of their number have also become small entrepreneurs. Despite the renewal of immigration from Greece, the arithmetic preponderance of the American-born generations has been inevitable. As of 1980, close to three out of every four Greek Americans are native to this country. The progeny of the early immigrants have moved, in the main, into middle-class vocations and into the suburbs. Although processes of assimilation have been undeniable, there has been a persistent attachment to "Greek identity," however hard to define that sentiment might be, well into many of the second and third generations. This, in broad strokes, is the social-demographic portrait of Greek America.

Greek American studies can be understood as the effort to relate academic research, intellectual understanding, and artistic expression to the collective experience of Americans of Greek ancestry. This is a manifold and ongoing experience faintly captured in the thumbnail sketch that opens this essay. Although Greek American studies as a formal subject area can hardly be said to exist, the outlines of cumulative scholarly undertaking are becoming discernible for the first time. My purpose here is to offer a preliminary reconnaissance of Greek American studies. Toward this end I will introduce the most relevant literature on Greek Americans, present an overview of the Greek historical experience in America, and indicate, as dispassionately as I am able, areas of competing interterpretations.

A prior issue, however, must first be introduced. The elementary question of the parameters of the Greek American population is a topic still barely explored. Even to estimate the total number of Greek Americans involves matters of definition as well as measurement. Is descent from Greek stock the determining variable? How does one count those of mixed Greek and non-Greek ancestry?[1] Is it more an issue of affiliation with Greek American communal institutions? Or is it a social-psychological sense of being ethnically Greek in American society? How does one categorize permanent residents with Greek citizenship, those on student visas, illegal aliens, and so forth? These are all issues that require more thought and study, though they will never be known with precision.

We can, however, present some provisional observations. The US census adopts a lineage definition of ethnicity. The 1970 census reports 177,274 Greek-born Americans (first generation) and 257,296 native-born Americans of fully Greek or mixed parentage (second generation), for a total of some 434,000 persons of "Greek ancestry" in this country.[2] These numbers have been challenged as undercounting Greek Americans, especially among the new immigrants. We also know little of the biological demography of Greek Americans. One can note, impressionistically, that the Greek American family has never been a large one. Among the earlier as well as the more recent immigrants, the outer limits tend to be three or

---

[1]The manner and degree in which cultural identity transmits across the generations through mixed marriages is one of the most intriguing, yet least understood, mechanisms of ethnic imprinting.

[2]US Bureau of the Census, *Census of the Population: 1970*, vol. 2, *Subject Reports*, "National Origin and Language," Final Report PC(2)-1A.

perhaps four children, and the American-born generations are barely reproducing themselves, if that.

Nevertheless, a more complete and current picture of the Greek American population can be offered by making some assumptions on the ratio of births to deaths since 1970, the rate of immigration from Greece and return back in the seventies, the probable size of the third and fourth generations, and by adding several score thousand Greek immigrants probably underreported in the census. On the basis of these calculations and guesses, a maximal estimate of the total Greek American population by 1980 would be:

first generation	350,000
second generation	450,000
third generation	350,000
fourth generation	100,000
TOTAL	1,250,000

The figure of a million and a quarter or so Greek Americans is based on a broad definition—the inclusion of all persons with at least one Greek grandparent. Even so, this is well below the two, three, or even four million sometimes claimed by Greek American community leaders. When we use more qualified, but more meaningful, definitions of who is a Greek American, the figures are expectedly even lower. On the basis of national survey items that allow for ethnic or religious background measures, we find—when extrapolated to the total American population—between seven and eight hundred thousand who identify themselves as either Greek American or Greek Orthodox.[3]

The Greek American population can also be described in terms of its regional distribution. A breakdown by states in the 1970 census shows the largest number of Greeks to be in

[3]The American Council on Education (ACE) national survey of college freshmen in 1972 included—on a one-time-only basis—a self-identifying ethnic measure. Among all respondents, .035 percent identified themselves as "Greek." A 1975 Gallup poll of American religious preferences found .031 percent who identified as Greek Orthodox. If the ACE and Gallup figures are extrapolated to a total US population of 222,000,000 (the census projection for 1980) and rounded off, there are approximately 800,000 self-identified ethnic Greeks in this country, and 700,000 who identify themselves as Greek Orthodox. The ACE and Gallup poll data were made available by special request of this writer.

New York—about one in four of all Greek Americans—followed by Illinois, California, Massachusetts, New Jersey, Pennsylvania, Ohio, and Michigan. To look only at the total number of Greeks by state, however, does not indicate the proportionate Greek American presence in these locales. New Hampshire, closely followed by Massachusetts, has the highest ratio of Greek Americans of any state in the union. Other states with disproportionately high ratios of Greek Americans are, in descending order, New York, Illinois, Connecticut, New Jersey, Maryland, and Michigan. Thus, though there has been some outward movement in recent years toward the Sun Belt, the main body of Greek Americans continues to be found in the states of the Northeast and the Great Lakes.

Prolegomenon on Greek American Historiography

Almost from the start of their large-scale arrival in this country, Greek Americans have been the subject of accounts rendered in the Greek language either by travelers from Greece or by immigrant commentators in this country.[4] Seraphim G. Canoutas, lawyer, journalist, and major figure in Greek American circles during the first decades of this century, issued a Ἑλληνο-Ἀμερικανικὸς Ὁδηγὸς (Greek American guide) from 1907 to 1915. This was an early effort to record systematically the number of Greeks, their settlements, and their economic activities in the United States. Canoutas, who visited virtually every state in the union to pursue his investigations of Greeks in America, published many works including Ὁ Ἑλληνισμὸς ἐν Ἀμερικῇ (Hellenism in America) in 1918

[4]This essay makes no pretense of covering all the Greek-language materials on Greek Americans, many of which are extremely difficult to locate. All references in the text to Greek-language materials are those that I have personally examined and are generally available in major university library collections. For more extensive bibliographical listings of Greek-language materials as well as primary sources on Greek Americana, the reader's attention is directed to Evangelos C. Vlachos, *An Annotated Bibliography on Greek Migration* (Athens: Social Science Centre, 1966); Michael N. Cutsumbis, *A Bibliographic Guide to Materials on Greeks in the United States, 1890-1968* (Staten Island, N.Y.: Center for Migration Studies, 1970); and Theodore Saloutos, *The Greeks in the United States* (Cambridge: Harvard University Press, 1964) 389-400. The most recent bibliographic compilation is by John G. Zenelis, "A Bibliographic Guide on Greek Americans," included as chapter 14 of the present volume (see below, pp. 231-72).

and Τὸ Πρόβλημα τοῦ Ἑλληνισμοῦ τῆς Ἀμερικῆς (The problem of Hellenism in America) in 1927.[5] Around the time of World War I, several visitors from Greece, mostly Athenian journalists, published their personal judgments on the conditions of Greek immigrants in this country. To be mentioned especially in this regard is Οἱ Ἕλληνες τῆς Ἀμερικῆς ὅπως τοὺς Εἶδα (The Greeks of America as I saw them) by Maria S. Economidou, the spirited wife of an Athenian publisher who took it upon herself to report on the plight of Greeks laboring in the American West.[6] Over the next half-century, other visitors from Greece would follow in this tradition and publish their impressions of Greek Americans for homeland readers.[7]

The most comprehensive of the secondary sources in the Greek language is Bobby (Charalambos) Malafouris' Ἕλληνες τῆς Ἀμερικῆς, *1528-1948* (Greeks in America, 1528-1948), privately published in this country in 1948.[8] Malafouris' book is often drawn upon, though not as often cited, by researchers of Greek America. Although not presented as a scholarly contribution, Malafouris' work is of special value in that it prints information on Greek American history and institutional life gathered at a time when many of the pioneer generation, the same cohort as Malafouris himself, were still alive. The volume concludes with a collection of photographs and capsule biographies of the Greek American businessmen and professionals, immigrants all, who contributed financially to its publication.

Elias K. Ziogas, who lived in New York from 1948 to 1964 before returning to Greece, has given us two books on Hellenism in America, the first published in 1958 and the second in 1977, both collections of popularly written essays.[9]

[5]Seraphim G. Canoutas, *Ho Hellenismos en Amerike* [Hellenism in America] (New York: Cosmos, 1918); Canoutas, *To Provlema tou Hellenismou tes Amerikes* [The problem of Hellenism in America] (New York: Herald Printing Syndicate, 1927).

[6]Maria S. Economidou, *Hoi Hellenes tes Amerikes hopos tous eida* [The Greeks of America as I saw them] (New York: D.C. Divry, 1916).

[7]See, for example, Alexandros Krikos, *He thesis tou Hellenismou en Amerike* [The status of Hellenism in America] (Athens: Blazoudake Brothers, 1915); Vasileios Valaoras, *Ho Hellenismos ton Henomenon Politeion* [Hellenism in the United States] (Athens: Typois P. Leone, 1937); Manoles Triantaphyllides, *Hellenes tes Amerikes* [Greeks in America] (Athens: no publisher indicated, 1952).

[8]Bobby (Charalambos) Malafouris, *Hellenes tes Amerikes, 1528-1948* [Greeks in America, 1528-1948] (New York: Issac Goldman Co., 1948).

[9]Elias K. Ziogas, *Ho Hellenismos tes Amerikes, autos ho agnostos*

Ziogas' books have special research value for their biographical vignettes of Greek American literary and artistic figures, many of whom the author personally knew. A perceptive and detailed history of the founding in 1911 of "Helicon," Greek America's first scholarly society, and a study of the struggle in this country between the supporters of the demotic and puristic forms of the Greek language can be found in Nikos I. Rozakos, Νεοελληνικὴ ἀναγέννησι στὴ Βοστώνη (Modern Greek renaissance in Boston) published in 1975.[10]

To be sure, there is much variability in the Greek-language accounts of Greek Americans, but two divergent patterns are discernible. The writings by visitors from Greece tend to document the privations of immigrant life in America, especially in the early decades, to stress the rupture between the immigrants and their patrimonial heritage, and to conclude that assimilation was proceeding rapidly among the Greeks in America, even within the immigrant generation. The accounts presented by Greek immigrant writers are more likely to give laudatory coverage of Greek American "success" stories, to stress the vitality of indigenous Greek American institutions, and to emphasize the endurance of a Greek cultural identity, even among the American-born generations.

Published research on Greek Americans has appeared in both quantity and quality in the English language. The first scholarly article in English was "A Study of the Greeks in Chicago" by Grace Abbott, which came out in a 1909 issue of the *American Journal of Sociology*.[11] Abbott, an associate of Jane Addams, was connected with Hull House, the settlement project adjacent to Chicago's Greektown, whose activities played an important role in the lives of early Greek immigrants. Abbott's study was pathbreaking also for its attention to Greek immigrant women, a topic which was slighted for decades to come. Two important books were published just before World War I describing the early immigrant settlements. One was the caustic but insightful *Greek Immigration*

[Hellenism in America, that unknown quantity] (Athens: Hellenic American Publication Agency, 1958); Ziogas, *Hoi Hellenes tes Amerikes* [The Greeks of America] (Athens: Iolkos, 1977).

[10]Nikos I. Rozakos, *Neoellenike anagennese ste Vostone* [Modern Greek renaissance in Boston] (San Francisco: Wire Press, 1975).

[11]Grace Abbott, "A Study of the Greeks in Chicago," *American Journal of Sociology* 15:3 (November 1909) 379-93.

to the United States (1911) by Henry Pratt Fairchild.[12] An
anthropologist, Fairchild displayed a good grasp of the economic motivations underlying Greek migration to this country. More flattering but perhaps less penetrating was *Greeks
in America* (1913) by Thomas Burgess, an Episcopalian prel-
ate sympathetic with Eastern Orthodox churches.[13] Appearing somewhat later was *The Greeks in America* (1922) by
J. P. Xenides, a Protestant clergyman born of Greek parents
in Asia Minor who had a long career as a teacher and relief
worker on both sides of the Atlantic.[14] The writings of Abbott,
Fairchild, Burgess, and Xenides were all informed by personal
contacts with early Greek immigrants. These pioneer studies
were part of a broader interest in social problems and were
closely related to the developing field of social work. They
exhibited the reformist belief that knowledge would help up-
lift the lot of the immigrants.

The number of major studies on Greek Americans that
appeared in the years just before and after World War I was
not to be matched until almost a half-century later. During
the four-decade period starting in the early 1920s, there appeared only a handful of articles in social science journals
along with several master's theses and privately published
monographs. Representative of the subject matter of this
literature are: welfare activities among the Greeks in Los
Angeles (1939) ;[15] the Greeks of "Bridgetown," a New England
mill town (1948) ;[16] the Greeks of Spartanburg, South Carolina (1949) ;[17] Greek American voluntary associations in
Boston (1949) ;[18] Greek immigrant associations in Chicago

[12]Henry Pratt Fairchild, *Greek Immigration to the United States*
(New Haven: Yale University Press, 1911).

[13]Thomas Burgess, *Greeks in America* (Boston: Sherman, French &
Co., 1913).

[14]J. P. Xenides, *The Greeks in America* (New York: George H. Doran
Co., 1922).

[15]Mary Antoniou, *Welfare Activities among the Greek People in Los
Angeles* (San Francisco: R and E Research Associates, 1974). The work
was originally written as a master's thesis at the University of Southern
California, 1939.

[16]Mayone J. Stycos, "The Spartan Greeks of Bridgetown," *Common
Ground* 8 (Winter 1948) 61-70; 8 (Spring 1948) 24-34; 8 (Summer 1948)
72-86.

[17]Rosamonde Ramsay Boyd, *The Social Adjustment of the Greeks in
Spartanburg, South Carolina* (Spartanburg, S.C.: Williams Printing Co.,
1949).

[18]Mary Treudley, "Formal Organization and the Americanization Pro-

(1950);[19] Greeks in the San Francisco Bay area (1951);[20] and cultural change among three generations of Greek Americans in San Antonio, Texas (1961).[21] Nearly all such studies were based on a single Greek American community and necessarily could not address broader questions of the Greek experience in the United States. In contrast, there were the chapters on Greek Americans which appeared in edited volumes—published, variously, in 1937, 1945, and 1952—dealing with America's diverse "nationality groups" (the contemporary term for what later were called ethnic groups).[22] These essays, though somewhat superficial and written to inform a general audience, had the advantage, nevertheless, of possessing a national perspective.

The most consistent source of commentary in the English language on Greek America for many years was *Athene,* an "American Magazine of Hellenic Thought." *Athene* came out of Chicago as a quarterly from 1941 to 1967 and contained articles on all aspects of Greek history, pieces on events in the Greek American community, as well as the advertisements of the Greek merchants who supported it. Painstakingly and lovingly edited by Demetrios A. Michalaros, *Athene* was innovative in that it regarded the culture of the Greeks in America as a continuing and dynamic part of the Hellenic tradition to be appreciated on its own terms. *Athene* remains to this day a lodestone of Greek American information, the regular con-

cess, with Special Reference to the Greeks of Boston," *American Sociological Review* 14:1 (February 1949) 44-53.

[19]Constantine Yeracaris, "A Study of the Voluntary Associations of the Greek Immigrants of Chicago from 1890 to 1948," unpublished master's thesis, University of Chicago, 1950.

[20]Demitra Georgas, *Greek Settlement of the San Francisco Bay Area* (San Francisco: R and E Research Associates, 1974). This work was originally written as a master's thesis at the University of California at Berkeley, 1951.

[21]Helen C. Lauquier, "Cultural Change among Three Generations of Greeks," *American Catholic Sociological Review* 22 (Fall 1961) 223-32.

[22]Michael Choukas, "Greek Americans," in *Our Racial and National Minorities,* eds. Francis J. Brown and Joseph S. Roucek (New York: Prentice-Hall, 1937) 339-57; Louis Adamic, "Americans from Greece," in *Nation of Nations,* ed. Louis Adamic (New York: Harper & Row, 1944) 266-86; M. J. Politis, "Greek Americans," in *One America,* eds. Francis J. Brown and Joseph S. Roucek (New York: Prentice-Hall, 1945) 242-57; and B. J. Vlavianos, "Greek Americans," in *One America,* eds. Francis J. Brown and Joseph S. Roucek, 3d ed. (New York: Prentice-Hall, 1952) 239-44.

tributions of Theodore N. Constant being especially notable in this regard.

While the scope of the literature on Greek Americans produced between the 1920s and 1960s did not approach the standards of the earlier work by Abbott, Fairchild, and Burgess, an important trend was becoming evident. Research on Greek Americans since World War I was increasingly the preserve of ethnic Greeks, whether immigrant or American born. This trend in Greek American studies has become more pronounced over the times and into the present.

A watershed event in Greek American studies was the 1964 publication of *The Greeks in the United States,* by Theodore Saloutos.[23] Issued by a prestigious university press, *The Greeks in the United States* was grounded in a thorough grasp of primary sources in both Greek and English while simultaneously capturing the broad sweep of the Greek immigrant experience. A work of monumental authority, *The Greeks in the United States* has been regarded as a model for historical researchers of other American ethnic groups. Though deeply sympathetic to his subject matter, Saloutos did not shy away from extended discussion of the political conflicts which were carried over from the old country and the imbroglios of contending church factions within Greek Orthodoxy in America. From a conceptual standpoint, Saloutos' work was significant in that it firmly placed the Greek ethnic experience in this country within the framework of American history. *The Greeks in the United States* had been presaged by Saloutos' *They Remember America* (1956), an account of Greek American immigrants who had returned permanently to Greece.[24] Subsequent to *The Greeks in the United States,* Saloutos continued to publish major articles on the history of Greek America.[25] Theodore Saloutos was clearly the dean of Greek American studies.

Since the mid-1960s, literature on Greek Americans has

[23]Theodore Saloutos, *The Greeks in the United States* (Cambridge: Harvard University Press, 1964).

[24]Theodore Saloutos, *They Remember America: The Story of Repatriated Greek-Americans* (Berkeley: University of California Press, 1956).

[25]Theodore Saloutos, "The Greek Orthodox Church in the United States and Assimilation," *International Migration Review* 7:4 (Winter 1973) 395-408; idem, "Causes and Patterns of Greek Emigration to the United States," *Perspectives in American History* 7 (1973) 381-437; idem, "Cultural Persistence and Change: Greeks in the Great Plains

grown at a rapid rate. In less than a decade and a half well over a score of studies dealing with Greek Americans have appeared. Topics covered include Greek American folklore;[26] social mobility and demographic change among Greek Americans;[27] ethnic and religious identification in the Greek American community;[28] Greek language and education in the United States;[29] and social and political attitudes of Greek Amer-

and Rocky Mountain West, 1890-1970," *Pacific Historical Review* 49 (February 1980) 77-103.

[26]Robert A. Georges, "Greek-American Folk Beliefs and Narratives," unpublished doctoral thesis, Indiana University, 1964; Gregory Gizelis, *Narrative Rhetorical Devices of Persuasion: Folklore Communication in a Greek-American Community* (Athens: National Centre of Social Research, 1974).

[27]Dimitrios I. Monos, "Upward Mobility, Assimilation and the Achievements of the Greeks in the United States, with Special Emphasis on Boston and Philadelphia," unpublished doctoral thesis, University of Pennsylvania, 1976; Toni Tripp Reimer, "Genetic Demography of an Urban Greek Immigrant Community," unpublished doctoral thesis, Ohio State University, 1977.

[28]See Robert James Theodoratus, *A Greek Community in America: Tacoma, Washington* (Sacramento, Calif.: Sacramento Anthropological Society, 1971), based on the author's doctoral thesis of 1961; James W. Kiriazis, "A Study of Change in Two Rhodian Immigrant Communities," unpublished doctoral thesis, University of Pittsburgh, 1967; Marie Helen Stellos, "The Greek Community in St. Louis (1900-1967): Its Agencies for Value Transmission," unpublished doctoral thesis, St. Louis University, 1968; Phyllis Pease Chock, "Greek-American Ethnicity," unpublished doctoral thesis, University of Chicago, 1969; Chrysie Mamalakis Costantakos, "The American-Greek Subculture: Processes of Continuity," doctoral thesis, Columbia University, 1971, since published in the American Ethnic Groups Series (New York: Arno Press, 1980); Donna Misner Collins, "Ethnic Identification: The Greek Americans of Houston, Texas," unpublished doctoral thesis, Rice University, 1976; Sandra Lee Schultz, "Intermarriage in a Greek-American Community: An Analysis of Ethnic Boundaries," unpublished doctoral thesis, University of Arizona, 1977; Andrea Judith Simon, "The Sacred Sect and the Secular Church: Symbols of Ethnicity in Astoria's Greek Community," unpublished doctoral thesis, City University of New York, 1977.

[29]David P. Seaman, *Modern Greek and American English in Contact* (The Hague: Mouton, 1972); Panos D. Bardis, *The Future of the Greek Language in the United States* (San Francisco: R and E Research Associates, 1976); George A. Lagios, "The Development of Greek American Education in the United States, 1908-1973," unpublished doctoral thesis, University of Connecticut, 1977; George Flouris, "The Self-concept and Cross-cultural Awareness of Greek-American Students Enrolled in the Monolingual and Bilingual Schools," unpublished doctoral thesis, Florida State University, 1978.

icans.[30] The quality of such studies is variable, as attested to by the relatively low number to be published in professional journals or by major presses. Nevertheless, there now exists a body of literature sufficient enough to warrant serious consideration as the basis for Greek American studies.[31]

Among doctoral dissertations and monographs in the social sciences, the following can be singled out either for their findings or the issues addressed. *Third Generation Greek Americans* (1980) by Alice Scourby grapples with the perplexities of the intertwining of Greek ethnic identity and Greek Orthodox affiliation among the grandchildren of the immigrants.[32] *The Assimilation of Greeks in the United States* (1968) by Evan C. Vlachos is a perceptive sociological study, not least because it anticipated for Greek Americans what was later to be known in the general literature as "ethnogenesis" —the reconstitution of ethnic consciousness over time.[33] *First and Second Generation Greeks in Chicago* (1971) by George A. Kourvetaris posits a shift in the ethnic anchor of the Greek American family from language maintenance among the immigrants to Greek Orthodoxy among the American born.[34] *Family and Mobility Among Greek Americans* (1972) by Nicholas Tavuchis found, contrary to accepted wisdom in the sociology of the family, that the upward class mobility of the children of Greek immigrants strengthened intergenerational and kinship cohesiveness.[35] "Education and Greek Immigrants

[30]Nicholas P. Petropoulos, "Social Mobility, Status Inconsistency, Ethnic Marginality, and the Attitudes of Greek-Americans toward Jews and Blacks," unpublished doctoral thesis, University of Kentucky, 1973; Marios Stephanides, *The Greeks in Detroit: Authoritarianism—A Critical Analysis of Greek Culture, Personality, Attitudes, and Behavior* (San Francisco: R and E Research Associates, 1975).

[31]See Cutsumbis, cited in note 4.

[32]Alice Scourby, *Third Generation Greek Americans: A Study of Religious Attitudes* (New York: Arno Press, 1980), originally written as a doctoral thesis for the New School for Social Research, 1967. See also Scourby, "Three Generations of Greek Americans: A Study in Ethnicity," chapter 5 of this volume.

[33]Evangelos C. Vlachos, *The Assimilation of Greeks in the United States* (Athens: National Centre of Social Research, 1968).

[34]George A. Kourvetaris, *First and Second Generation Greeks in Chicago* (Athens: National Centre of Social Research, 1971). Also by Kourvetaris, see "The Greek American Family," in *Ethnic Families in America*, eds. Charles H. Mindel and Robert W. Habenstein (New York: Elsevier, 1976) 168-91; and "Greek-American Professionals: 1820's-1970's," *Balkan Studies* 18:2 (1977) 285-323.

[35]Nicholas Tavuchis, *Family and Mobility among Greek-Americans*

in Chicago" (1974) by Andrew T. Kopan traces in meticulous detail all aspects of Greek ethnic education from before the turn of the century into the contemporary period; this study is also valuable for its history of the important Greek community of Chicago.[36] "Ethnic Impact on United States Foreign Policy" (1979) by Sallie M. Hicks presents a balanced and informed study of the makeup of the so-called "Greek Lobby" which appeared in the wake of the 1974 Turkish invasion of Cyprus.[37]

Toward the end of the 1970s, three books appeared which in contrasting ways sought to present a comprehensive picture of the Greek experience in America.[38] None could purport to supersede the historical depth of Saloutos' *The Greeks in the United States. Hellenic Presence in America* (1976) by Stephanos Zotos, though uneven and unfootnoted, nevertheless contains some insight on the manner in which Greek American communal institutions transferred from the immigrant cohort to the American-born generations.[39] A useful though eclectic compendium of dates, events, and documents is *The Greeks in America, 1528-1977* (1978) edited by Melvin Hecker and Heike Fenton.[40] My own *Greek Americans* (1980) seeks

(Athens: National Centre of Social Research, 1972). Also by Tavuchis, see "Naming Patterns and Kinship Among Greeks," *Ethnos*, no. 30 (November, 1971) 152-62.

[36]Andrew T. Kopan, "Education and Greek Immigrants in Chicago, 1892-1973: A Study in Ethnic Survival," unpublished doctoral thesis, University of Chicago, 1974.

[37]Sallie M. Hicks, "Ethnic Impact on United States Foreign Policy: Greek-Americans and the Cyprus Crisis," unpublished doctoral thesis, American University, 1979.

[38]Derivative works with little original research or insight are: Jayne Clark Jones, *The Greeks in America* (Minneapolis: Lerner Publications, 1969); and Demetrius Mazacoufa, *The Story of the Greeks in America* (Atlanta: Argonne Press, 1977). The "Yankee City" series, edited by W. Lloyd Warner and published by the Yale University Press during the 1940s, makes frequent mention of Greeks in a New England mill town. Though regarded as a sociological classic, the volumes are singularly uninformative for either data or ideas on Greek Americans. In a different category is George J. Leber, *The History of the Order of AHEPA* (Washington, D.C.: Order of AHEPA, 1972). Although containing no interpretation, the book is valuable as a primary source of information on Greek America's leading voluntary association.

[39]Stephanos Zotos, *Hellenic Presence in America* (Wheaton, Ill.: Pilgrimage Press, 1976).

[40]Melvin Hecker and Heike Fenton, comps. and eds., *The Greeks in America, 1528-1977* (Dobbs Ferry, N.Y.: Oceana Publications, 1978).

to impart the human flavor as well as the sociology of the
ethnic experience and interprets, and arguably overstates,
Greek American social history as essentially a process of em-
bourgeoisement.[41]

As befits its centrality in the Greek American community,
the Greek Orthodox Church has been the subject of special-
ized attention. Relevant though only periodic commentary can
be found in various issues of such theological journals as the
Greek Orthodox Theological Review, Diakonia, and *Logos.* A
succinct and well-informed history of the Greek Orthodox
Archdiocese in America, written from the vantage of a biography of Patriarch Athenagoras I, is *From Mars Hill to Manhattan* (1976) by George Papaioannou.[42] A convenient collection of primary sources reflecting the changing concerns of
the Archdiocese is *Encyclicals and Documents of the Greek
Orthodox Archdiocese of North and South America* (1976),
edited by Demetrios J. Constantelos.[43] The emergence of a
reflective scholarship within Greek Orthodoxy in America is
clearly evident.[44] Such scholarship as yet, however, has failed
to address the intellectual contributions of leading American
writers in the sociology of religion.[45]

[41]Charles C. Moskos, Jr., *Greek Americans: Struggle and Success*
(Englewood Cliffs, N.J.: Prentice-Hall, 1980).

[42]George Papaioannou, *From Mars Hill to Manhattan: The Greek
Orthodox in America under Athenagoras I* (Minneapolis: Light and Life
Publishing Co., 1976). See also Alexander Doumouras, "Greek Orthodox
Communities in America before World War I," *St. Vladimir's Seminary
Quarterly* 11:4 (1967) 177-9; and Peter T. Kourides, *The Evolution of
the Greek Orthodox Church in America and Its Present Problems* (New
York: Cosmos, 1959).

[43]Demetrios J. Constantelos, ed., *Encyclicals and Documents of the
Greek Orthodox Archdiocese of North and South America: The First
Fifty Years, 1922-1972* (Thessaloniki: Patriarchal Institute for Patris-
tic Studies, 1976). See also by Constantelos, "The Greek Orthodox
Church in the United States," unpublished paper, Stockton State College
(New Jersey), 1976.

[44]A partial list of Greek Orthodox theologians and commentators who
strongly reflect the American experience includes: Constantine Cavarnos,
Anthony M. Coniaris, Demetrios J. Constantelos, James Steve Counelis,
Alexander Doumouras, Stanley S. Harakas, Harris P. Jameson, Andrew
T. Kopan, George Papaioannou, Nicon D. Patrinacos, Harry Psomiades,
John Rexine, and Nomikos M. Vaporis. The *Greek Orthodox Theological
Review,* published in the United States, has become a recognized journal
in general Christian thought as well as in Eastern Orthodoxy.

[45]One would be hard pressed to find citations in the writings on Greek
Orthodoxy in the United States of such contemporary figures in the

Another genre in Greek American historiography is regional studies. By far the best example of such studies, and an indispensable source on the Greeks, warts and all, in the Rocky Mountain region is Helen Zeese Papanikolas' *Toil and Rage in a New Land* (1974).[46] The Greeks of Oregon have been described in Thomas Doulis' *A Surge to the Sea* (1977).[47] Lesser efforts, but still useful, are George T. Frantzis' *Strangers at Ithaca* (1962), the story of the Greek spongers of Tarpon Springs, Florida;[48] *The Greek Texans* (1974);[49] and a 1977 account of the Greeks in Wyoming by Dean P. Talagan.[50]

Although Greek American studies seem to be approaching a point of crystalization, significant research lacunas are apparent. This is especially evident with regard to certain major historical topics. It is remarkable that the Greek community of New York City, the largest in the country, has never been the subject of a comprehensive history. The political left is an important dimension of the Greek experience in the United States, and scholarly balance requires it be included in an understanding of Greek America. We know a fair amount about the early Greek male immigrants, but not nearly as much about the women who arrived a decade or two later.[51]

On the contemporary scene, it would be unfortunate if the recently arrived immigrants from Greece were not accorded the same research attention given to those who came to this

sociology of religion as Robert N. Bellah, John Murray Cuddihy, Charles Y. Glock, Andrew M. Greeley, and Martin E. Marty.

[46]Helen Zeese Papanikolas, *Toil and Rage in a New Land: The Greek Immigrants in Utah*, 2d ed. (Salt Lake City: Utah State Historical Society, 1974).

[47]Thomas Doulis, *A Surge to the Sea: The Greeks in Oregon* (Portland, Ore.: privately printed, 1977).

[48]George T. Frantzis, *Strangers at Ithaca: The Story of the Spongers of Tarpon Springs* (St. Petersburg, Fla.: Great Outdoors Publishing Co., 1962).

[49]*The Greek Texans* (San Antonio: University of Texas at San Antonio, Institute of Texan Cultures, 1974).

[50]Dean P. Talagan, "Faith, Hard Work and Family: The Story of the Wyoming Hellenes," in *Peopling the High Plains*, ed. Gordon O. Hendrickson (Cheyenne: Wyoming State Archives and Historical Department, 1977) 149-68.

[51]Greek immigrant women in the West are treated at some length and with insight, however, in Papanikolas, *Toil and Rage in a New Land.*

country three-quarters of a century ago.[52] The overarching question is in what ways do the experiences of the newcomers resemble or differ from that of their earlier counterparts. Some very specific research avenues can be mentioned to indicate the range of Greek American studies from the perspective of the behavioral sciences. Psychiatric studies of Greek Americans are informative, though one must be wary of generalizations based on descriptions of what are, presumably, atypical groups.[53] We need to know something of the rudimentary youth gangs that have surfaced in the older Greek neighborhoods in both New York and Chicago. The phenomenon of "second settlements" of Greek Americans—the move to suburbia—has never been conceptualized, much less studied. The Greek American press lends itself to examination by the very nature of the printed media, but Greek-language television and radio programs ought also to fall within our purview. Greek American voting behavior is a subject about which there is little systematic knowledge.[54] Studies of Greek Americans and their position in the American economy are

[52]HANAC Staff, *The Needs of the Growing Greek-American Community in the City of New York* (New York: HANAC, 1973).

[53]Psychiatric observations of newly arriving Greek immigrant wives have identified a "Persephone syndrome"—neurotic symptoms of anxiety and depression brought about by the geographical separation of grown daughters in America from their mothers in Greece. Extreme mother-daughter attachment regarded as normal in Greece becomes pathological when the daughter is, in a manner of speaking, "abducted" to the United States by her husband. See Nicholas Dunkas and Arthur G. Nikelly, "The Persephone Syndrome," *Social Psychiatry* 7 (1972) 211-6. See also Dunkas and Nikelly, "Group Psychotherapy with Greek Immigrants," *International Journal of Group Psychotherapy* 25:4 (October 1975) 402-9.

Clinical studies of mentally disturbed second-generation Greek American children found the children came from families where an extremely traditionalist Greek form of child rearing was attempted. See John Papajohn, "The Relations of Intergenerational Value Orientation Change and Mental Health in an American Ethnic Group," unpublished paper, Brandeis University, 1977.

[54]Survey data collected during the 1970s reports the party identification of Greek Americans as follows: 48 percent Democratic, 24 percent Republican, and 29 percent independent (total adds to 101 percent due to rounding computations). See Mark Siegel, "Ethnics' A Democratic Stronghold?" *Public Opinion* (September-October 1978) 48. See also Craig R. Humphrey and Helen Brock Louis, "Assimilation and Voting Behavior: A Study of Greek Americans," *International Migration Review* 7:1 (Spring 1973) 34-45.

as yet fragmentary.[55] In this regard a study of Greeks and restaurants should by no means be regarded as frivolous.

The social history of Greek America also includes literary and cultural materials. Out of the Greek immigrant experience came a rivulet of fiction, satire, and poetry. Written in Greek, possessing varying literary qualities, these works mirrored the yearning for the old country and the encounter with the new. They offer a peek into the main body of the immigrants with their *nostalgia*—the Greek word is an exact cognate of the English—and *xenitia*, the sense of sojourning in foreign parts. Of all the Greek-language fiction writers in this country, none warrants our attention as much as Theano Papazoglou Margaris. Most of her stories deal with the dissipation of the originally strong Greek atmosphere that used to characterize individuals and neighborhoods in the immigrant milieu. Margaris' work forms a portion of American literature, albeit in a language which prevents it from having other than a restricted readership.

Poised between the constricted world of the immigrant and the horizons of American literature, the novels of the children of the immigrants present an expansion of the picture of Greek American life. At least fifteen novels by second-generation Greek Americans have been published over the past three decades. The best of them, such as the works of Harry Mark Petrakis, gain their strength from showing an authentic knowledge of the immigrant world while managing to keep a measure of distance. Standing as a slice of the Greek experience in America, these works of fiction are dominated by a theme and countertheme. The theme claims that Greeks seek to preserve their national identity in a new land. The countertheme responds that the individual struggling against his or her environment must give way, at least partly, to the inexorable process of assimilation. This perception of the cultural and generational dialectics of ethnicity appears in almost all serious Greek American fiction.

By the 1970s, Greek American literature had developed sufficiently to become the subject of informed study. Our understanding of the Hellenic word in the United States, whether written in English or Greek, is especially indebted to two Greek American literary critics. M. Byron Raizis has for

[55]See, however, Helen H. Balk, "Economic Contributions of the Greeks to the United States," *Economic Geography* 19 (1943) 270-5.

some time performed the essential task of relating Greek American writers to each other and to the literary scene in Greece. Alexander Karanikas has given us *Hellenes and Hellions* (1980), a complete survey of Greek characters in American fiction from the early nineteenth century to the present.[56] A work of impressive scholarship, *Hellenes and Hellions* has permanently expanded our knowledge of the ethnic experience by uncovering the diverse literary images of the Greek presence in America.

Research time and resources are scarce commodities. Necessarily there must be some priorities of where to invest scholarly commitments. Greek American studies must be cleanly separated from inflated claims of Greeks as "world-beaters." Such ethnic indulgences are faintly self-denigrating in that they assume the court of native American opinion has the right to pass judgment as to whether or not Greek Americans merit acceptance and respect. Greek American studies must also be informed by the ongoing scholarship and insights of the broader human condition, lest it stumble into the pitfalls of claustral introspection. If any field such as Greek American studies is to thrive, it will be from the collaborative efforts of persons from diverse academic specialties and with contrasting perspectives as to the meaning of Greek America. The components of Greek American studies will be objective and subjective, statistical and artistic, macroscopic and microscopic. At its core, however, there must be a general sensitivity to historical materials and trends.

New research material, of course, can also raise as many problems as it solves. It can reveal such a variety of phenomena that generalization is often made harder. It becomes much more difficult to say anything about Greek America when research reveals the diversity hidden by that term and that perhaps there is no such thing as *one* Greek America. Extant research can be placed, nevertheless, in a variety of paradigms which, even if competing, will facilitate the intellectual development of Greek American studies.

---

[56]Alexander Karanikas, *Hellenes and Hellions: Modern Greek Characters in American Fiction, 1825-1975* (Urbana: University of Illinois Press, 1980).

The Greek American Experience: An Overview

The Greek experience in America started before the founding of the United States and will continue into the indefinite future. An overview of this experience requires making some judgments on how to divide Greek American history. Five more or less distinct stages are proposed: (1) a time of false starts and early beginnings in the period before 1890; (2) the era of mass migration, from 1890 to 1920; (3) the formation of Greek American institutions from 1920 to 1940; (4) an era of consolidation, from 1940 to 1965, within Greek America; and (5) the contemporary period since 1965 of increasing Greek American diversity. No historical divisions, of course, can be as neat as those indicated here. Basic social patterns overlap across several of the periods, and in each there were countervailing tendencies against prevailing trends. Nevertheless, each of these historical stages had certain unique and dominant qualities that serve to demarcate one from the other. Specifying such stages in historical development, moreover, does help us master our bearing and thereby makes it easier to grasp the Greek American experience.[57]

False Starts and Early Beginnings (before 1890). The first Greek known for sure to have set foot on American soil was one Don Teodoro or Theodoros. A ship caulker serving aboard a Spanish expedition, Don Teodoro was killed by Indians in 1528 near what is now Pensacola, Florida. There are many reports of Greek captains and sailors manning Spanish vessels exploring the New World. Though plausible, no firm historical evidence has been uncovered to support such claims. More fanciful reconstructions of history have purported to prove that Christopher Columbus himself was of Greek parentage.[58]

We are fortunate that the historian E. P. Panagopoulos

---

[57]The capsule history of Greek Americans given here, in addition to my own research materials, relies on the works of Theodore Saloutos, Helen Zeese Papanikolas, and George Papaioannou. Of course, all interpretations and emphases are my own responsibility.

[58]Seraphim G. Canoutas, *Christopher Columbus: A Greek Nobleman* (New York: St. Mark's, 1943). Canoutas' treatise is not the first on the subject. In 1937 Spyros Cateras of Manchester, New Hampshire, privately printed a small book entitled *Christopher Columbus Was a Greek Prince and His Real Name was Nicolaos Ypsilantis from the Greek Island of Chios*, mentioned in Adamic, *A Nation of Nations*, 266.

has given us a full and absorbing account of the first large migration of Greeks to America.[59] The story begins in 1763, when Florida passed from Spanish into British hands. Andrew Turnbull, a Scottish doctor married to the daughter of a Greek merchant in London, became intrigued with the idea of establishing a colony in the newly acquired territory by bringing in Greek settlers. Toward this goal he secured a royal land grant about seventy-five miles south of Saint Augustine. Turnbull named his colony New Smyrna, after the Asia Minor birthplace of his Greek wife, Maria Gracia Rubini. Along with Italians and Minorcans, Turnbull recruited some four hundred Greeks, principally from Mani on the southernmost tip of the Greek mainland. The settlers, really indentured laborers, arrived in Florida in 1768 only to encounter appalling conditions. An unsuccessful rebellion broke out, within two years half of the original colonists were dead, and by 1777 the remnant abandoned New Smyrna for Saint Augustine. In Saint Augustine some of the Greeks seem to have prospered, but by the middle of the nineteenth century the first Greeks in the New World had disappeared with barely a trace.

Other "firsts" in early Greek American history can be briefly noted. The first Greek American scholar was John Paradise. Persuaded to come to this country by Benjamin Franklin and Thomas Jefferson, whom he met in Europe, Paradise, in 1787, married into the Ludwell family, one of Virginia's most distinguished. Coming to America by the back way, so to speak, of the Bering Strait was Eustrate Delarof, a native of the Peloponnesus. From 1783 until 1791 Delarof was in charge of all Russian trading operations in the Aleutians and Alaska and is considered by some reckoning to have been the first de facto governor of Alaska. The first Greek American marriage we know of occurred in 1799 in New Orleans when Andrea Dimitry, a native of the island of Hydra, married Marianne Celeste Dracos, the daughter of a well-to-do merchant who had come to New Orleans from Athens around 1766. With indisputable Greek lineage from her father's side (her mother was of mixed French Acadian and American Indian ancestry), Marianne Celeste, who was born in Louisiana on March 1, 1777, may qualify as the Greek American Virginia Dare.

[59]E. P. Panagopoulos, *New Smyrna: An Eighteenth Century Greek Odyssey* (Gainesville: University of Florida Press, 1966).

Passing out of the mists of Greek American antiquity, we come to a remarkable episode in Greek-American relations. The Greek War of Independence (1821-1828) against the Ottoman Turks had gained the sympathy of many American and European philhellenes. One outcome of American philhellenism was to bring to the United States several score Greek orphans. Most of these orphans went on to become professionals in their adopted country.[60] Among those whose later careers can be documented are John Zachos, an educational pioneer among freed blacks after the Civil War and an early proponent of equal education for women, who served as the curator of the Cooper Union School in New York; Evangelos Sophocles, who became professor of Greek at Harvard University; and Lucas Miltiades Miller, US Representative from Wisconsin (1891-1893), the first Greek American Congressman. Several of the orphans went on to distinguished careers as officers in the US Navy. Coming to the United States at a later date, in 1867, at the behest of the philhellene Dr. Samuel Gridley Howe, was Michael Anagnos. He was to marry Howe's daughter and succeed his father-in-law as head of the Perkins Institution for the Blind in Boston.

About the time the Greek war orphans were making their mark, another group of Greeks appeared on the American scene. Starting in the 1850s, a small number of Greek merchants began to locate their import-export businesses in port cities such as New York, Boston, San Francisco, Savannah, Galveston, and New Orleans. It was in New Orleans that the first Greek Orthodox church in America was established in 1864. The founding nucleus were Greek cotton merchants, Nicholas Benakis being the prime mover. Maintaining its existence into the present, Holy Trinity in New Orleans can rightfully claim to be the oldest Greek church in the western hemisphere.

Another trickle of Greeks to come to this country in the nineteenth century consisted of sailors who came off ships arriving in American ports. Most of these Greek sailors gravitated to loading vessels and worked on ships in the Great Lakes and on steamboats plying the Mississippi River and its

[60]Two of the more prominent of the nineteenth-century Greek Americans have been the subject of extended study. See Franklin Sanborn, *Michael Anagnos, 1837-1906* (Boston: Wright and Potter, 1907); and Eva Catafygiotou Topping, "John Zachos: American Educator," *Greek Orthodox Theological Review* 21: 4 (Winter 1976) 351-66.

tributaries. A few became oyster fishermen in the Gulf states. The number of such Greeks—probably several hundred—working and residing in the United States was sufficient enough to merit the attention of a *New York Times* story in 1873.[61]

Neither the educated Greek Americans of the orphans' generation, nor the Greek merchants, nor the Greek sailors were, of course, typical of the waves of Greek immigrants who were to come to these shores in a later age. The establishment of Greek American communal institutions was to be the accomplishment of the poor and uneducated, but energetic and resourceful, immigrants who came to this country from the villages of rural Greece.

The Era of Mass Migration (1890-1920). The world of the Greek peasant at the turn of the century was a desperately poor one. Whatever the glories of its classical monuments and the beauty of its seas and mountains, it was a harsh land from which to wrest a living. But, more importantly, the Greeks of the countryside knew they were poor. They made invidious comparisons with the small bourgeoisie and the petty government functionaries of their homeland. The notion of moving to a better place—anticipated in the Greek maritime tradition and Greek entrepreneurship in the cities of the old Ottoman Empire—was already part of a common worldview.

It cannot be overstated that the overriding motive for Greek migration to the United States was economic gain. The intent of the overwhelming majority of immigrants was to return to Greece with sufficient capital to enjoy a comfortable life in their home villages. At the least, they expected to ensure the proper marriages of their daughters and sisters by building up dowries with their American earnings. It is hard to recapture the power of the lure that was America—except that even today, in Greece, that lure still holds forth, though in much-reduced form.

During the 1880s about two thousand Greeks came to America, mostly from Sparta. During the 1890s more than 15,000 Greeks, drawn from a wider regional base, departed for the United States. A flood of Greek immigrants occurred in the first two decades of the twentieth century. Between 1901 and 1910 some 167,000 Greeks came to these shores.

---

[61]"The Greeks in America," *New York Times* (August 4, 1873), reprinted in Hecker and Fenton, *The Greeks in America*, 61-64.

From 1911 through 1920, despite the interruption of World War I, more than 180,000 Greeks migrated to America. These figures refer only to Greeks born in Greece proper and, therefore, do not include immigrants of Greek stock who came from outside the Greek state. We do not have accurate statistics as to how many Greeks came from such "unredeemed" areas, but 100,000 would be a cautious estimate. Thus, all in all, upwards of 450,000 Greeks—the vast majority males—arrived in the United States between 1890 and 1920.

Many immigrants accomplished exactly what they had set out to do—make money and return to Greece. Estimates are that about 40 percent of all Greeks admitted to the United States before 1920 went back to their homeland; some after only a short stint in America, others after five or ten years here. We do not know how many of these early returnees eventually decided to come back to America and stay for good. For sure, many Greeks counted as "repatriated" were simply returning to the old country to bring back relatives or newly acquired wives to America. Certainly the number of such double immigrants in the early decades of this century was considerable.

Once the initial immigrants had settled in America, they wrote to their home villages, usually with passage money enclosed, to encourage their male relatives to follow. Those without relatives in America to bring them over were often recruited by labor agents scouring the Greek hinterland with promises of jobs in America. However he acquired his passage money, the immigrant's trauma began before he arrived in America: wrenched from familiar surroundings, consigned to the nether regions of an oceanic ship, crossing in cramped quarters, fearing that a cough or blemish might cause one to fail the physical examination required for entry into America.

Once through the processing of Ellis Island and admission to the United States, the newly arrived immigrant would head by train toward his destination: the relatives who had preceded him, or the job promised him by the labor agent. If he had no firm destination he would seek out a place where some of his fellow villagers could be found. The flood of Greek immigrants who arrived in America before 1920 can be traced along three major routes: (1) Greeks going to the western states to work on railroad gangs and in mines; (2) Greeks going to New England mill towns to work in the textile and shoe factories; and (3) Greeks who went to the large northern cities—especially New York and Chicago—who, in addition to working in factories, found employment as peddlers or in the service trades. All of these movements shared many similarities, but each was also different from the others and requires separate comment.

The first sizable group of Greeks to arrive in the American West came as strikebreakers. A 1903 strike of coal miners in eastern Utah was broken by Greeks brought in from the East. Though the Greeks in the main were not stirred by the workers movement gaining strength in the West in the years before World War I, they took a leading role in some strikes: notably, the 1912 copper strike in Bingham Canyon, Utah, and the 1913-1914 coal strike at Ludlow, Colorado. By the time of World War I there were at least fifty thousand Greek workers in the mines and smelters and on the railroad gangs throughout the West. Greek railroad laborers were especially concentrated in California, where, in 1910, there were more Greeks proportionate to the total state population than anywhere else in America. In time, some of the immigrants left the mines and railroads to become small businessmen, but this should not obscure the fact that many Greeks in the West remained blue-collar workers for all of their lives. An explosion in 1924, in the Castle Gate mine near Price, Utah, caused the death of 172 men, including 50 Greek miners.

As in other parts of the country, the Greeks in the West were to confront a virulent nativistic reaction. But it was in the West, where their relative numbers made them more visible, that the Greeks faced the most serious incidents. In McGill, Nevada, three Greeks were killed in an antiforeign melee in 1908. When the Ku Klux Klan was active in Utah, Greeks were singled out as a special target. The most publicized anti-Greek assault took place in 1909 in the city of South Omaha, Nebraska, on whose outskirts was a shantytown of several thousand Greek laborers, a number swollen by unemployed railroad workers waiting out the winter. Following a shooting incident between a Greek and a policeman, a mob, with the acquiescence of local authorities, rampaged through the Greek quarter, burning most of it to the ground and driving all Greeks from the city.

A second major destination of Greek immigrants was the textile and shoe factories in the mill towns of New England. In the first decades of this century, sizable Greek colonies could be found in Manchester and Nashua in New Hampshire;

Bridgeport, New Britain, and Norwich in Connecticut; and Chicopee, Haverhill, Lynn, Peabody, New Bedford, and Springfield in Massachusetts. Early on there was a major Greek concentration in Boston. The settlements of Greek workers in New England had counterparts in the factory towns of Ohio, Pennsylvania, and upstate New York. But for Greeks the foremost mill town was Lowell, Massachusetts, a community that has a special significance in the history of Greek America. In 1906 the first Greek Orthodox church in America with a Byzantine motif was erected in Lowell. By 1910 Lowell, with a total population of about 100,000, had at least 20,000 Greeks. Even as late as 1920, Lowell was the third-largest Greek city in America, trailing only New York and Chicago.

The living conditions of the early Greek immigrants in the mill towns were, to say the least, frugal. Extreme parsimony was the operating principle, the object being to save as much money as possible to send back to Greece. Usually a half-dozen or so men would rent a cheap apartment and collectively share expenses. Modern hygiene and a balanced diet were not commonly practiced. Tuberculosis was a frequent scourge (it has always been a special dread in the Greek American community). Most of the Greek immigrants in New England were to remain in the mills for at least a decade or two, if not for their entire working lives. To compound matters, the reception accorded the Greek arrivals, from immigrants of other nationalities as much as native Americans, was generally hostile.

The third major destination of the Greek immigrants was the big cities of the Middle Atlantic and Great Lakes states. On the eve of World War I there were at least several thousand Greeks each in such cities as Philadelphia, Pittsburgh, Buffalo, Cleveland, Toledo, Detroit, Gary, and Milwaukee. But the preeminent Greek American cities were to become New York and Chicago. By 1920, New York and Chicago each possessed at least fifty thousand Greeks. Chicago's "Halsted Street Greektown" was the most geographically concentrated of any in the country and developed into a distinctive ethnic enclave. Even though New York never produced a concentrated Greektown like Chicago's, it became the home of the leading Greek American newspapers and the headquarters of the Greek Orthodox Church in America.

Along with those who found work in meat-packing plants, steel mills, and factories, many Greek immigrants in the big cities started out as busboys, pushcart vendors, and peddlers of fruit, candy, and flowers. Unique to New York City was a major Greek furrier industry. A mainstay in the early immigrant economy was the shoeshine or bootblack business. Throughout the North there were literally scores or even hundreds of Greek-owned shoeshine parlors in each of the big cities. Some of the owners of these parlors employed a "padrone" system, which was little more than indentured labor for recently arrived boys from Greece. For many years bootblacks and Greeks were synonymous in our large urban centers.

Only a small number of Greek immigrants headed toward the South. Of all the Greeks who came to America before 1920 fewer than one in fifteen settled in the states of the old Confederacy. There is a small community in the South, however, which does occupy a singular position in Greek America —Tarpon Springs, Florida. In 1905 more than five hundred Greek spongers from the Dodecanese Islands were brought to Tarpon Springs. From that time until World War II, Tarpon Springs had a majority Greek population, a situation without parallel in any other town in the United States.

It was the arrival of Greek women in sufficient numbers that anchored the Greek community in this country. Before the turn of the century only a very few Greek women entered the United States, each of whom must have been a pioneer in her own right. Between 1900 and 1910 women made up less than one in twenty of the Greek immigrants, and only one in five between 1910 and 1920. The preferred way for a Greek woman to come to America was to be accompanied: if married, with her husband; if single, in the company of brothers or cousins. But since marriages were frequently arranged across the ocean, many "picture brides" had to travel to America on their own.

By and large, Greek immigrant women—married and unmarried—did not work outside the household. There were, however, some exceptions to the general pattern. For a woman to work in the family store was acceptable, though even this was not a rule. In the West in the early years, moreover, many married women ran boarding houses for Greek laborers. But it was in New England where the likelihood of women working was highest. A large proportion, some say a majority, of the Greek immigrant women in the mill towns were operatives in the textile and shoe factories. But even there most women did not continue working once they were married or after their husbands had secured a modicum of economic stability. The clearly dominant standard—and the one that was in the main adhered to—among early Greek immigrants was for women not to be in gainful employment.

A very few years after the start of the mass migration, there also began within the Greek American population a process of internal social stratification that is characteristic of American society as a whole. Though many Greek immigrants would remain in the laboring class for their entire lives, the beginnings of a Greek American middle class can be detected by, say, 1910. Certainly, by the 1920s there was a considerable number of Greeks who had become owners of small businesses. The entrepreneurial capacity of the Greek immigrant was remarked upon by almost all observers of the early immigrant scene. The new businesses tended to concentrate in certain enterprises: confectioneries or sweet shops, food service, retail and wholesale produce, pool halls, floral shops, hatters, dry cleaners, and shoe repair shops. The Greek presence in America was putting down commercial roots.

Greek American Formal Organizations (1920-1940). The transformation of the Greek immigrant colony into a Greek American community was presaged by the passage of restrictive immigration legislation culminating in the Reed-Johnson Act of 1924. The Greek quota was set at one hundred immigrants per year. This contrasted with the 28,000 Greeks who came to this country in 1921, the last year of relatively open immigration. In 1929 the annual Greek quota was raised to 307, where it remained for most of the next three decades. Nonquota immigrants, however, were allowed—principally through the mechanism of wives joining husbands in America —and Greek entry into the United States averaged about two thousand yearly between 1925 and 1930.

The halt in mass migration had two profound consequences on Greek America—one immediate and the other long-term. First, there was a frantic scramble to acquire American citizenship on the part of those already in the United States. In 1920 only one in six Greek male immigrants had acquired American citizenship. By 1930 half of these immigrants had become naturalized Americans. Second, without the transfusion of new arrivals from Greece, American-born Greeks would eventually replace the immigrants as the core Greek

American population. In 1920 only one in four Greek Americans was born in this country, but by 1940 American-born Greeks were in the majority.

The prototype of formal organization in the early immigrant colonies was the *kinotis*, or "community," which served as the basis for subsequent Greek Orthodox churches. By 1916 there were 60 Greek churches in the United States and about 140 by 1923. The significant point of the appearance of Greek Orthodox churches in America was that they originated from the actions of the immigrants themselves, not the ecclesiastical authorities. The early Greek Orthodox churches in this country, although independent for all practical purposes, were under the spiritual aegis of the Patriarchate of Constantinople (Istanbul in Turkey). In 1908, however, the Patriarchate formally placed the Greek churches in America under the authority of the Church of Greece. Hopes were sadly misplaced that putting the Greek Orthodox churches in America under the authority of the Church of Greece would bring order. The Holy Synod in Athens, however, became embroiled in a game of musical chairs as the royalist supporters of King Constantine I and the liberal backers of Venizelos alternated in power. The royalist-Venizelist schism, which embroiled Greece from before World War I into the 1920s, cleaved the Greek community in this country as well.

In 1918, the Metropolitan of Athens, Metaxakis, promised to establish a bona fide American Archdiocese. However, Metaxakis, a Venizelist, was deposed in 1920 as head of the Church in Greece and replaced by a royalist. Metaxakis came to the United States, claiming to be the rightful head of the Church of Greece and, as such, assumed the administration of the Greek churches in this country. In 1921 Metaxakis convened the first clergy-laity conference of the Greek communities in the United States and laid the basis for the formal incorporation of the Greek Archdiocese of North and South America. Shortly after founding the Archdiocese, Metaxakis was elevated to the Patriarchate and transferred the Archdiocese in America to dependency on Constantinople. Archbishop Alexander was appointed head of the new Archdiocese. Throughout his archbishopric—from 1922 to 1930—Alexander was bitterly opposed by royalist congregants. Although the royalist-Venizelist schism cut across class and regional lines, there were some discernible patterns. The most traditional and working-class Greeks—especially in New England—were most likely to be found in the royalist camp, while the more assimilationist and middle-class elements—especially in the Middle West—were most likely to be supporters of Venizelos and Archbishop Alexander.

By the close of the 1920s, the Greek Orthodox churches in the United States—now numbering about two hundred—were in a state of acute demoralization. The time for reconciliation was overdue. After a period of negotiation among the disputants, it was agreed that the feuding bishops would accept reassignments in Greece. Further, the respected Athenagoras was selected to head the Archdiocese in America. Athenagoras' long tenure as Archbishop—from 1931 to 1948—proved to be of major significance in the development of the Greek American community. Athenagoras' first task—in which his patience and tact served him well—was to defuse the royalist-Venizelist collision in this country. His second goal was to centralize the administration of the Greek churches in the Archdiocese. In this endeavor he was ultimately successful, but not before setting off another round of intercommunal fighting. The permanency of the Church in this country was confirmed by the founding of a Greek Orthodox seminary, Holy Cross, in 1937. This laid the basis for American-educated Greeks to enter the clergy in significant numbers and indicated the transition from a Greek immigrant to a Greek American church.

The internecine events occurring within the Greek Orthodox Church were mirrored on the secular side. The Greek-language press in America was quick to take sides between contending factions. With origins going back to the first waves of mass migration, the Greek press was to have its golden age during the 1920s. The influence of the Greek-language press was remarkable because so few of the early immigrants brought with them the habit of reading newspapers. Reading a newspaper regularly was something they learned to do in the United States. Two newspapers, in particular, both dailies and both coming out of New York City, were destined to play a powerful role in the immigrant community for many decades. The *Atlantis,* ardently royalist in its early years, continued to take conservative positions on political matters in Greece and backed the Republican Party in this country; the *National Herald* ['Εθνικὸς Κῆρυξ] supported Venizelos and identified with liberalism in Greece and later the New Deal in America.

The high fecundity rate of Greek newspapers was matched

by a plethora of Greek fraternal societies. The large majority of these associations were *topika somateia,* societies whose members came from the same region or village in the old country. The idea of a national association that would embrace all Greek immigrants was periodically voiced. A Pan-Hellenic Union was founded in 1907. Suffering from financial mismanagement and accusations that it was an agent of the Greek government, the Pan-Hellenic Union withered away by the time of World War I.

The pattern of fragility and localism of Greek American voluntary associations was broken in 1922. In that year, a group of Greek businessmen founded the American Hellenic Educational Progressive Association—usually referred to by its acronymn as AHEPA. A fraternal association with Masonic influences, AHEPA was to become the leading Greek American lodge. AHEPA represented the social aspirations of a growing Greek middle class. Most importantly, AHEPA acknowledged the wrenching reality that most Greeks were in this country to stay. Even though its official face was one of assimilationism, however, in a conscious effort to outflank antiforeign American nativism, AHEPA was always committed to Greek identity, albeit within an American context. Because it adopted English as its official language, AHEPA was viewed by its critics as an instrument of de-Hellenization. Proponents of preserving as much as possible of Greek life in the United States formed their own organization in 1923—the Greek American Progressive Association, or GAPA. The GAPA leadership was sincerely dedicated to its cause, but was fighting a rearguard action against the tide of Americanization. In later years, unlike AHEPA, GAPA would find it difficult to make the transition from an immigrant to an American-born membership, and the lodge became increasingly moribund.

The Greek advance into the American middle class was abruptly set back by the Depression. The thirties were grim years for most Americans and Greek Americans were not an exception. Marginal Greek-owned businesses went under in dismaying numbers. Working-class Greeks witnessed a sickening drop in earning power, even when fortunate enough to have jobs. Greek American voluntary associations declined in membership, and the Greek-language press saw its circulation and advertisements shrink. The Greek Orthodox Church was sorely pressed to find the funds to maintain itself. For the only time in history, the outflow of Greeks back to the old country exceeded the number coming over to America. From a political standpoint, the Depression moved the large majority of the Greek community into the Democratic party. Whereas the Greek commercial element was strongly Republican in the 1920s, small businessmen came to identify as closely with New Deal recovery measures as did working-class Greeks.

The Depression also gave an added impetus to the Greek American socialist constituency. Since the time of World War I there existed in this country a radical press in the Greek language. The Industrial Workers of the World had an active Greek branch starting in the early 1920s. Various Marxist groups and communist workers clubs emerged, changed form, and reappeared throughout the interwar period. The most significant left-wing Greek group was Local 70 of the Fur Workers Union in New York City. During the thirties and forties the communist hold on the furriers—then affiliated with the CIO—seemed unbreakable. In its heyday in the years just before and during World War II, the Greek furriers could be counted upon to give some mass to Greek American leftist demonstrations. Whether the left was a major or marginal component of the Greek experience in America is an issue of debate. In any event, what can be termed the "old" Greek American left was to suffer mightily in the years following World War II—a victim of sectarian infighting, the McCarthyite atmosphere, and the repressive legislation of the Smith Act.

The Depression was a traumatic event in Greek America. Nevertheless, a certain amount of resiliency and maturity was also evident. The core of the Greek American population had shifted from immigrant bachelors to family members. Somehow, the Greek American community found the wherewithal to establish an extensive network of Greek-language afternoon and Saturday schools. In this way many of the second generation were to become familiar with, and often speak quite well, the language of their forebears. Old country regionalisms and politics were giving way to a more composite Greek American subculture. It was apparent by the end of the 1930s that Greek American energies were increasingly drawn from and focused upon the American scene.

The Period of Consolidation (1940-1965). The Italian invasion of Greece in the fall of 1940 brought Greece into World

War II. The initial successes of the Greek army in throwing back the Italian invaders had an exhilarating effect on the Greek American community. In a matter of days a Greek War Relief Association was formed in this country and raised substantial sums of money, uniting Greek Americans in an unprecedented fashion. Once the United States itself entered World War II, Greek American support for the war effort was wholehearted. In their common struggle against the Axis powers, Greek and American interests were joined as never before. The heroism of the Greek resistance—the communist-dominated EAM/ELAS—during the German occupation was so exceptional that it evoked admiration from Greek Americans of all political stripes. But even before the Germans were defeated, political differences in Greece were being felt in the Greek American community. The communist-led resistance in Greece and the British-supported government in exile were each girding for control of a liberated Greece. A vicious civil war broke out between the government and the communists that lasted until 1949. One of the historic consequences of the Greek civil war was that, under the mantle of the 1947 Truman Doctrine, American military aid and advisers were crucial in the final defeat of the insurgent forces. The Truman Doctrine initiated a military alliance between Washington and Athens that over the next generation led to increasing American influence in Greek political and economic life.

Within Greek America, the consequences of World War II were important for another reason. The prosperity generated by the war brought about a major economic ascent exceeding even that of the 1920s. The Greek American occupational structure in the main body of immigrants was now dominated by small businessmen. Among the American born, the majority were in white-collar occupations or the professions. Notable as the overall economic improvement of Greek Americans had been, there are important qualifications to be made. A minority, principally old bachelors, were still trapped in poverty. There still was an immigrant proletarian segment in the factory towns of the North, but it was shrinking in both absolute numbers and relative weight. The general picture was indisputable. By the 1950s it could be said that Greek Americans had arrived in American society.

The fifties were also a time of general serenity within the Greek American community. To be sure, the social base of the most traditional immigrant associations was approaching dissolution, but those incorporating the American born—such as AHEPA—were displaying sufficient appeal to ensure their long-term viability. The Greek Orthodox Church enjoyed a period of unaccustomed equanimity. The leadership of the Greek Archdiocese had passed to Archbishop Michael in 1949, following Athenagoras' elevation to the Patriarchate of Constantinople. Under Michael's stewardship, the Church took the first steps toward an accommodation of second and third-generation Greek Americans. The Greek Orthodox Youth of America, an organization in which English was the official language, was established in 1950 and grew rapidly over the next few years. At the time of Michael's death in 1958, there were about 250 Greek Orthodox churches in this country, all of which were in the fold of the Archdiocese. Michael also pressed for public recognition of Eastern Orthodoxy as a major religious faith—along with Protestantism, Catholicism, and Judaism—in this country.

The post-war period was also one in which Greek immigrants again began to arrive in this country. The Greek quota had been set at 307 annually since 1929, but under special refugee legislation in 1948 it was made possible to borrow from the future. By 1952 the Greek quota was mortgaged to the year 2014! Hopes for less-restrictive immigration policies were set back by the McCarran-Walter Act of 1952. Legislation passed in 1953 and 1954, however, permitted nonquota Greeks to enter either as displaced persons or through preferences given to close relatives. Another element were Greeks who came under student visas and eventually managed to become permanent residents and, later, citizens. All told, about seventy thousand Greeks—either by borrowing on future quotas, by qualifying for displaced persons status, by utilizing provisions enabling citizens to bring over relatives, or by entering as students—came to the United States between the end of World War II and 1965.

If the numbers of the postwar arrivals were nowhere near those of the era of mass migration, they were still sufficient to have a retarding effect on the assimilation of the Greek American community. The fresh wave of immigrants replenished Hellenism in America. Greek Orthodox membership grew, the circulation of the Greek-language press revived, travel to and from Greece expanded, and Greek food and other items were increasingly marketed. Although the new arrivals meant the Greek American community would not be completely cut off from the wellsprings of Greek culture, however, this does not imply that the processes of Americanization were being reversed. The American-born ascendancy was undeniable. There were no longer any Greektowns in which young children were brought up to speak Greek as their first language. Throughout the United States, the community was moving from one made up of Greeks with American citizenship to one consisting of Americans of Greek ancestry.

A thoughtful observer in the early 1960s would have predicted a lingering sort of Greek ethnic consciousness within an overarching American social identity. The power of the immigrant past was fading. This seemingly natural progression of events, however, was not to come to pass—at least not at its expected speed. Instead, Greek America entered a period of growth and turbulence. Some of this was a result of the new ethnic pride in the descendants of the immigrants, which was to become part of the American mood in the sixties and seventies. Much more direct, there was the reopening of the immigration doors to large numbers of Greeks.

A Time of Diversity (1965-present). The Immigration Act of 1965 abolished the country-of-origin basis of selecting immigrants. From 1966 to 1971, during the first flush of the new legislation, about 15,000 Greeks came to America annually. Since the mid-1970s, the figure has stabilized at around 8,000 Greek immigrants per year. A projected 175,000 Greeks will have legally arrived in this country in the fifteen years since the passage of the new immigration law.[62] The new Greeks located in all parts of the United States, but especially in communities where relatives had previously settled. New York City and Chicago, however, attracted by far the largest number of recent arrivals. Both cities have witnessed the reappearance of Greektowns—the Astoria section in Queens and the Western-Lawrence area on Chicago's northwest side—swelling neighborhoods where the newcomers overlaid earlier concentrations of Greek Americans. The New York community grew at such a rapid rate that a publicly funded network of social services, the Hellenic American Neighborhood Action Com-

[62]Over the past two decades, an estimated 30,000 Greek seamen have jumped from their ships and disappeared somewhere in America.

mittee, was founded in 1972 to meet the needs of that city's Greek population.

In comparison with the earlier Greek immigrants, the recent arrivals were more likely to be better educated and more urban (though perhaps closer to a rural background than they would have liked to let on). The really significant difference between the older and new immigrants was in family composition. Unlike the demography of the original immigrants, there were almost as many women as men among the recent arrivals. Moreover, many of the new Greeks were coming to this country as married couples in the company of their small children. A large number of the newly arriving Greek women would themselves enter the labor force, principally in light factory work, in contrast with the stay-at-home Greek women of the earlier immigration.

Many of the recent Greek immigrants followed the path of their predecessors and went into the food-and-drink business. An impressive number of the newcomers have become owners of restaurants, nightclubs, bars, coffee shops, and short-order establishments, more than replacing the declining cohort of older Greek restauranteurs and tavern keepers. The new Greeks also were becoming proprietors of tailor shops, shoe repair shops, dry cleaners, grocery and produce stores, and, in New York especially, owners of taxicabs. Most of the new immigrants, however, were not small businessmen, but worked for someone else. Some went into factories, but more moved into construction, painting, and maintenance work. A large number also became waiters or grillmen in Greek-owned restaurants.

Among the main body of the American-born generations the clear trend was away from the working class, away from the small entrepreneur, and toward white-collar or upper-middle-class vocations. In appraising the social standing of second-generation Greek Americans, the salient point of reference is to use native white Americans as the "norm." The 1970 census is informative. Greek Americans were twice as likely as the native white population to have completed college.[63]

[63]US Bureau of the Census, *Census of the Population: 1970*, 2:21, 51, 114, 161. On the economic and social ascent of Greek Americans, see also Leonard Broom, Cora A. Martin, and Betty Maynard, "Status Profiles of Racial and Ethnic Populations," *Social Science Quarterly* 12:4 (September 1971) 379-88. The unusually strong emphasis on upward mobility among Greek Americans is documented and discussed in Bernard C.

Looking at income levels, second-generation Greek Americans enjoyed earnings 31.6 percent higher than the average of native whites. In the contemporary period, more than a few Greek Americans have done uncommonly well in the corporate world, professions, arts, education, entertainment, and politics. Following the Turkish invasion of Cyprus in 1974, second-generation Greek Americans played a key role in making United States foreign policy adhere to its own laws by instituting an arms embargo on Turkey. The successes, albeit partial and temporary, of the so-called "Greek Lobby" over the opposition of the Administration and much of the national press was a stunning achievement for a community heretofore not organized for political action.

The Greek Orthodox Church in this country is, for all practical purposes, coterminous with the Archdiocese.[64] Since 1959, Archbishop Iakovos has been primate of the Archdiocese, which oversees some 440 churches and a panoply of educational and charitable activities. About 300,000 family members are dues-paying members of the Archdiocese. It would be reasonable to estimate, however, that about four in five of those who identify as ethnic Greeks regard themselves as Greek Orthodox—whether as active congregants or only nominally. A process of Americanization of the Church is evident. For some time the majority of new priests have been American-born graduates of the Holy Cross School of Theology. Perhaps the ultimate in the Americanization of the Church is the growing number of non-Greeks who are becoming a part of it. In the 1960s, mixed couples accounted for three out of ten church marriages, and by the mid-1970s the figure was about half. In the epoch-making Clergy-Laity Congress of 1970, following the personal appeal of Iakovos, an English liturgy was permitted (not required) depending upon the judgment of the parish priest in consultation with his local bishop. The progression to English would have been inevitable and relatively smooth had it not been for the large influx of new immigrants from Greece. The Greek Orthodox Church was more ready, in effect, for English in 1960 than it would be two decades later. By the late 1970s, a kind of local option system was evolving: churches in the immigrant neighbor-

Rosen, "Race, Ethnicity, and the Achievement Syndrome," *American Sociological Review* 24:1 (February 1959) 47-60.
      [64]A handful of Greek Orthodox churches of dubious canonicity operates outside the Archdiocese.

hoods of the large cities offered their services entirely in Greek; churches in the suburbs had services increasingly in English.

The conflict and potential in the Greek Orthodox Church in this country arise from a clash of two cultures. The new culture emerged with the ascendancy of the American born. Proud of its Greek ethnicity, it is nevertheless receptive to the vision of an open church, holding itself out to all baptized Orthodox. The old culture, fortified by recent immigrants, rejects these premises. It looks back to a church serving as the repository of the Greek language and national survival. It favors a fortress church amidst the battering of Americanism. The internal situation of the Church today can only be appreciated against the background of this cultural struggle.

Over the past decade and a half the Greek American media has become more diversified. Following the demise of the venerable *Atlantis* in 1972, the only remaining Greek-language daily was the *National Herald*. But in 1977 and 1978, two new dailies began to serve the Greek immigrant readership of New York City. Immigrant audiences also listened to a variety of Greek radio and television programs broadcasted in the major metropolitan centers. Faced by diminishing numbers of Greek newspaper readers, the Greek American press has searched for a wider audience among the American born. By the late 1970s, slightly more than half of the Greek press readership was accounted for by papers published exclusively in English, about a third had a bilingual format, with the remainder being completely in Greek. There was also the periodic appearance of illustrated magazines published in English which covered in about equal measure events in Greece and in Greek America.

The Greek American left has experienced a revival since the late 1960s. Unlike the old Greek American left, whose hard-core members were communists and others sympathetic to the Soviet Union, the new left is more ecumenical in its socialism and reflects, in large part, the diversity of the political left in Greece. To somewhat oversimplify, the Greek American left today draws disproportionately from three identifiable groups: a segment of the new immigrants of working-class background, Greek-born university students and intellectuals, and second-generation academics. No one quite knows the relative weight to assign to each, but collectively they bring together a constituency that strives to foster critical thought in this country and to move the Greek American community toward identification with anti-capitalistic movements within Greece. The Greek American left was given special impetus by the 1967 military seizure of power in Greece and American complicity during the period of the Greek dictatorship. The advent of the Junta in Athens, however, revealed much about the prevailing ideological currents in Greek America. Acquiescence, if not outright support, of the Greek military regime characterized the bulk of the older immigrants, the American-born generations, as well as mainline Greek American organizations. Support for the Junta noticeably weakened in its last stages, but candor requires one to admit that widespread opposition never developed within the Greek American community. Some corroboration of the dominant ethos of middle-class Greek Americans can be gleaned from a 1972 national survey of college freshmen.[65] Compared to the national norm, Greek American students, nearly all of whom can be presumed to be either second or third generation, were found to be significantly more conservative in their political views, less sympathetic with criminal rights, and much more likely to regard higher education in instrumental rather than intellectual terms.

The focal point of Greek American cultural interests has undergone a change since the 1960s. Where formerly there was a somewhat affected focus on classical Hellas, the contemporary awareness is much more in tune with the culture of modern Greece. Hopes for developing a nationally based and sustained interest in Greek society and culture came a long way toward realization with the formation of the Modern Greek Studies Association in 1968. The appearance of Greek American publishing enterprises in the 1970s has been an important instrument in the introduction of Greek writers to an English-reading audience. The *Journal of the Hellenic Diaspora*, published since 1974, has evolved into a high-quality review of modern Greek literature and critical commentary on current Greek issues. By the late 1970s modern Greek studies were beginning to take root in more structured aca-

---

[65]Thus, by way of illustration, 74 percent of Greek American freshmen identified their political preference as middle of the road or conservative, compared to 64 percent of a national sample. See the 1972 survey of college freshmen conducted by the American Council on Education.

demic settings, though facing the problems of raising funds from outside donors and persuading reluctant university administrators to release money or teaching time.

Interest in Greek American studies as a separate topic also appeared in the late 1970s. A national symposium on "The Greek Experience in America," the first of its kind, was held at the University of Chicago in 1976. Also in 1976, the Maliotis Cultural Center was established on the Hellenic College/Holy Cross campus in Brookline, Massachusetts, with the purpose of presenting cultural work—lectures, films, art exhibits—pertaining to the Greek American as well as Greek and Orthodox heritages. In 1978 the Greek Theater of New York and the *Journal of the Hellenic Diaspora* announced a playwriting competition on the Greek experience in America, the winning play to be produced in both Greek and English versions. In 1978, as well, the National Endowment for the Humanities allocated $797,000, contingent upon matching funds, to produce a documentary television series on the Greeks in America.

Greek Americans in the contemporary era lend themselves less to generalization than in times past. The Greek American experience today is a diverse one. It consists of a declining cohort of older immigrants. It is the still-unfolding experience of the new immigrants from Greece. It is the story of the adult children of the immigrants. And there are the third and fourth generations who are still half-sketched figures in the unfinished canvas of Greek America. Between, and to a lesser degree within, each of these groups there are major differences in class position, loyalties to the old country, commitment to Greek Orthodoxy, language use, life style, and politics. Yet in some important ways these differences should not obscure the larger steadiness of the Hellenic presence in America.

Contrasting Perspectives on Greek America

Few subjects are more likely to stir up passions among Greek Americans than talking or writing about Greek Americans. The cognitive maps one has about Greek America almost always have prescriptive implications. In one way, to approach Greek American studies resembles the situation of modern Greeks who are now laboriously trying to untangle their own social history and see themselves clearly. In another way, closer to home, it confronts the basic paradigms of ethnic studies in America. The contending views about Greek Americans can be reduced to two main questions. Is there more or less variability within Greek America than between Greek Americans and other Americans? Is there more or less variability between Greek Americans and Greeks than between Greek Americans and other Americans? To pose such questions is a necessary first step toward a conceptualization of Greek American studies.

Commonalities versus Differentiation. The prevailing interpretation of Greek Americans is to understand them in terms of cohesiveness and commonalities. From this standpoint one can see the ascent of many of the immigrants into the middle class and the high economic and educational standing, relative to native-born Americans, of Greek Americans of the second and third generations. Such a perspective also emphasizes the paramount place of Greek Orthodoxy in shaping the patterns of Greek ethnic identification in this country. While one might recognize ethnic differences between, say, a Greek American raised in Lowell, Massachusetts and one in Orange County, California, the more salient observation might be how interchangeable the two would probably be with regard to church membership, Greek American outlook, and a strong, rather conservative, feeling for the family. The old country localisms of the immigrants, moreover, tend to be worn down among their progeny into a common Greek American identity. Paradoxically enough, American-born Greeks have become more like each other in their common middle-class standing, social values, and communal participation than are the Greeks of Greece, where class, regional, and political lines are more sharply drawn. The "melting pot" metaphor has been a better describer of the homogenization of American-born Greeks with regard to each other than it is of their absorption into the general American population.

A contrasting interpretation is to emphasize the differences and conflicts within Greek America. A sizable number of the early immigrants, probably a majority, never escaped from the working class. Census data shows that Greek immigrants, taken collectively, have consistently trailed about 10 percent behind the average income levels of native-born American whites. Too much focus on the mainline, predominantly middle-class, Greek American organizations obscures the fact that large numbers of Greek Americans are not part of them. There is some evidence, especially among the American born, that those at the very top of the success ladder and those locked in blue-collar employment are most likely to remove themselves from participation in Greek American social activities. An anticlerical element—at odds with the mainstream, where Greek Orthodoxy holds sway—represents another differentiating feature in the Greek experience in America. Even Greek Orthodoxy in this country is not homogeneous. Beyond cultural differences between the generations, the Church is buffeted by religious currents, notably a charismatic movement, which introduces a subjectivism that temperamentally and sociologically runs against the grain of what is essentially an ethnic and sacramental church.

A preliminary appraisal of Greek American variability must take into account certain specific demographic, economic and cultural factors. Those immigrants who prospered in America were the most likely to remain in this country and establish families here. Not all who returned permanently to Greece did poorly in America, of course, but the proportion of returnees who were economic failures was certainly greater than those who put down roots in the United States. Even among those who did not do well but settled in America, a large number remained bachelors, thereby reducing the potential number of blue-collar parents. Overall, then, the Greek immigrants advancing into the middle class were the most likely to reproduce themselves and pass on values supportive of the Greek American "establishment" to their children. The fundamental question today is to what degree the experiences of the new immigrants and their children will replicate those of their predecessors. It is also very important to remember that about two out of every three Greeks who ever came to the United States were from the Peloponnesus, the region which in modern Greek history is the most conservative in social and political matters. (By way of contrast, the Peloponnesus makes up about 15 percent of the population of contemporary Greece.) Indeed, it would not be too far afield to propose that Greek American culture is an overlay on a Peloponnesian-American base.

The immigrants who came to the United States in the first two decades of this century—and to some degree those of later eras—were products of a cultural ambience and educational system whose *Weltanschauung* understood society in excessively nationalistic terms. The Greek mind, so attuned to national rather than class categories when carried over to this country, worked to blur stratification lines within the immigrant community; it likewise inhibited identity with non-Greeks of the same class position in the broader society. Socialist organization, especially that which looked outward toward the American milieu, was always difficult for the Greek immigrants. The *kafenion* or coffeehouse, the workers' most common grouping, drew minds away from America with nostalgic memories of the old country. Moreover, in the early decades of the century, it seemed unwise to align oneself with "unpatriotic" causes at the very time Greeks were questing for American acceptance. Yet, even under adverse conditions, a Greek American left did appear early on and displayed enduring qualities through the 1940s. Since the 1960s, the Greek American left has again come to represent a distinctive component in Greek America.

That there would be some tension between the new immigrants from Greece and the Greek Americans already here was perhaps inevitable and understandable. Between the old and the new immigrants there would be differences in willingness to take part in existing Greek American associations, and invidious characterizations of moral qualities, political beliefs, and work habits. But it was between American-born Greeks and the newcomers that relations tended to be most strained when not just socially distant. Much of this derives from the contrast in class composition between the earlier and contemporary Greek American populations. In the initial era of mass migration, all Greeks were in the same position of starting at the bottom. Today, on the contrary, there is an uneasy coexistence between, on the one hand, a middle-class grouping of older immigrants and their American-born progeny and, on the other, the large number of new immigrants who are still on the underside of the American social structure. Furthermore, the early arrivals had to stand together simply because all Greeks were looked upon with much the same hostility. In the more tolerant era of the present, it may be that the imperatives for Greek Americans to feel bonded with each other are neither as operative nor as necessary as before.

In almost all of its facets, the Greek American community has been one in which infighting and jealousy are not unknown. Here and there one can find petty personalities in positions of leadership, now and again a drop into vitriolic clashes over organizational resources, language use, and political matters. But to make too much of this can be misleading. One must understand Greek American communal life as part of the general rule that people are at their most involved when acting with those they know intimately rather than for abstract causes or faceless classes. This is also how we are to understand the intensely personal politics of Greek American organizations.

Hellenic Diaspora or American Ethnics. The intellectual quandary of Greek American studies is its relation to modern Greek studies.[66] Two versions of the Greek experience in America compete. One is that Greek Americans are to be understood as part of a homeland extension, a *homogenia,* a Hellenic diaspora. The other approach is to see Greek Americans as entrants and then participants in American history. Which of these—to be sure overstated—versions are we to accept? There is no simple answer, for each contains part of the truth.

The paradigm of the diaspora is that one's cultural roots and political sensitivities must be nourished by a responsiveness to contemporary Greek realities—even if at a distance. The diaspora understanding, paradoxically enough, is one in which Hellenic traditionalists and many Greek American leftists find some agreement. The underlying presumption is that, whether residing or even born in the United States, Greeks in America share a destiny somehow connected with other people who call themselves Hellenes. The fact that most of the early immigrants continued to maintain strong emotional and personal ties to Greece—and that a sizable fraction actually returned to the old country—speaks clearly to the diaspora persuasion. Among the new immigrants, as well, there was a strong undercurrent to come to America on a trial basis. If things turned out well, they were prepared to remain; if not, they would pack up and return to Greece. Even among the American-born generations there are some who put their "Greekness" at the very center of their social identity. The diaspora perspective also raises the problems of crisscrossing, perhaps conflicting, loyalties toward Greece and the United

---

[66]In an important sense, one of the accomplishments of scholars of modern Greece was to assert the legitimacy of their subject matter by differentiating it from classical Greek and Byzantine studies. In a parallel fashion, it can be argued, Greek American studies will remain undeveloped unless it is separated from modern Greek studies.

States, problems normally hushed in the Greek American community. Among its more analytical proponents, the diaspora view implies that the Greek immigrant phenomenon—to America and elsewhere—is better grasped as a profound outcome of the political economy of modern Greece than as a minor theme in the American historical experience.[67]

A quite different view is that Greek Americans must be placed in the broad context of the ethnic experience in the United States. Whatever the fulness of their traditional heritage and allegiances to the old country, the Greek immigrants who came to these shores inevitably reordered their lives; initially, to the imperatives of the economic and social structure of the United States and, later, to some degree of conformance with American cultural norms. Among those born in this country, it seems clear that one's identity is not that of a transplanted Greek, but rather the sensibility of an American ethnic. The ethnic perspective, however, is not without its own controversy. It has long been assumed that immigrant nationalities would pass through successive generations in progressively diluted form until a point was reached where they would disappear as recognizable entities. This position has been strongly challenged by a renewed appreciation of the endurance, even if modified, of distinctive ethnic subcultures.

A useful distinction has been made between acculturation and assimilation. Acculturation refers to the acquisition by the immigrants and their descendants of the cultural behavior —language, norms, customs—of the host society. Assimilation implies the entrance of the ethnics into the very fabric—the social cliques, business life, civic activities, and, eventually, the families—of the receiving society.[68] Usually acculturation proceeds faster than assimilation. The Greek American case, however, shows a more obdurate pattern. Acculturation has probably lagged behind assimilation. This is the only way to understand continuing Greek Orthodox affiliation and the

[67]The Hellenic diaspora viewpoint is not a homogeneous one, however. Compare, for example, the neo-Marxian interpretation of Nicos P. Mouzelis, *Modern Greece: Facets of Underdevelopment* (New York: Holmes and Meier, 1978) with the demographic-cum-ecological perspective in William H. McNeil, *The Metamorphosis of Greece since World War II* (Chicago: University of Chicago Press, 1978).

[68]The most influential statement of this thesis is found in Milton M. Gordon, *Assimilation in American Life* (New York: Oxford University Press, 1964).

baroque structure of organized Greek America in the face of such assimilative measures as economic ascendancy, political representation, and even intermarriage. There has been the further assumption, moreover, that twentieth-century ethnic persistencies were mainly to be found in working-class ethnic neighborhoods.[69] But such an understanding has little applicability to upwardly mobile and geographically dispersed ethnics, such as American-born Greeks, for whom ethnic identification is more a matter of cultural choice than a constraint of the social structure.

A more productive formulation of ethnicity pulls together the analytically separable variables of descent, culture, and self-identification.[70] By looking at the changing interaction of these factors over the time elapsed from the initial arrival of the immigrants, one can ascertain not so much the degree of continuity of the immigrant heritage, but, more centrally, account for the appearance of new forms of ethnic consciousness that may alternately wane and wax in relation to the common American culture. The brand of Hellenism in America, therefore, should not be confused with that of the homeland or of recent immigrants. Rather than viewing Greek American ethnicity as an increasingly pale reflection of an old country culture, we would be better advised to consider and respect it in its own right.

Some of the issues in sorting out the different conclusions between and within the Hellenic diaspora and American ethnic perspectives could be illuminated by looking at Greek immigration to other countries.[71] Close to a hundred thousand Cypriot Greeks reside in England, along with a smaller number of immigrants from mainland Greece.[72] Several hundred

[69]See, for example, Herbert J. Gans, *The Urban Villagers* (New York: Free Press, 1962) ; Stanley Lieberson, *Ethnic Patterns in American Cities* (New York: Free Press, 1963) ; and William L. Yancey, Eugene P. Ericksen, and Richard N. Juliana, "Emergent Ethnicity," *American Sociological Review* 41:3 (June 1976) 391-403.

[70]Andrew M. Greeley, *Ethnicity in the United States* (New York: John Wiley and Sons, 1974) 290-317.

[71]A compendium of overseas Greek communities and migration statistics is *Apodimoi Hellenes* [Greeks abroad] Athens: National Centre of Social Research, 1972).

[72]Of the approximately 110,000 Greeks residing in England in the late 1970s, about 90 percent were Cypriots. A useful, though somewhat dated, study is A.D. Christodoulis, *Ekthesis epi tou Provlematos tes en M. Bretannia Hellenikes Parekias* [Report on the problems of the Greek

thousand Greeks labor in the Federal Republic of Germany as *Gastarbeiter* or "guest workers."[73] A Greek community of indeterminate size has existed in what is today the Soviet Union from tsarist times.[74] Smaller numbers of Greeks are found in the Near East, Africa, Eastern Europe, and Latin America. But the most salient comparisons of the Greek American experience are to be made with the Greeks of Canada and Australia, the two other predominantly Anglo-Saxon continental countries which have received large numbers of Greek immigrants. In point of fact, Greek Canadians and, especially, Greek Australians, though less in total number, make up a larger proportion of their respective countries than do Greek Americans. Some research has been done on Greek Canadians and Greek Australians, though, up to now, it has not been placed within a comparative framework.[75] Even a cursory

colony in Great Britain] (Nicosia, Cyprus: mimeographed, 1967). In 1978, Robin Oakely was completing a major research study on Cypriot migration and settlement in England.

[73]A theoretical statement and some of the bibliography on Greek laborers in Northern Europe can be found in Demetrios G. Papademetriou, "European Labor Migration," *International Studies Quarterly* 22:3 (September 1978) 377-408. The results of attitudinal surveys of Greek workers in Germany and other Northern European countries are given in Elie Dimitras, *Enquêtes sociologiques sur les émigrants grecs*, vols. 1 and 2, and volume 3 of that same series, by Elie Dimitras and Evangelos C. Vlachos, *Sociological Surveys on Greek Immigrants* (Athens: Naitonal Centre of Social Research, 1971).

[74]Large numbers of Greeks settled along the northern coast of the Black Sea and in the nearby Caucasus during the eighteenth and nineteenth centuries. In 1944, Stalin, in one of his most ruthless actions, deported en masse the Greeks—along with other minorities—to central Asia. See Aleksandr M. Nekrich, *The Punished Peoples* (New York: W. W. Norton, 1978) 104-5. A quite different group of Greeks in the Soviet Union are the several score thousand guerillas and their families who sought haven following the communist defeat in the Greek Civil War in 1949. As late as 1960, there were some 300,000 reported Greeks in the USSR, of whom about 40 percent regarded Greek as their mother tongue. See S.V. Vtechin, *A Concise Encyclopaedia of Russia* (New York: E. P. Dutton, 1964) 210.

[75]On the Greeks in Canada, see the excellent study of the new migrants in Judith A. Nagata, "Adaptation and Integration of Greek Working Class Immigrants in the City of Toronto, Canada," *International Migration Review* 4:3 (Fall 1969) 44-69. An interesting examination of the effects of cultural determinants on Greek economic achievement in Canada is Peter D. Chimbos, "Ethnicity and Occupational Mobility," *International Journal of Comparative Sociology* 15:1-2 (March-June 1974) 57-67. Dated and unscholarly but useful is George D. Vlassis,

glance at Greek Canada and Greek Australia, however, reveals both parallels and contrasts with the Greek experience in America.[76]

In sum, Greek American studies must take debate about its own nature as part of its recognized subject matter. It may

The Greeks in Canada (Ottawa: privately printed, 1953). Despite their promising titles, there is not much information to be found in Peter Stathopoulos, The Greek Community of Montreal (Athens: National Centre of Social Research, 1971); or Efrosini Gavaki, The Integration of Greeks in Canada (San Francisco: R and E Research Associates, 1977).

All interested in Greek Australians must make reference to Charles Price, ed., Greeks in Australia (Canberra: Australia National University Press, 1975). See especially the social history given by Mick P. Tsounis, "Greek Communities in Australia," in ibid., 18-71. A perceptive account of Greek factory workers is Petro Georgiou, "Migrants, Unionism and Society," Australia and New Zealand Journal of Sociology 9: 1 (February 1973) 32-51. On Greek Australian political struggles, see Mick P. Tsounis, "The Greek Left in Australia," Australian Left Review, no. 29 (March 1971) 53-60; and Christina Holbraad, "Ethnic Culture and Political Participation: A Study of Greeks in Australia, 1926-1970," unpublished doctoral thesis, Australian National University, 1978. On the Greeks in New Zealand, see J. Baddeley, "The Church and the Coffeehouse," Urban Anthropology 6:3 (Fall 1977) 217-36.

[76]It is estimated that in 1980 there were over 300,000 Greek Australians and around 140,000 Greek Canadians, or about 2.1 percent and .6 percent of the total populations of their respective countries—compared to about .5 percent of Greek descent in the United States. The Hellenic presence in these two countries is especially visible because the overwhelming majority live in major cities: Melbourne and Sydney in Australia, Toronto and Montreal in Canada. Relative to the United States, that is, Greeks are much more geographically concentrated in Australia or Canada.

The conflicts within Greek Australia and Greek Canada parallel but are much more pronounced than those in Greek America. The older, more established Greeks along with their progeny often find themselves at odds with the more proletarian new migrants. But unlike in the United States, the numerical preponderance in Australia and Canada clearly lies with the new arrivals. Especially in Australia, Greek leftist groups contend with the Greek Orthodox Archdiocese for leadership within the Greek community.

Greek Australians and Greek Canadians are certainly much more "Greek" than are Greek Americans, though much of this can be laid to the recency of their arrival. A look at the demographics, however, indicates some constriction in the Greek immigrant population. The mass migration of the 1960s has crested and since the mid-1970s the outflow back to the old country may be approaching the number of Greeks coming in. Although repatriation has been a major feature of Greek immigrants in the United States, impermanency in the new country appears

seem disappointing to some readers that I make no unequivo-
cal assertions one way or the other about the outcomes of
Greek America. Only two general truths emerge from a dis-
passionate look at the Greek American experience. One is that
assimilation tends to occur much more, and more quickly, than
Greek traditionalists think. The other is that Greek ethnic
persistencies change much less, and more slowly, or are recon-
stituted more than assimilationists might think. Both truths
tend to operate in such a way that Greek Americans will always find what happens somewhat surprising.

to be much more characteristic of Greek migrants in Australia and
Canada. Among native-born Greek Australians and Greek Canadians,
processes of assimilation and outmarriage are at least as evident as
among second-generation Greek Americans.

CHAPTER 3

THE GREEK POPULATION OF
NEW YORK CITY

BY

EVA E. SANDIS

It is somewhat surprising to find the dearth of published work on the Greek population of New York City as compared with that about Greeks in Lowell, Massachusetts, Detroit, Chicago, Denver, or San Antonio, Texas. This is particularly so when one considers that for many of the immigrants who have headed toward places such as these, New York City has been the port of disembarkation, and for many more, their final destination. Some general works, it is true, have incorporated data on Greeks in New York, and during the last decade, unpublished doctoral theses have begun to deal with aspects of Greek life in the metropolis. The objective of the present study is to pull these materials together and attempt a brief assessment of the state of our knowledge about the metropolis' Greek population. It concludes with some suggestions for research strategies which may be usefully employed in future investigations.

Early Greek Settlement of New York

"New York was their first settling place," observed the philhellene Anglican clergyman Thomas Burgess, writing about the first Greek immigrants of the 1880s who arrived from the Peloponnesus. By 1895, he noted, they had settled

65

"by hundreds" in the city.[1] The earliest settlements were located on the East Side, in Chelsea, and in the South Bronx.[2]

Numbers. The primacy of New York City and State by 1913 over the rest of the country in the number of Greeks is shown by Canoutas. According to his estimate, out of a total of 253,100 Greeks in the United States in 1913, New York State led in the number of resident Greeks with 32,000, followed by Massachusetts (31,000) and Illinois (30,000). The breakdown by cities within New York State at that time, as estimated by Canoutas, is given in the following table:

New York, incl. Brooklyn	20,000
Albany	400
Buffalo	1,000
Schenectady	500
Yonkers	300
all other places	10,000
TOTAL	**32,200**[3]

Occupations. The Greeks, like other immigrant groups in New York, pursued their economic goals along two routes: they cultivated the commercial needs of their own ethnic enclave, while, at the same time, they vied for control over the city's larger commercial and manufacturing interests. Thus, at the turn of the twentieth century, Greeks, Italians, and Jews competed for the wholesale food business, produce hauling, and the trucking and moving industries. All of these groups met on the corner stands where they tried to outsell each other as street peddlers, fruit and vegetable vendors, and florists.[4]

Statistics bear out the fact that New York City became "the citadel of the florist trade" in the United States.[5] The approximately 150 Greek florist establishments in New York

[1]Thomas Burgess, *Greeks in America* (New York: Arno Press, 1970; originally published in Boston, 1913) 34.

[2]HANAC Staff, *The Needs of the Growing Greek-American Community in the City of New York* (New York: HANAC, 1973) 87.

[3]Burgess, 231, citing statistics compiled by Canoutas.

[4]Andrea Simon, "The Sacred Sect and the Secular Church: Symbols of Ethnicity in Astoria's Greek Community," unpublished doctoral thesis, City University of New York, 1977, pp. 16-19.

[5]Theodore Saloutos, *The Greeks in the United States* (Cambridge, Mass.: Harvard University Press, 1964) 260.

City seemed to constitute "a kind of monopoly," Burgess noted, adding that "Mayor Gaynor of New York, on his daily walk to City Hall, gets his boutonniere from a Greek flower girl's stand."[6]

Greeks in New York were second only to those in Chicago in the development of the confectionery business.[7] The year 1885 saw the establishment of one of the earliest Greek restaurants on Roosevelt Street on New York's Lower East Side. By 1912 there were about two hundred.[8] Although first catering to Greeks, the restaurants subsequently began to cater to the quick-lunch crowds in the densely populated parts of lower New York. Profitable businesses developed as a result of low overhead costs and family labor.

Finally, the fur industry was an important source of employment for Greeks in New York City from early on.[9]

Church, School, Social Life. As soon as Greeks had arrived in New York City, they went about the task of establishing their churches, schools, and regional associations. The first Greek Orthodox Church of New York City was established in 1892. As Saloutos describes it, "during 1892, about 500 Greeks met in a small hotel on Roosevelt Street where they organized the Society of Athena" and determined to secure a priest and establish a church. Eventually, an archimandrite, Paisios Ferentinos, was sent by the Holy Synod of Greece. He arrived from Patmos to serve as the first priest of the new parish, Holy Trinity. Soon dissension split the parish, and eventually a new one, that of the Annunciation, was formed, with a priest from the theological school at Chalkis, Callinicos Dilbaes. He had been sent by the Ecumenical Patriarchate, unaware of what was going on.[10]

In 1918, the recently elevated Metropolitan of Athens, Meletios Metaxakis, on his first trip to the United States to organize the Greek Orthodox churches, visited New York City and designated Alexander, his assistant in the Athens see, and like him, a Venizelist, as his first American bishop. In 1922, during the Metropolitan's second stay in the United

[6]Burgess, 36.
[7]Ibid., 35; Saloutos, 262.
[8]Burgess, 34, 37.
[9]Charles C. Moskos, Jr., *Greek Americans: Struggle and Success* (Englewood Cliffs, N.J.: Prentice-Hall, 1980) 24.
[10]Saloutos, 123.

States—after being deposed as head of the Greek Church upon the 1920 royalist restoration—Metaxakis "laid the groundwork for the formal incorporation, under the statutes of the State of New York, of the Greek Archdiocese of North and South America."[11] Subsequently, upon his elevation to the throne of the Ecumenical Patriarchate, he appointed Alexander as first Archbishop, and transferred the dependence of his Archdiocese to the Patriarchate.[12]

Closely associated with the development of the Greek Church was the development of Greek schools, for the preservation of the children's language and religion. As early as 1911, Burgess records the purchase of "a large and suitable building" in the Bronx, costing $35,000, for this purpose.[13]

That event foreshadowed developments of the twenties and thirties, when new US immigration legislation made entry of persons from Southern and Eastern Europe difficult. Greek immigration was decimated. Those who now came, came to be reunited as families, and came to stay. This contrasted with the years prior to World War I, during which the migratory pattern had been one of males who planned to return to Greece after accomplishing their economic goals in America. Between 1908 and 1912, 40,718 aliens departed for Greece, and between 1913 and 1917, 58,365 emigrant aliens gave Greece as their intended residence, according to the US Commissioner General's Reports. Among those Greeks who stayed and married in the United States, intermarriage was not uncommon. A study by Drachsler found that 22 percent of Greek marriages in New York City were with non-Greek wives in the period 1908-1912.[14]

From the beginning, the immigrants had a predilection for forming regional, or "home-town," societies. As early as 1900, in New York alone, there were thirty such societies in existence.[15] An incomplete list of twenty-four Greek societies in New York City in 1911, furnished by Burgess to show the "number and variety" of these associations, includes nineteen regional societies, as well as two business associations, an

[11]Moskos, 35-6.
[12]Saloutos, 289.
[13]Burgess, 76.
[14]Julius Drachsler, *Intermarriage in New York City* (New York: Columbia University Press, 1921).
[15]Saloutos, 75.

athletic association, a ladies charitable group, and a volunteer military company.[16]

Politics, Political Clubs, and Newspapers. "Politics," in the minds of the early Greek immigrants to New York, meant Greek politics. Royalist and Venizelist sentiments, rather than American political issues, absorbed their attention and were the subject of their political debates.

Fewer than 20 percent of the Greeks were naturalized American citizens by 1917. As America turned increasingly isolationist in the post-World War I period, the Loyalty Leagues of New York launched a naturalization campaign designed to prevent hostilities from being vented against Greek aliens. As Saloutos describes it, on May 1, 1919, "200 filed out of Evangelismos Church and went to City Hall to declare their citizenship intention."[17]

As the immigration gates closed and the immigrants settled down in the United States to form Greek communities, their political concerns began to include some American issues. By the 1920s, Greek political clubs existed in New York, as in all major Greek communities. Fragmentary information suggests that sizable segments of the politically active in New York and New Jersey worked on behalf of the Democratic Party.[18] The two New York dailies took opposing political stances. The Democratic-oriented *National Herald* supported Franklin D. Roosevelt in his campaign for President in 1932. The *Atlantis,* on the other hand, professed Republican principles.

In 1894 Solon J. Vlastos, a New York community leader of Cretan descent who had come to the city as a youth in 1873, started to publish the *Atlantis* as a triweekly.[19] By 1912, it was a daily with a circulation of twenty to twenty-five thousand and was read throughout the country.[20] Whereas the *Atlantis* was a defender of Greek royalist policies, the *National Herald,* first published in New York City in 1915, was pro-Venizelist. Over the years, while other papers had short-lived histories, these two New York papers enjoyed a loyal following and a nationwide circulation.

[16]Burgess, 61.
[17]Saloutos, 185, 234.
[18]Ibid., 243.
[19]Ibid., 89.
[20]Burgess, 67.

The Greek Population of New York City Today

Numbers, Distribution, and Social Characteristics. A breakdown by states in the 1970 census shows that the primacy of New York State in terms of number of Greeks continues from the early days. Approximately one in four of all Greek Americans resides in the Empire State. Illinois is second in the number of Greeks, followed by California, Massachusetts, and New Jersey. In the 1970s, New York State also had the third-highest ratio of Greek Americans to the total state population, exceeded only by New Hampshire and Massachusetts.[21]

New York City's Greek American population during the 1970s has been estimated at about 300,000, based on projections from census and Archdiocesan data, as well as the educated estimates of knowledgeable sources.[22] These estimates are in sharp contrast to the official United States census figure for New York City's Greek stock in 1970: 63,854.[23] On the other hand, the estimates are conservative relative to some figures that have been put forward. The numbers vary, of course, according to who is included in the definition of a "Greek."

The US census uses national origins (Greece) plus descent (the cutoff is the second generation) as the basis for its ethnic stock count. The census category "foreign stock"—which comprises "all first and second-generation Americans"—includes the foreign born (first generation) and the native born of foreign or mixed parentage (second generation).[24] Not included in the census count are third and fourth-generation Greeks, those born in areas of the Greek diaspora—such as Asia Minor, Egypt, and Bulgaria, who consider themselves Greek despite non-Greek nationality—and underreported immigrants, both legal and illegal.

In May 1973, the Hellenic American Neighborhood Action Committee (HANAC) undertook a handcount and analysis of census tract 115 in Astoria, Queens, to better assess the influence of factors such as these on the 1970 census count. Whereas the census had counted 409 Greeks in tract 115, HANAC's

[21]Moskos, 65.
[22]Ibid.; HANAC, 14.
[23]See New York City, Department of City Planning, *1970 Census.*
[24]US Bureau of the Census, *Census of the Population 1970*, vol. 2, *Subject Reports*, "National Origin and Language," appendix C.

total was 838. Extrapolating from this discrepancy, and on the basis of additional considerations, HANAC estimated the city's Greek population to be close to 333,000, and to be composed of the following population groups:

GROUP	NUMBER	%
borough population	180,000	54
new immigrants	78,391	24
illegal aliens	62,842	19
refugees	11,723	3
TOTAL	332,956	100[25]

The category of "new immigrants" also includes students and temporary workers and their families who have adjusted their status. The projections include adjustments for internal growth of the immigrant community.

Despite the undercount of the Greek population by the census, these statistics are in accord with Archdiocesan and other data about the ongoing concentration of the city's Greek population in Queens, as well as the continuing existence of substantial Greek sectors in Manhattan and Brooklyn, with some scattered groupings in the Bronx and on Staten Island. In all boroughs except Richmond, the Greek-born population has tended to outnumber the second generation. This has been particularly true in Manhattan, and somewhat less so in Queens, Brooklyn, and the Bronx. The percentages of foreign born are given in the accompanying tabulation.

GREEK FOREIGN STOCK BY BOROUGH : 1970

BOROUGH	NUMBER GREEK FOREIGN STOCK	% FOREIGN BORN
Manhattan	11,678	57.4
Queens	32,298	56.3
Brooklyn	13,249	52.4
Bronx	5,513	50.1
Richmond	1,116	34.5
TOTAL	63,854	54.8[26]

[25]HANAC, 14.
[26]NYC, *1970 Census*, table PS-2, New York City & Boroughs.

The Astoria section of Queens has become the largest Hellenic settlement outside of Greece or Cyprus. With the influx of immigrants since the late sixties added to Greek Americans already residing there, it is estimated to have a population of from sixty to seventy thousand Greeks.[27] Initial Greek migration into Astoria did not begin until the early 1920s, after lengthy stays in Manhattan. Neither the Greek community nor Astoria experienced much growth in the thirties and forties, during the Depression and the war years. Only in the post-World War II years did the trend reverse itself. As Simon points out, the recent arrivals who came to Astoria to live, directly upon their arrival in this country in the late sixties and early seventies, gave a new lease on life to a section of the city just as it was beginning to feel the pinch of the more widespread problems of urban decay and suburbanization.[28]

Even in the most populated Greek enclaves in Queens, it is notable that the population has remained outnumbered by those of Italian descent. In each of these tracts, first and second-generation Italian Americans accounted for 23 to 29 percent of the population. In tract 115, for example, which according to the census had 409 persons of Greek stock in 1970 (and according to HANAC's 1973 recount, 838), the Italian stock numbered 905—or 29 percent of the tract's population of 3,112—and this may well have involved an "Italian" undercount on the part of the census.

The Greek population of Brooklyn has tended to be more residentially dispersed than the Greek population of Astoria. This has also been the case in Manhattan. Here, Greeks are not infrequently found in the same tracts as Cubans—for example, in the Washington Heights area.

With respect to demographic characteristics such as age and sex, the 1977 registered alien count of the US Immigration and Naturalization Service provides some data. It gives the age distribution of the 18,239 Greeks in New York City who were either permanent or temporary residents (94 and 6 percent respectively). The modal age category was 25 to 34 years, as would be expected of an immigrant group. The next most frequent age category was 45 to 64 years, presumably the result of immigration legislation (of 1965) favoring family reunification, e.g., with parents.

[27]Moskos, 56.
[28]Simon, 72-109.

More trend-indicative information about the age distribution of the Greek population in the New York metropolitan area is provided by the 1970 census. A "Standard Metropolitan Statistical Area" (SMSA), according to the census, is a county which contains at least one "central city" of fifty thousand or more inhabitants. In addition, contiguous counties are included in an SMSA if they are socially and economically integrated with the central city. According to the 1970 census, the New York SMSA comprised, in addition to the five boroughs with their 7.9 million people, the counties of Nassau, Suffolk, Rockland, and Westchester, with a population of 3.6 million.[29] A comparison of the ages of foreign-born Greeks, second-generation Greeks, and the native-born population of native parentage residing in the New York SMSA shows that the age distribution for males and females of Greek descent tends to approximate that of the native-born population as one moves from the first to the second generation. Whereas only 8.7 percent of the foreign-born Greek males and 11.0 percent of the females are under 18 years of age, at least one-third of both males and females of Greek descent of the second generation fall into this under-18 age category. On the other hand, there is a drop in the proportion of those over 65 years old as one moves from the foreign-born to the second generation.

AGE DISTRIBUTION OF GREEK NEW YORKERS
BY SEX AND GENERATION

MALES	FOREIGN-BORN GREEK	SECOND-GENERATION GREEK	WHITE NATIVE-BORN OF NATIVE PARENTAGE
under 18	8.7%	37.7%	44.8%
18-64	72.2	61.0	50.6
65 and over	19.1	1.3	4.6
	(n = 21,435)	(n = 19,730)	(n = 2,587,825)

FEMALES			
under 18	11.0	33.3	39.4
18-64	70.7	65.7	54.0
65 and over	18.3	1.0	6.6
	(n = 18,257)	(n = 19,709)	(n = 2,765,044)[30]

[29]US Bureau of the Census, *1970 Census of Population and Housing*, PHC (1)-145, New York, N.Y. SMSA, part 1.
[30]US Bureau of the Census, *Census of the Population: 1960*, vol. 1,

The sex distribution also shows characteristic differences between the first and second generation, according to both the 1960 and 1970 census data for the New York SMSA. According to both decennial counts, males predominated among the first-generation Greeks (58.6 and 54.0 percent respectively), but by the second generation the sex ratio was balanced.

Educational and Occupational Mobility, Mobility Orientations, and Integration of New Immigrants Into the Labor Market. According to all indications, New York's Greeks have shown remarkable educational mobility. Tavuchis made a perceptive study of the social mobility and kinship patterns of a nonrandom sample of fifty second-generation Greek American males. All those included in the sample were native-born Americans of Greek or mixed parentage, married, who had graduated from high school, were employed full time, and were residents of the New York metropolitan area. Most respondents were located through the help of the Archdiocese and many belonged to the same parish.[31]

Tavuchis found that although 80 percent of all parents and parents-in-law had the equivalent of an eighth grade education or less, 68 percent of the respondents were at least college graduates. The educational level of the respondents' brothers and brothers-in-law was only slightly below their own.[32] On the other hand, substantial sex differences in educational level remained. Only 18 percent of the wives and 19 percent of the respondents' sisters had completed college or gone beyond.

The 1970 census data for the New York SMSA corroborates the intergenerational educational mobility of the Greeks. It also indicates a substantial narrowing of the educational gap between males and females from the first to the second generation. According to the census, the median of years of school completed for natives of Greek or mixed parentage in 1970 was 12.6 years for males and 12.5 years for females. These medians are higher than those for native-born whites of native parentage, both males and females.[33]

Characteristics of the Population, "General Social and Economic Characteristics, New York," table 99; and *Census of the Population: 1970,* vol. 1, PC1-C34, "General Social and Economic Characteristics, New York."

[31]Nicholas Tavuchis, *Family and Mobility among Greek-Americans* (Athens: National Centre of Social Research, 1972) 28-9.

[32]Ibid., 49 (n.1), 133.

[33]*Census of the Population: 1970,* PC2: table 15.

With respect to jobs, Tavuchis found that the overwhelming majority of respondents had achieved occupations substantially higher than their fathers or fathers-in-law. Whereas most first-generation males' jobs were in the managerial or service workers category, with very few professionals or clerical workers, among the second generation, most (82 percent) were professionals or managerial executives.[34] Sons, for example, who were engineers, attorneys, or advertising agency owners had fathers who were florists, owned diners, or worked as countermen, waiters, or cooks.

The findings also suggested that the respondents held a "slight edge" over their siblings and siblings-in-law with regard to occupational achievement, and that the rate of mobility had not been the same for all kin of orientation.[35] Kin utilized a variety of mechanisms to keep such differences from straining family ties. Other, extraclass criteria were sometimes employed to define the success of a person, such as the quality of his marriage, e.g., whether he had married a Greek partner, or the comparisons were simply viewed as "irrelevant." Other mechanisms mentioned by Tavuchis were commitment to kinship values, and vicarious identification with successful kinsmen.[36]

With respect to mobility orientation, the study found "abundant evidence" of a strong commitment to mobility values among the respondents. This was evidenced both by the "strong emphasis placed upon education" as a means of rising in the class structure, and by the "recognition of the potential significance of acculturation"—e.g., the changing and modification of surnames—as a factor in social mobility.[37]

The 1970 census data for the New York SMSA tends to support Tavuchis' finding of Greek intergenerational occupational mobility. Whereas the occupational distribution of foreign-born Greek males showed a heavy concentration in the crafts (21.1 percent) and service work (33.6 percent), second-generation Greek males evinced a predominantly white-collar occupational distribution, with sizable concentrations in the professions (19.7 percent) and in managerial jobs (16.7 percent). In fact, they exceeded the percentage of native whites of native parentage found in these, as well as in the "sales"

[34]Tavuchis, 48.
[35]Ibid., 52.
[36]Ibid., 61, 170.
[37]Ibid., 42.

job, categories. First-generation Greek women in the New York labor force were mainly operatives (46.6 percent), whereas in the second generation, the majority (53.8 percent) were clerical workers, in proportions even exceeding the native whites of native parentage.[38]

The 1970 census data for the New York SMSA also shows that although the median family income of the Greek-born ($8,631) was considerably below that of native-born white New Yorkers ($11,300), that of second-generation Greeks was substantially above it ($12,958), again suggesting rapid intergenerational economic mobility.

Simon's study—of religious practices of Greeks in New York as related to their perceptions of social class and their actual positions—provides some interesting comparative data on the issue of intergenerational mobility. Simon's nonrandom sample included sixty-five members of St. Demetrios' Church in Astoria, mainly first-generation Greeks who had come to the United States in the early post-World War II years and had moved to Astoria in the sixties after first gaining an economic foothold in Manhattan; and thirty members of St. Markela's "rebel" Church, also in Astoria, most of whom were more recent immigrants of the late sixties and early seventies who had come to live in Astoria directly upon their arrival in the country.[39]

On the basis of her study, in which she used interviews and participant observation techniques, Simon concluded that some Greeks pursue "a strategy of assimilation" and upward occupational mobility for themselves and their children; others follow "a strategy of incapsulation." Both strategies are derived from their "positions in the class hierarchy."[40] Most of the Greeks from St. Demetrios, she noted, viewed themselves "as members of the middle class or on their way into it." They either were independently employed, were working in managerial positions, or were professionals. "Their American-born children often held occupations which established clearly" their parents' claims to middle-class positions.[41]

The Greek members of St. Markela's, as Simon describes them, were not necessarily in working-class jobs, but they

[38]*Census of the Population: 1970*, PC2: table 16.
[39]Simon, 121, 163.
[40]Ibid., 235.
[41]Ibid., 148, 194.

were, and perceived themselves to be, economically powerless.[42] Many had arrived just before the United States recession in 1972. Some were downwardly mobile occupationally. Few were self-employed men, and they often worked for non-Greeks. Most were employed in the restaurant business, as waiters, busboys, and dishwashers.[43]

While both groups of Greeks wanted their children to be socially mobile, to those pursuing the strategy of assimilation —regardless of own occupational level—this meant white-collar careers for their children, preferably in the professions. To those pursuing a strategy of incapsulation, family interest came first, in practice. In a couple of cases, boys had left school to help their families earn enough money to return to Greece.[44]

Employment opportunities for the newest immigrants, indeed, have often been associated with the traditional food business, with shoe repairing, dry cleaning, and the like. However, as Moskos has noted, arrivals since the late-sixties, in New York especially, are to be found as pizza parlor operators, taxicab drivers, and pushcart vendors of frankfurters, ice cream, and hot chestnuts.[45]

HANAC discusses some of the exploitative practices facing Greek "greenhorns" and especially illegal aliens: "off the books" employment, underscale wages, and work without benefits such as paid sick leave, health insurance, or paid vacations.[46]

An examination of the occupational breakdowns of Greek immigrants who entered the United States in 1977 shows that almost nine out of ten (88.3 percent) entered on relative preferences, that is to say, without a job offer.[47] According to their occupational background in Greece, the largest number of those who had held jobs were craftsmen.[48] Judging by their initial job opportunities in places like New York, some downward occupational mobility appears to be a characteristic experience for many recent Greek immigrants, at least initially, as they enter service or operative jobs. Over half the entering

[42]Ibid., 206.
[43]Ibid., 183.
[44]Ibid., 177-8.
[45]Moskos, 55.
[46]HANAC, 42.
[47]US Department of Justice, Immigration and Naturalization Service, *1977 Annual Report*, table 7A.
[48]Ibid., table 8.

immigrants (55.6 percent) have been housewives, and for many of these, entry into the New York labor market, as an operative or sales clerk, is their first experience of work in a nonfamily connected business outside the home.

Changing Family and Kinship Patterns. There is widespread agreement that Greek American families exhibit a trend toward a less patriarchal structure and the development of characteristics similar to those predominant in American society as a whole. The dislocation of traditional patterns is noticeable in such developments as the lessening of male dominance among spouses, the diminution of parental discipline over children, and the increasing selectivity of kin relations.[49]

Tavuchis' finding that 90 percent of his New York area households consisted of either a husband and wife living alone or with unmarried children suggests that "second generation Greeks do in fact exhibit conformity to the conjugal family ideal." On the other hand, a vast majority of the respondents lived within easy reach of their parents and parents-in-law, siblings and spouses' siblings.[50] The study found a relatively high level of interaction between respondents and their parents, with respect to most categories of mutual aid—instrumental, including gift giving and extending professional services like recommending a dentist; performance of personal services such as child care, in-home repair, and help in emergencies like sickness; and affective aid, such as giving advice and discussing problems.

An interesting observation by Tavuchis is that despite the stereotype of the authoritative Greek father, little advice was passed on from father to son. He explains it thus: "For our own respondents as well as a large but unknown proportion of second generation Americans, the father emerges as a shadowy, distant figure throughout childhood and adolescence." The result of the menial jobs of these fathers, combined with long hours of work, was that sons and daughters "simply lacked the opportunity to develop those close and intimate ties with their fathers until late in life." Therefore, instrumental

---

[49]See Chrysie M. Costantakos, *The American-Greek Subculture: Processes of Continuity,* American Ethnic Groups Series (New York: Arno Press, 1980) ; Moskos, *Greek Americans;* and Evangelos C. Vlachos, *The Assimilation of Greeks in the United States* (Athens: National Centre of Social Research, 1968).

[50]Tavuchis, 73, 135.

and expressive activities tended to be fused in the mother.[51]

Tavuchis' data also showed extensive interaction between siblings and siblings-in-law, both face-to-face and by telephone. All the respondents and their siblings gave to or received from each other some form of assistance.[52] Although no data was available on interaction with godparents—a very important relationship among Greeks—we would hypothesize a relatively high level of interaction with godchildren, including reciprocal mutual aid, as a continuing pattern among the second generation.

The interaction patterns of the second-generation Greek Americans with their parents (and parents-in-law) and with their siblings and siblings-in-law were in accord with their felt obligations toward both those of the older generation and those of their own. In response to the question, "What obligations do you think people have to parents?" three major themes were universally stressed by Tavuchis' respondents: financial or instrumental aid, affective or socioemotional support, and deference or respect.[53] Obligations to siblings were viewed as somewhat more diffuse, partly because there were no status differences involved. Nevertheless, one owed siblings "unqualified support" in the instrumental and expressive spheres. Toward a sister, brothers expressed the additional obligation of "protection" until marriage. Siblings-in-law were simply viewed as "friends" in terms of obligations.[54]

Costantakos' doctoral thesis dealt in detail with the question of continuing subcultural continuity among Greek Americans. The community selected to investigate this issue was that of the Three Hierarchs, in the Bay Ridge section of Brooklyn, which in 1970 was estimated to have about six thousand Greeks, with a continuing influx of newcomers from Greece.[55] Costantakos' nonrandom sample included 33 pre-World War II immigrants ("old"), 39 immigrants who arrived after World War II but mainly before the changes in the 1965 immigration legislation ("recent"), 90 second and 40 third-generation Greek Americans, and a residual group of nine others of Greek background ("other").[56] The "third gen-

[51]Ibid., 121.
[52]Ibid., 156, 158.
[53]Ibid., 91.
[54]Ibid., 137, 140, 142.
[55]Costantakos, 145.
[56]Ibid., Apendix, table 41.

eration" group included respondents of intergenerational status—those who derived third-generation status from the mother and second-generation status from the father.[57] The rationale for deriving third-generation status from the mother was that she "is the socializing agent."[58]

In her conclusion, Costantakos hypothesized that continuing subcultural identity is manifested by the "modified extended kin family," neolocal, but with close affectional ties and economic assistance patterns between the generations.[59]

Simon's study again presents interesting contrasts between Greek New Yorkers with upwardly mobile, assimilationist goals and those pursuing incapsulationist strategies. Among the former, increased equality in husband-wife and parent-child statuses was apparent, and there appeared to be an overlap in traditionally sex-defined spheres of activity. Wives were encouraged to go out and work, provided children were cared for; evenings out were "couples' evenings out." Residence after marriage was expected to reflect children's ability to decide their own locus of residence and style of life, although there was some reciprocal feeling that it would be "good" to live close to home. Social life included friends as well as kinsmen, and business relations were considered "too critical" to involve relatives.[60]

On the last point, some of Tavuchis' successful second-generation respondents had also expressed reluctance to engage in financial transactions with relatives, for fear of being a "burden" on kin. Others, however, felt no qualms on this score, and had reported good experiences with relatives in this sphere of interaction.[61]

Among immigrants of St. Markela's, equalitarianism was not a characteristic of family relations, either between husbands and wives or between parents and children. Shared spheres of activity between marital partners were rare, and women tended to "defer to male decisions." The inferior position of daughters, Simon noted, "remained intact." Marriage was an important area of their children's lives which parents

[57]Ibid., 572.
[58]Ibid., 571.
[59]Ibid., 521.
[60]Simon, 139, 140, 145, 146.
[61]Tavuchis, 93.

felt should be in their control. Kinsmen were preferred over friends for social visits and mutual aid.[62]

One pattern reported to be on the increase is intermarriage. In the mid-1920s, mixed couples accounted for two out of ten Greek Orthodox church marriages; by the 1960s, three out of ten; and by the mid-1970s, about half of these marriages.[63] It should be remembered that these figures do not include the indeterminate number who have married outside the Greek Orthodox Church. Among those more likely to take this step, as Saloutos has noted, would be Greek Americans without close family ties in the home country, and those without expectations of inheriting property in Greece and therefore under no constraint to be a member in good standing of the State Church.[64]

An examination of Archdiocesan data for the five boroughs of New York City reveals that the percentage of mixed marriages was 34.4 percent for the year 1979—a percentage essentially unchanged from 1969. This percentage is also substantially below that for the United States as a whole, which, according to the 1980 Archdiocesan Yearbook, was 51.1 percent for 1978-79.[65] However, the figure for New York City undoubtedly "hides" the increasing number of intermarriages in suburban areas of New York, such as Long Island and Westchester. It is worth noting that the most sizable increase in mixed marriages has occurred in Brooklyn, where many second-generation Greek American families live. There, the rate of intermarriage has gone up from 34.8 percent in 1969 to 43.3 percent ten years later. This is still below the rate reported for the parish of the Three Hierarchs by Costantakos at the end of the sixties—close to 50 percent. Among her own respondents, however, only 9.3 percent had intermarried, the percentage rising to 13.1 among the second generation.[66]

A quick preliminary survey of the religious affiliation of partners to mixed marriages in New York City indicates that they are likely to be Roman Catholics. Of the mixed marriage

[62]Simon, 170, 177-80.

[63]Moskos, 73.

[64]Theodore Saloutos, "The Greek Orthodox Church in the United States and Assimilation," *International Migration Review* 7:4 (Winter 1973), 404.

[65]Greek Orthodox Archdiocese of North and South America, *1980 Yearbook*, 76.

[66]Costantakos, 499, 588.

records interspersed chronologically among the first 575 marriage records filed with the Archdiocese in 1979, all were with Roman Catholic partners except two: one between a Greek Orthodox woman and an Episcopalian, and one between a Greek Orthodox male and a Methodist. There was no indication that Greek Orthodox males entered mixed marriages more frequently than females, or vice-versa. Costantakos' survey of mixed marriages in the Three Hierarchs parish from 1932 to 1970 indicated only a slightly greater propensity of females than males to enter mixed marriages. Out of 235 mixed marriages contracted during this period, 56 percent were entered into by Greek American women, the rest by Greek American men.[67]

Although Archdiocesan figures on divorce are recorded by state rather than by municipality, it seems evident from the figures for New York State that the number of divorces has remained quite stable, both for endogamous and for mixed marriages. Since approximately 90 percent of the state's divorces occur within the five boroughs of New York City, this suggests that the divorce rate for the city itself has been stable during the past decade. The most characteristic development during these years has been the drop in the number of recorded church marriages, both endogamous and mixed, in the five boroughs. Suburbanization of the second and third-generation Greek Americans is a partial explanation; another is the increasing number of couples who evidently marry entirely outside the Greek Orthodox Church.

Religion. Although Greek Orthodoxy and Greek ethnicity are significantly intertwined up to the present day, "they do not completely overlap," as Moskos has noted.[68] In the United States as a whole, approximately four out of five ethnic Greeks are at least nominally Greek Orthodox. This figure (79.4 percent) was supported for the Brooklyn subcommunity studied by Costantakos.

Since 1959, Archbishop Iakovos has been primate of the Greek Orthodox Archdiocese of North and South America. Its administration has been headquartered in New York City since its inception in 1922, as previously noted. There is general consensus that as a Greek American institution the Arch-

[67]Ibid., 598, table 44.
[68]Moskos, 67.

diocese is unmatched, both in membership and in "national visibility."[69]

In the five boroughs of New York, the distribution of parishes is: Manhattan, 11; Queens, 5; Brooklyn, 4; Bronx, 1; and Richmond, 1. Also, a dozen more parishes are distributed throughout Westchester and Long Island.[70]

The total registered membership at the end of 1979 was an estimated 17,100. Since each member represents about five persons in a family,[71] this signifies approximately 85,500 registered members of the Greek Orthodox Church in the metropolitan area. Of these, slightly over 20 percent are suburbanized Greek Americans who have moved out to Long Island communities like Hempstead and Greenlawn, or outlying communities north of the city like New Rochelle and Yonkers.

An interesting phenomenon in recent years is the springing up of churches not affiliated or recognized by the Greek Orthodox Archdiocese of North and South America. According to HANAC there were reportedly "eleven such churches in Queens and as many as twenty throughout the city" by the early 1970s, made up mainly of new Greek immigrants but also of some who had broken away from Archdiocese-affiliated churches.[72]

In her study of "The Sacred Sect and the Secular Church," Simon described one such nonaffiliated church in Astoria. On a typical Sunday, 150 to 200 Greeks, mainly women, especially older ones, attended the church, with new immigrants serving as ushers. The outstanding characteristics of this church, according to Simon, were its emphasis on spiritual matters, emotional expression in ritual performance, and hierarchy in social relations—between priest and laity, male and female, the spiritual and the secular realm.[73]

On the other hand, the Archdiocesan parish church in Astoria displayed a contrasting set of emphases: ecumenism in theology coupled with a concern for secular matters, order in ritual performance, and equality in social relations—be-

[69]See, for example, Costantakos; Moskos; Saloutos, "The Greek Orthodox Church in the US and Assimilation"; and Alice Scourby, *Third Generation Greek Americans: A Study of Religious Attitudes*, American Ethnic Groups Series (New York: Arno Press, 1980).

[70]Greek Orthodox Archdiocese, *1980 Yearbook*, 128-31.

[71]HANAC, 89.

[72]Ibid., 88.

[73]Simon, 110.

tween clergy and laity, men and women, etc. There was concern with the establishment of social programs, and the introduction of English into the church liturgy. The church reflected the assimilationist, mobility-oriented strategy of the long-time Greek immigrants and their American-born children.[74]

Studies of the church allegiance of second and third-generation Americans in the New York area have found that it appears to remain strong. In her study of subcultural continuities among Brooklyn Greek Americans, Costantakos suggested that the Greek Orthodox Church "remains strong as a unifying force," despite problems associated with assimilationist tendencies in response to the conflicting needs of the Church's various constituencies.[75]

In response to Costantakos' question as to whether the Church should be "more Americanized," twice as many of the pre-World War II immigrants and of the second and third-generation Greek Americans than of the post-World War II immigrants answered in the affirmative. Also, far fewer of the recent immigrants than of the others thought it "absurd to insist" on using the Greek language in church.[76] Saloutos observed that the decision of the 1970 Clergy-Laity Congress —approving the substitution of English for Greek in the liturgy —brought "sharp" reactions from dissidents in Greek communities "especially in New York where Greek was chiefly spoken."[77]

Scourby, in her 1967 doctoral thesis, investigated the religious attitudes of seventy-one third-generation Greek American high school and college students. Her nonrandom sample was secured through names supplied by two Greek Orthodox churches in Brooklyn and Nassau County and four colleges— three located in New York City and one in Nassau County. All the youths' parents (with the exception of one father) were Greek Orthodox, and one or both parents were native born (93 percent of the mothers and 65 percent of the fathers). Scourby found the youths' attitudes—as measured by the Thurstone-Chave Scale—on the whole were favorable toward the Church.[78]

[74]Ibid., 137.
[75]Costantakos, 475ff.
[76]Ibid., 238, 239.
[77]Saloutos, "The Greek Orthodox Church," 406.
[78]Scourby, 37, 86.

Language and Culture Maintenance: Parochial and Public Schools. The Archdiocese has a parochial school system, which has developed out of the efforts of Greek immigrant parents to pass on the Greek heritage, especially knowledge of the Greek language, to their offspring. In New York City, there are twelve day schools run by the Archdiocese, with an enrolment of just under four thousand pupils. Although one school dates back to the pre-World War I decade, the rest were all founded since the late 1940s. Most have classes ranging from kindergarten through the eighth or ninth grade, although a couple go all the way through high school, and two—the most recently established—are for nursery age to fifth-grade children.[79] In addition, there are the Archdiocesan afternoon schools for language classes. In New York, there are twenty-two such schools, with an enrolment of 3,032 pupils.

A third source of Greek language and cultural instruction in New York City in recent years has resulted from the Bilingual Education Act of 1968. However, according to the HANAC report, "existing programs for Greek-speaking children are extremely limited."[80] Only 4 percent of non-English speaking children were being reached by the bilingual programs existing in New York City five years after passage of the act. At the time, the city had approximately 5,500 Greek-speaking pupils, almost half of whom had moderate to severe difficulty with the English language.[81]

One reason for the limited application of the Bilingual Education Act to alleviate language difficulties of Greek American students is that the program itself has not been accorded an overwhelmingly enthusiastic reception by Greek Americans. Especially in its first years of operation, philosophical disagreements existed among educators, community leaders, and Greek American parents in New York City as to whether or not a bilingual approach is the best one for children of Greek background with English-language problems.[82]

With respect to higher education, modern Greek studies programs have been implemented at Columbia University and Queens College of the City University of New York. On the other hand, programs of Greek American studies are still

[79]Greek Orthodox Archdiocese, *1980 Yearbook*, 102-6.
[80]HANAC, 54.
[81]Ibid., 56.
[82]These obstacles to bilingual education have been reported by both Moskos and HANAC.

mainly in the planning stage, in New York and in the rest of the country.[83]

Associations. In addition to ties of family and religion, Greek Americans in New York City have a variety of associational ties. It is through these, it has been suggested, that second and third-generation Greek Americans in particular become identified with their ethnicity.[84] The most numerous, and perhaps, the most characteristically "Greek," are the hometown, or regional societies, of which there were at least sixty in New York City at the end of the seventies. An incomplete listing follows:

Aetoloakarnanian Mutual Society
Aghios Philippos of Andros Society
Allilovoithitikos Syllogos Cyprion "Zenon"
Arcadian Association of America "O Geros tou Morea"
Association of Hellenes from Egypt in America, Inc.
Athenians' Society
Benevolent Society of Macedonians "Aliakmon"
Cassian Benevolent
Cephalonian Association "Aenos," Inc.
"Cephalos" Cephalonian Society of America
Chian Federation of America
Cretans' Association "Omonoia," Inc.
Cyprus Federation of America
Erikousa Kerkyras Brotherhood
Evrytanon Society of America "Evrytania"
Federation of Dodecanese Societies of America
Federation of Karpathian Societies of America
Greek American Cyclades Islands Federation of
    America and Canada
Greek Rumanian Association of America
Hellenic Society of Constantinople
Hydras Society
Kalavrytinon Brotherhood "To Lavaron tou '21"
Kastelorizoton Society
Lacedaemonians Association
Lacedaemonians Ladies Auxiliary
Messinian Benevolent "Aristomenis"

[83]Moskos, 88-9.
[84]Ibid., 148.

Monemvasioton Society
Naupaktians Brotherhood
Naxos Society
Nisyrian Society "Gnomagoras"
Nisyrian Youth Organization
"Panagia Proussiotissa" Syllogos Evrytanon
Panahaian Benevolent "Agia Lavra"
Panchiaki "Koraes" Society, Inc.
Pan-Coan Society "Hippocrates"
Pan-Elian Federation
Pan-Epirotic Federation of the U.S.A. and Canada
Pan-Euboean Society
Panimbrian Benevolent Society
Panlemnian Society "Hyfestos"
Panlesvian Society of America
Pan-Macedonian Association, Inc.
Panthessalian Federation
Pan-Zakynthian Brotherhood "Dionysios Solomos," Inc.
Pontion Society "Komninoi"
Pyrrhus Benevolent Society and Daughters of Epirus
St. Athanasios Association of Perista
"St. John Theologos" Society, Inc. (Nisyrian)
Samos Society "Pythagoras"
Skopeliton Society "Agios Reginos"
Society of Epirotes Anagenesis-Souliotissai
Spetsioton Association "Spetsai"
Syros Society of New York
Thessalonikians Society of New York
Theveon Society "Epaminondas"
United Cyprians of America[85]

As can be noted, there is no particular geographical concentration evident.

Other types of associations of Greek Americans in the New York area are professional/community groups, charitable organizations, and cultural and recreational groups. Professional associations include the Hellenic Medical Society, the Hellenic Universities Graduates Association, the Hellenic-American Educators Association, and the Panhellenic Seamen's

[85]The list was compiled from the Greek Archdiocese's *1980 Yearbook*, 180-2; and Melvin Hecker and Heike Fenton, comps. and eds., *The Greeks in America, 1528-1977* (Dobbs Ferry, N.Y.: Oceana Publications, 1978) 134-6.

Association. Important cultural associations in the city include the Hellenic Cultural Circle "Filiko," the Hellenic University Club, and the Parnassos Society of New York.

Virtually every Greek community in the United States has branches of the following national organizations or federations, as Costantakos observed in her analysis of the organizational structure of the Greek American community of the Three Hierarchs in Brooklyn: the prestigious AHEPA—the American Hellenic Educational Progressive Association—and its auxiliaries; the Daughters of Penelope, the Sons of Pericles, and the Maids of Athena; the Church-related Ladies Philoptochos Society (Friends of the Poor) and GOYA (Greek Orthodox Youth of America); and GAVA (the Greek American Veterans Association).[86]

Last, but not least, mention must be made of HANAC, the Hellenic American Neighborhood Action Committee, founded in 1972 and serving the Greek population of New York City, especially those newly arrived, with language classes, job placement, youth counseling, etc.

Politics, Newspapers. Despite the proliferation of organizations in the New York area, there is "not a single" one that can act as "a political coordinator or liaison" between the Greek population and the city government, according to HANAC's pessimistic assessment only a few years ago.[87] It noted the general philosophical distaste of Greek Americans for reliance on "outsiders"—government bureaucracies and public agencies—to serve their needs, coupled with the absence of Greek civil servants in government agencies.[88]

Some support for the latter contention is given by the census data for the New York SMSA. The tabulation below compares the proportion of workers in government service in the New York area by nativity and sex, according to the 1970 census.

[86]Costantakos, 146.
[87]HANAC, 93.
[88]Ibid., 90.

WORKERS IN GOVERNMENT SERVICE IN THE NEW YORK
SMSA BY NATIVITY AND SEX

	males	*females*
foreign born	2.9%	3.4%
native born of Greek/mixed parentage	13.2	16.0
native born white of native born parentage	15.8	16.5[89]

The tradition of self-reliance and circumvention of government, rather than participation in it, has been noted frequently. Discussing Greek ethnic politics in Astoria in the 1970s, Simon reported that "individualism was the accepted route to success," and resulted in the ideological demise of Greek political effort. Within the Greek community, Greek politicians were found to have "little leverage," and the local Democratic clubs to be "hardly more supportive of aspiring candidates than the community."[90]

Simon observed that among the more recent immigrants of the late-1960s and 1970s, there was conspicuous avoidance of impersonal linkages, whether with city agencies or political bureaucracies. When the assistance of politicians or public administrators was needed, "personal links were called upon to serve some personal need." On the other hand, the more assimilated Greek Americans, according to Simon, resented patronage tactics by local Greek American political hopefuls. Although they "recognized" that much of New York politics operates as a patronage system of personal politics, they "objected to the denial of party politics and meritocracy."[91]

Although the Greek population of New York has had at its disposal Greek-language newspapers of various political persuasions to help shape its views on political issues of the day, these issues have rarely dealt with local political matters. Today, two Greek-language dailies serve the city's Greek population: one of long standing, the *National Herald,* and one founded in 1977, the *Proine.*

An overview of a sample of fifty-two issues of *National*

[89]*Census of the Population: 1970,* PC(1): New York, N.Y. SMSA, table 16.
[90]Simon, 95.
[91]Ibid., 182, 149.

Herald for 1979 reveals that the lead stories focused on major foreign policy issues involving Greek-American relations: the question of resuming American foreign aid to Turkey and Greece's entry into the Common Market. Feature stories typically dealt with educational and art events ,as well as human interest stories. Headlines such as the following testify to this: "Exhibition of ancient Greek art at Metropolitan Museum"; "Mrs. .... Gets Ph.D. in Education at Fordham University"; "Greek American destroys tires of 49 New York City Police Tow Trucks after own car is Towed Away Fourth Time."

It should be noted that these feature stories, and the calendar of events, while often about New York City, also include eastern seaboard cities, since the paper caters to a nationwide audience and has a readership in the capital and other major American cities with Greek populations. Classified advertisements promote buying and selling in the various boroughs of the city, especially of restaurants. They also call attention to the availability of apartments and lots for sale in Greece, for those with money to invest. And for those who might be discouraged or homesick, there are advertisements, in English, for "jobs, jobs, jobs" in Greece: as cooks, countermen, waiters, carpenters, plumbers, etc.

Concluding Comments

On the basis of this brief review of the available data on Greek life in the metropolis, how shall one assess the state of knowledge and suggest strategies for future investigations? Clearly, the available data is insufficient in quantity, despite encouraging signs of scholarly endeavor over the last decade. As for the quality of the data, despite its generally high level, some problems exist. First, the nonrandomness of the survey samples which have been utilized, while not necessarily invalidating the findings, must at least be taken into account. Secondly, the operational definitions of some key variables, like immigrant "generation" and "recency" of arrival, have not been comparable, and great care must be taken in comparing findings about, let us say, "recent" immigrants or "third generation" Greek Americans.

For example, Costantakos' "recent" first-generation migrants are roughly equal in time of arrival to Simon's first-generation Greeks of the St. Demetrios parish (1946-1960), but they are considerably earlier in time of arrival than Simon's first-generation "recent" immigrants attending St. Markela's (late 1960s and early 1970s). Furthermore, Scourby's and Costantakos' "third-generation" Greek Americans of intergenerational status are comparable to second-generation foreign stock as defined by the US census. Incidentally, an important theoretical and empirical question, for purposes of deriving generational status, is to what extent mothers are the critical socializing agents of their children from the standpoint of assimilation.

In addition to the quantity and quality of the data, there is a certain lack of continuity in research. The many significant unfinished issues opened up by researchers at the end of their investigations have not yet, in many instances, been picked up by other researchers. There is a wealth of material for Ph.D. students and postdoctoral researchers to follow up on the pioneer work of such investigators as Tavuchis, Costantakos, Scourby, Moskos, Simon, Kourvetaris,[92] and others.

This suggests the possibility of a threefold research strategy: first, following up on the research questions posed by earlier investigations; second, incorporation of theories and concepts from related areas which throw light on the Greek case; and third, systematic analysis of variations among the Greek American population, especially regional ones.

With respect to continuity of social research in the area of Greek American ethnic studies, there are gaps in at least two areas already alluded to. In family sociology, little is known about sibling interactions, or about interactions with godparents, as Tavuchis has pointed out. Kourvetaris has noted that very few studies exist on the actual role relations within Greek American families, especially among immigrants, as compared with the cultural norms and ideas of a "patriarchal" structure and a "large" kin network. In the sociology of religion, Scourby and Simon have both called for more investigations of the interplay between ethnicity, class, and religious behavior. Scourby has also called for investigations of reciprocal expectations of priests and laity, and the relationships be-

[92]George A. Kourvetaris, "The Greek American Family," in *Ethnic Families in America,* ed. C. H. Mindel and R. W. Habenstein (New York: Elsevier, 1976) 168-91.

tween feelings of group superiority or inferiority and the maintenance of religious cohesiveness.[93]

Greek American ethnic studies would also benefit from making use of theories in related areas of ethnic studies rather than inflexibly concentrating on assimilation theory in attempting to understand Greek American life. In these other fields, investigators are making use of network theory, middleman theory, dual labor market theory, and a variety of other approaches which are giving them new productive insights into the workings of ethnic groups. Even in the area of assimilation, studies in other fields have come up with findings that put the Greek case in a new light. For example, recent investigations of both the Chinese and Indian middle-class immigrants show that among them, too, social assimilation precedes cultural assimilation, and not vice-versa.[94]

Finally, it would be useful to attend to regional variations in the characteristics of the Greek population in this country. Most studies have concentrated on the population as a unitary phenomenon, even though the empirical bases of the studies were geographically specific. All the studies based in the New York area were of this type. Although this is perfectly legitimate, the author of one of these studies herself called for "a comparative study of regional differences of Greek-American subcommunities in the United States."[95] The evidence to date from these and other studies of ethnic groups certainly suggests that the social context in which a population is situated —such as the characteristics of the labor market and the ethnic concentration of the population—affect its own experience: its occupational profile, social mobility rate, and intermarriage rate and the religious denomination of the partner.

Studies of these three types would add to our knowledge of the Greek population of New York and the nation and, at the same time, integrate Greek American ethnic studies with the field as a whole, enriching both.

[93]Scourby, 88, 89.
[94]See Eva E. Sandis, "Some Sociological Observations on Voluntary Organizations among Recent Immigrants in New York," *Journal of Voluntary Action Research* 6 (June 1978) 98-101.
[95]Costantakos, 537-8.

CHAPTER 4

GREEK AMERICAN INVOLVEMENT IN CONTEMPORARY POLITICS

BY

PETER N. MARUDAS

Greek American involvement in contemporary politics, while a relatively new development, has surprisingly captured significant public attention in recent years. This public focus seems attributable to several factors: first, the increasing prominence and numbers of Greek Americans in high elective offices, and second, the interest generated over the past six years by the controversial legislative struggles on the Cyprus and related Turkish embargo issues. As one who has been privileged to participate in and observe both situations, I shall try to share some observations, impressions, and conclusions about this interesting development. However, I wish to caution my readers that this presentation will resemble more a mosaic rather than an organized paper, since it is based primarily on a "fleeting empiricism" rather than studious and painstaking research. I do hope that my efforts here today will spur enterprising scholars to research this intriguing topic with greater detail and insight—particularly while so many pioneer and original sources are still available.

Visible and vigorous Greek American political participation, both individual and collective, has largely evolved over the past twenty-five years. Actually, the first Greek American ever elected to high public office in the United States was Lucas Miltiades Miller of Wisconsin, who served for one term— 1892-1894—in the US House of Representatives. An orphan of the 1821 Greek War of Independence, he was adopted by the

93

philhellene American Colonel J. P. Miller, and, like other children of that heroic struggle who were brought to America, his adult life was spent in devoted public service to his adopted land. But for our purposes, Congressman Miller was a historical aberration far outside the pale of this presentation, although again ambitious scholars should prepare a study of his life if none yet exists. Miller's career preceded the great influx of Greek immigrants to America, and the political story we seek to tell today is about those immigrants and the subsequent generations who walked in their path.

I was vividly reminded of this focus earlier this week when I consulted with my chief political mentor, who is not, with all due respect, Senator Sarbanes, but someone in the Greek tradition much more senior—my ninety-year-old maternal grandfather. Nicholas Leventis came to America in 1907 from the rugged mountain village of Zatouna in the country of Gourtenia, Arcadia, a location made infamous as the lonely exile selected by the Military Junta for the Greek composer Mikis Theodorakis. I seek your indulgence for this brief biographical diversion, but I believe that my grandfather's life style, as such, was typical of that generation and its approach to American society and politics. He was a successful small businessman who supported his parents, dutifully earned dowries for three unmarried sisters in Greece, and simultaneously reared six children, all married and part of a family that now includes sixteen grandchildren and twelve great-grandchildren. During his early and middle years, he volunteered and returned to Greece to fight in the Balkan wars, helped found and build a new Greek Orthodox church in his home city of Detroit, was an active member and founder of the Pan-Arcadian Federation, a member of the Odd Fellows Fraternal Order, an ardent royalist and a fanatic follower of Franklin Delano Roosevelt, whose philosophy he still eloquently espouses.

This biographical description, I believe, accurately represents characteristics that marked thousands of Greek American lives and households throughout America in the early part of this century, and helped to differentiate the Greek American community from other ethnic groups. I further believe that these particular cultural, social, and economic factors inhibited political participation in earlier stages of Greek community life while paradoxically fostering it in later phases. These communal traits are familiar to most informed students of the Greek American community, but their political implications are not as readily apparent. For, unlike other prominent ethnic groups, the Greeks immigrated to the US in relatively small numbers, rarely congregating in permanent ghettos and at first economic chance moving away from their neighborhood of entry. There were exceptions, but the rule was that relatively small numbers of Greek immigrants usually spread themselves out residentially within an area. Thus, by avoiding the pressures and hardships associated with large overcrowded working-class neighborhoods, Greek Americans were not compelled to organize politically either to advance individual gain or for collective community protection. Most significantly, they were not, as the Irish, Italians, the large Slavic groups, or even the Germans, at an earlier period, pitted directly against existing political, economic, or social arrangements.

This fact was further reinforced by the small-business economic ethos which overwhelmingly prevailed in the Greek immigrant community. Like all immigrants, the Greeks initially worked for someone else, but most sought and eventually succeeded in owning their own enterprises. Therefore, they rarely looked to government—except in the narrowest instances of licensing or immigration matters—for jobs or public assistance as part of normal patronage largesse bestowed as a reward for ethnic political involvement. Again, unlike the Jewish community—sometimes viewed as comparable because of its business orientation—the Greeks were fewer and had little need to organize politically for protection against traditional bigotry and persecution. And as Greek workers quickly moved out of the nation's factories and mines to operate their own enterprises, they were immunized from the growing politicizing process of the trade union movement.

This commercial independence was further augmented by the social isolation stemming from the inward aspect of the Greek American community. The preoccupation with family, Church and *topika* (localized social clubs), as opposed to non-Greek neighbors and institutions like the PTA and Rotary, created this barrier. In fact, the extreme homogeneity of the Greek community fostered by the ethnic-religious life centering around the Greek Orthodox parish and extensive use of the Greek language discouraged interaction with other groups. This stands in sharp contrast again to the Irish, Italians, Poles, and other Slavs, who as Roman Catholics frequently attended church with different nationalities and often sent their children to be educated in heterogeneous parochial schools.

In addition, an obsessive preoccupation with old country politics in the 1920s and 1930s tended to dissipate political energies within the community, as witnessed by the prolonged bitter royalist-Venizelist struggles, rifts which undermined the community's social and religious unity and again precluded organized political activity in American society. This isolation was further aggravated by the Great Depression, which for most Greek Americans was a time of struggle for survival with little time for the luxury of political activity.

Thus, we can safely assert that the Greek community in its first four decades of identifiable community life in America (1910-1950) was inner-directed, concentrating on individual economic success and strengthening the Church, family, and other institutions that nurtured religious and social conformity. Political activity was viewed primarily, and almost exclusively, as a civic obligation exercised by voting proudly and regularly. To be sure, there were organizations and forces that encouraged outside involvement. AHEPA fostered such activity, as did membership in clubs such as the Masons, the Odd Fellows, and other non-Greek fraternal groups, but these associations were rarely political in nature or consequence.

However, it is a mistake to believe that political life was absolutely dormant in the community. Greek American political organizations were formed in many areas. This past November I attended an election rally sponsored by the Greek American Political Club of Stark County, which was first organized in 1917 in Canton, Ohio. More importantly, individual Greek Americans were laboring courageously and quietly in the political vineyards. During the late forties and early fifties, this hardy breed finally emerged in the public limelight with several becoming powerful national figures—though most were leaders or activists with regional or local political influence.

For lack of a better description, I have termed these durable, occasionally flamboyant but dedicated pioneer Greek politicians as the "insiders." Many have passed from the scene; some are still with us, but virtually all broke ground for broader Greek American political participation. Depending on the circumstances, these individuals in communities throughout the nation were the tenuous or strong connection between the body politic and the Greek American community.

They were for the most part Democrats, as most Greeks voted Democratic or lived in Democratic districts, but there were many Republicans as well.

Some of them come to our memories quickly. George Vournas, great AHEPA leader, venerable patriarch of liberal Greek American politics and the confidant of Presidents; Tom Pappas, a power broker in national Republican politics during the Eisenhower and Nixon years; John Maragon, whose name may not evoke immediate recognition today, but who at the height of his notoriety operated at the inner recesses of the Truman Administration; William Helis, the New Orleans oil tycoon and another Greek American with great influence. There were others: Dean Alfange, who in 1942 was the American Labor Party candidate for Governor of New York; Charles Maliotis of Massachusetts, a close friend of the Kennedys and Speaker Tip O'Neill; Bill Collins of Minneapolis, a long-time friend and supporter of the late Hubert Humphrey; the late George Johnson, the prominent California Democrat who passed away only recently; Angelo Geocaris, who, as a student, spearheaded the campaign for Senator Paul Douglas of Illinois and is still a positive and important influence in that state's Democratic politics; and Andrew Fasseas, also of Illinois, a Republican who held high appointed office.

Countless others operated unheralded and unknown outside of their local community. They were the likes of Charlie Diamond, a Greek American activist in Detroit who served as the link to the Democratic Party; and Gus Pecunes in Baltimore, who relentlessly assisted and prodded young Greek Americans into political activity. An extraordinary and diverse group of political operatives, these insiders lobbied for Greek American appointments to the service academies, beseeched immigration authorities to speed the union of families, and urged the community to participate politically. Some gave large amounts of money to the parties and their candidates, others served on ethnic committees, and some plied the precincts to pump the Greek vote for the preferred candidate. While a few acted out of less-than-noble reasons, most were motivated by a genuine and fervent desire that Greek Americans participate fully in the American political system. They viewed political participation as a practical need for the community and as a civic obligation owed to the American nation.

In the course of this discussion, certain events or personalities stand out as important symbols, landmarks if you will, in the Greek American political saga. One of these persons is Michael Manatos, now retired and living in Washington, the father of the Honorable Andrew Manatos, former administrative assistant to Senator Thomas Eagleton and Assistant Secretary for Congressional Affairs at the US Department of Commerce in the Carter Administration. Mike Manatos is important because he was the first Greek American appointed to the White House staff, accorded that honor in 1960 by President Kennedy, who designated him as Administrative Assistant for Congressional Relations. This was a position quite amenable to Manatos, who served for many years on the staff of five Democratic Senators from Wyoming, where earlier his Cretan forebears had settled. Manatos came to Washington in 1937 and is believed to be the first Greek American to work on Capitol Hill. Today, many young Greek Americans hold junior and senior staff positions, among them the "dean" of Greek American staffers, James Pyrros, who has served as administrative assistant to Representative Lucien Nedzi of Michigan for the last eighteen years.

Wyoming would seem an odd place to produce a leading Greek American political personality, being a small state with a very small Greek population. But Manatos proved that even in Wyoming an energetic and astute young Greek American, supported by his community, could obtain an influential position on Capitol Hill leading to an important White House appointment. Mike Manatos had fulfilled the fondest dreams of those "insiders" who had preceded him and brought great pride and distinction to the Greek American community. In fact, he was the only Kennedy staffer to be retained by Lyndon Johnson and served the entire eight years (1960-1968) of the Kennedy-Johnson Administrations. He was the vanguard of others, like Harold Pachios, who served in the Johnson White House and recently won the Democratic nomination for the first congressional district of Maine, a seat once held by a fellow Greek American, Peter Kyros; Tom Korologos, who held a similar post in the Nixon and Ford Administrations; Peter Peterson of Nebraska, the former President of Bell-Howell and the first Greek American to hold a cabinet post— Secretary of Commerce; John Nassikas, Chairman of the Federal Power Commission; and numerous Greek Americans who successfully sought important staff positions at all governmental levels. Manatos' appointment, in a sense, was the culmination of the efforts of Greek American political insiders in the same manner as George Christopher's election as Mayor of San Francisco in 1955 and John Brademas' as Congressman in 1958 from Indiana were beacons to aspiring Greek American politicians. As with the pioneer insiders, we have the pioneer elected officials—those daring individuals who broke the barriers of elective office and, in the process, helped to write some very interesting American political history.

It would be impossible and even disrespectful to discuss our subject without mentioning the role of George Christopher, the quintessential Greek American politician. Christopher was the first Greek American elected as a big-city mayor and, for a long time, the most important elected officeholder in the Greek American community. Born in Arcadia, Greece and brought as an infant to America, Christopher grew up in one of San Francisco's toughest neighborhoods. He was a successful businessman who accomplished what many Greek American politicians did so well after him: winning a major election without an ethnic political base. He could not rally thousands of fellow ethnics to his cause, but instead had to work skillfully and effectively to build a victorious coalition, an effort even more impressive since he was a Republican in an overwhelmingly Democratic city. Christopher also smashed other barriers as well. He was the first Greek American to seek a statewide nomination for senator and one of the first to run for governor (he lost to Ronald Reagan in the primary). Although unsuccessful in each race, he widened the horizons and excited the imagination of fellow Greek Americans. He also gained national prominence by leading the successful effort to bring the New York Giants baseball team to San Francisco and by his historic confrontation with the visiting Russian ruler, Nikita Khrushchev.

Equally as important as Christopher's achievement was the election of thirty-one-year-old John Brademas as the first Greek American Congressman of the modern period. Unsuccessful in two previous efforts, Brademas, a Democrat, persevered, and this Harvard-educated Rhodes scholar and former assistant to Adlai Stevenson succeeded in 1958 in winning election from Indiana's third congressional district. He occupied that seat until 1980, and in 1977 became chief majority whip, a position third in the House leadership, exceeded only by the Speaker and the majority leader. Brademas was defeated in the elections of 1980 and has since been appointed President of New York University. He is presently serving in that capacity.

What Christopher symbolized at the local and state level, Brademas exemplified at the national. He was the first of a growing number of American-born politicians who were now primed to participate fully in American politics. They were for the most part either successful businessmen or well-educated professionals who through sheer determination and political skill were able to win impressive political victories without the support of a large ethnic voting bloc. With few exceptions, the young Greek American politician had to rely on an appeal to the general voter based on his intellectual ability, political acumen, and personal character.

To appreciate fully the explosion of Greek American elective involvement, let us examine Greek American political success in elections occurring in a twelve-year period from 1966 to 1978. It should be stressed that this in no way represents a complete accounting of Greek American activity, but clearly demonstrates the astounding involvement of Greek Americans in politics at all levels.

A recapitulation of this early activity shows George Christopher elected in 1955 as Mayor of San Francisco, and in 1958 John Brademas as the first Greek American elected to Congress in a modern period. In that same year, Peter Pitchess was elected Republican Sheriff of Los Angeles County, and shared with Brademas the record for Greek American political longevity. The 1960 elections produced two Greek American mayors. George Vavoulis, a Republican, was elected Mayor of Saint Paul, Minnesota, a position he held until 1966, and George Chacharis, a Democrat, won the mayoralty in Gary, Indiana, a position he gave up two years later because of criminal charges. The early sixties were generally devoid of prominent Greek American political activity, although many younger individuals were running for local and state office. Most notable was the outstanding California state senator, Nick Petris, who first entered the State Assembly in 1958, and moved up to the Senate seat he presently holds in 1967.

Curiously, Brademas had to wait until 1966, nearly a decade later, before he was joined by other Greek Americans in Congress. That year Nick Galafianakis, an attorney from Durham, North Carolina and a Duke University law professor, and Peter Kyros of Maine, a Naval Academy graduate and Harvard-trained lawyer, won House seats. Spiro Agnew, a

Republican of Maryland, made his auspicious entrance in 1966 as the nation's first Greek American governor while Paul Sarbanes, a Democrat and young Greek American lawyer, became the first of his community elected to the Maryland State Legislature.

In 1968 the nation was stunned when the relatively unknown Agnew was tapped by Richard Nixon to be Vice President and overnight the name Spiro became a household word. Gus Yatron of Reading, Pennsylvania, a successful small businessman and Democrat, was also elected to the House in that same year, bringing the Greek American congressional delegation to four. The ranks were further swelled in 1970 as Sarbanes, a Princeton graduate, who like Brademas was a Rhodes scholar and like Kyros a Harvard law graduate, won a House seat from Baltimore. Greek Americans made impressive gains locally that year as John Rousakis, a Democrat, was elected Mayor of Savannah, Georgia, and Lee Alexander, another Democrat, was elected Mayor of Syracuse, New York. Both men put together impressive coalitions, still serve in office, and Alexander is a past President of the US Conference of Mayors. In 1971, they were joined by another Greek American mayor, the dynamic and colorful George Athanson, a Democrat who won the hearts of hometown citizens in Hartford, Connecticut, and has served longer in that office than any other mayor.

The following year the Greek American delegation in Congress added and lost a member. The addition came with the election of Republican L.A. "Skip" Bafalis, a transplanted New Hampshire businessman, who won election from Florida's tenth congressional district. The loss was Nick Galafianakis, who had stunned political observers by his primary victory over long-time incumbent Senator Everett Jordan. However, Galafianakis' hopes to be the first Greek American Senator were dashed in the Nixon-Agnew 1972 landslide, which elected Jesse Helms Senator from North Carolina. At the state and local level, Michael Bakalis, among others, including several judges around the country, won an important state-wide office as he was overwhelmingly elected State Superintendent of Education in Illinois. Bakalis, it will be recalled, ran for the governorship of Illinois in 1978 as the Democratic nominee and lost to present Governor James Thompson.

Greek American political activity continued in the 1974 elections, particularly in Massachusetts with the election of

Michael Dukakis, a Democrat, a classmate of Sarbanes at the Harvard Law School and the son of a highly respected immigrant physician, as governor. Paul Tsongas, also a Democrat, another son of immigrants, and a Yale Law School graduate, won at the young age of thirty-three the House seat from his native Lowell, a center of Greek population. That same year Theodore Venetoulis, a Democrat and former congressional administrative assistant and a widely respected political operative, launched his own candidacy and was elected Baltimore County Executive, the same post that fellow Greek American Spiro Agnew held from 1962 to 1966. In 1975 two more Greek Americans joined the ranks of mayors, one of them a Republican, John Apostol, elected Mayor of Annapolis, Maryland's capital city, and Mrs. Helen C. Boosalis, a Democrat, who won election as Mayor of Lincoln, Nebraska's capital city. Both have since been reelected for additional four-year terms.

In the American bicentennial year of 1976, Paul Sarbanes of Maryland set a precedent by his election as the first Greek American United States Senator. Sarbanes, the son of immigrants from Laconia, Greece, grew up in the family restaurant in Salisbury on the eastern shore and received enthusiastic support from Greek Americans both in Maryland and throughout the nation. It may have taken decades for the first Greek American to serve in the Senate, but only two years elapsed before the election of a second, as Paul Tsongas, against great odds, defeated the powerful incumbent Senator Edward Brooke. In that same year, Massachusetts continued to be a center of Greek American political success as Nick Mavroules, the Democratic Mayor of Peabody, won a seat in the House of Representatives from his Eastern Massachusetts district. Further north, Olympia Bouchles Snowe was elected to the House from Maine. Mrs. Snowe, a graduate of St. Basil's Academy, was the first Greek American woman elected to Congress, and her election gave Maine the distinction of having sent to Washington a Greek American Republican in Snowe and a Greek American Democrat in Peter Kyros, who served from 1966 to 1974.

Throughout this period, Greek Americans continued their quest for elective office at all levels. The four-hundred-member New Hampshire Legislature usually numbered five to ten Greek Americans in its ranks, including the minority leader, Democrat Chris Spyrou. In nearby Rhode Island, George Panichas, another Democrat, was elected and still serves in that state's legislature. State Senator William Gekas of Harrisburg, Pennsylvania, made an unsuccessful run for the Republican nomination as lieutenant governor in 1978, but is still a member of the State Senate. In neighboring Ohio, Harry Meshel, Chairman of the powerful State Senate Finance Committee, is mounting a strong effort to obtain the Democratic nomination from his congressional district in Youngstown and is given a good chance to retake the seat from its Republican occupant. Also in Ohio, the Stark County Sheriff (which includes Canton) is a Greek American Democrat, George Papadopoulos, and the Canton City Solicitor, another Democrat, is the thoughtful and highly respected Harry Klide. At one point in the sixties, the State of Michigan numbered four local elected prosecutors of Greek American background, including George Paris, Prosecuting Attorney from Macomb County, the state's third-largest jurisdiction. In the Illinois State Senate there are three Greek Americans: two Democrats, Sam Maragos and Steve Nash of Chicago, serving along with the veteran Republican Adeline Geocaris of Waukegan. Chris Victor Semos, the popular Greek American leader and Democrat from Dallas, has long been a stalwart in the Texas Legislature. Senator Petris was joined in the California Legislature in the seventies by two outstanding assemblymen and fellow Democrats, Louis Papan and Art Agnos. Greek Americans have been serving on city councils and county boards throughout the nation (at one time there were two Greek Americans serving as aldermen in Atlanta) and have been elected as mayors in Wethersfield and Waterbury, Connecticut; Newburyport, Massachusetts; Tenafly, New Jersey; Elkhart, Indiana; and Daly City, California. They also have occupied high party offices and top-level appointed positions.

This brief survey is presented not only to provide a factual report on Greek American politicians, but to demonstrate the rapidity of their entrance to the highest echelon of American political life. The period from 1966 to the present presents a remarkable picture of political progress. In that span, eight Greek Americans were elected to the House of Representatives, two to the US Senate, two as governors, five as mayors, and one as Vice President. This in addition to the hundreds of local and state officials who were elected and others who filed as unsuccessful candidates.

Perhaps no other Greek American was more publicly and erroneously identified with this development than Spiro Agnew, whose meteoric rise and demise stirred the nation. Agnew, however, was an atypical Greek American in that his community ties were at best tenuous and casual. However, once he achieved the governorship, after serving four years as elected Executive of Baltimore County, a large Baltimore suburban jurisdiction, he sought and received support from the Greek American community. Greek Americans generally responded favorably to Agnew when he assumed the Vice Presidency and he, in turn, to prove the legitimacy of his ethnic roots, represented the Nixon Administration in a controversial trip to Greece, where he lavished praise on the then-entrenched military dictatorship. But Agnew, like most successful Greek American politicians of that time, relied minimally on the support of the Greek American community for votes. What the community lacked in numbers, however, it made up in its accessibility to the people and in financial support.

The preoccupation with small business which forty years earlier prevented the early immigrants from outside involvement now became a vehicle for influencing hundreds of public officials and meeting thousands of their fellow citizens. One could safely guess that there are few major American communities without a prominent restaurant, tavern, or other business operated by a Greek American who is well known and respected by the local population or neighborhood. This phenomenon bolsters my impression that the Greek American has generally been treated by the press and public more gently and favorably than members of other ethnic groups. For instance, there is no word in the popular culture that negatively describes a Greek American. Whereas the vernacular is regrettably filled with perjorative names for Germans, Italians, Jews, Poles, and others, on the other hand, a prominent Greek American will frequently be referred to as the Golden Greek or the Galloping Greek, and even gamblers of Greek extraction will be warmly referred to as Nick the Greek or Jimmy the Greek, a context which generally earns little approbation.

Greek Americans were, therefore, critically placed in professions and businesses that provided unlimited opportunity for meaningful public exposure. This evolving Greek American political pattern, comprised of successful elective politics, growing economic strength, and public respect, set the stage for the next chapter of the fast-developing Greek American political story—massive political participation provoked by the outbreak of hostilities on the island of Cyprus and the subsequent Turkish invasion.

For the first time since the patriotic frenzy of World War II, the Greek American community united around a single issue. It was not difficult to arouse the community on a question that combined both morality, old country loyalty, and American policy. In the summer of 1974, at the height of the crisis, thousands of Greek Americans angrily protested the use of American weapons by Turkish invasion forces on Cyprus. They came from all over America to march in Washington and to demand that their government conduct a foreign policy of equality and justice for Cyprus and stability for Greece. This movement brought into American political life for the first time large numbers of Greek Americans who, up to that time, were either apathetic or too busy to participate. Even more impressive was the involvement of Greek-born professionals and academicians, who along with less sophisticated newly arrived immigrants visited Congress, sent telegrams, and organized rallies to plead their cause. First, second, and even third-generation Greek Americans who generally did not identify with "Greek issues" felt impelled to participate in this mass effort.

This grassroots movement was then coupled with the strength and influence of the Greek American delegation in Washington and with the presence of Greek American elected officials at other governmental levels as well. The Greek press, always a lively and vital component of the Greek American community, played a salutary role during this period of intense political involvement. One could assert that the Cyprus crisis brought together, in an unexpected and unprecedented manner, independent political trends in the Greek American community and fused them into a unity hitherto believed to be impossible. With the demise of the Junta in Greece, Greeks of all political persuasion were able to put aside their feelings about the dictatorship and now rally behind a democratically governed Greece. Also, the departure of the discredited Spiro Agnew meant that Greek Americans could now politically function free of his divisive influence.

The unexpected and impressive legislative victories that the Greek American community and its friends achieved in Congress despite powerful opposition from the executive and the congressional leadership demonstrated that political involvement could be beneficial and effective. New and viable organizations were spawned by this development and older groups were revitalized or made more politically conscious. The American Hellenic Institute, a vigorous lobbying group under the leadership of Eugene Rossides, an outstanding attorney and fervent Greek American, brought new focus and effectiveness to the political effort in Washington. The United Hellenic American Congress, organized by a Chicago businessman, Andrew Athens, greatly improved communication and activity among Greek American leaders, as did the Free Cyprus Committee. AHEPA, along with other traditional Greek societies, increased its public affairs involvement and mobilized its members throughout the nation. Individuals like Dr. James Kellis of Connecticut, Charles Maliotes of Massachusetts, George Livanos of New York, former Mayor Christopher, and others worked nationally to harness the political energy triggered by this tragic moment in Greek history. What the Greek Americans discovered from the Cyprus crisis was that well-organized political action, combined with able leadership and the right issue, could affect national policy. Not that Greek American political activity was the sole reason for success in Congress; there were, as scholars of the issue point out, other trends working against the Administration, but without the basic ingredient provided by the internal cohesion of the Greek American community these victories would have been impossible. In churches, at social club meetings, in family groups, and on campuses, Greek Americans reinforced each other and, as Senator Sarbanes has stated, established "an American lobby for the rule of law" and challenged our government to implement in its foreign policy the nation's finest principles.

After nearly six years of struggle on the issues of Cyprus and peace in the Eastern Mediterranean and following twelve years of steady political growth, the question now is what form, if any, this new-found political consciousness will take. This assertion raises more questions than answers. As the Cyprus issue fades or eludes solution, will the community's political staying power diminish? Will the changes in American politics such as the breakdown of party regularity and old coalitions affect such development? As the community becomes more "Americanized," will this erode unity or undermine this new "Greek American" consciousness? If neutralist or anti-western political forces gain control of the Greek parliament and government, will that bring disunity to the community here or cause an estrangement between Greece and the United States—and between Greeks and Greek Americans? Admittedly, these forces and trends are to a great extent out of the control of the community or its leaders, but they pose interesting challenges as we enter the political era of the eighties.

At a more basic level, will the obvious success of Greek Americans in achieving electoral office continue? There is no question that the Cyprus issue, on top of the successes of politicians like Brademas, Yatron, Sarbanes, and Tsongas in winning and holding high office, has encouraged and in some instances mesmerized budding Greek American politicians. Some, lured by the hope of raising large amounts of money from Greek communities, have made faulty political judgments that have led to inevitable defeats. This requires the community to make sophisticated and careful decisions about candidates who ask for support. With a few exceptions, Greek Americans elected to public office have been of generally superior or outstanding quality. It is, therefore, not merely a potential candidate's Greek background that should guarantee him or her automatic support, but qualities consistent with high political standards. It is the community's responsibility to exercise careful scrutiny of prospective candidates, lest they foolishly squander political resources or, once in office, embarrass the community. One veteran politician proposes a litmus test for determining a Greek American politician's commitment to the community's shared ideals and goals. He suggests its application after the official retires and the test is related to one's continuing interest in those issues affecting the Greek American community. On this basis, he argues, George Christopher and others like Nick Galafianakis represent the paragon of concern, while Spiro Agnew is the archetype opportunist.

Another area of activity and study will be the progress of politics in the new large Greek neighborhoods, most notably in Astoria and northwest Chicago. Will these large numbers of Greek Americans be transformed into a local political power or will many of these new immigrants remain unregistered, uninvolved, and in some instances barely connected to American society? This is a great challenge to Greek American institutions, and in New York it has been imaginatively confronted by the Hellenic American Neighborhood Action Committee (HANAC). And will the new political momentum carry over into support for non-Greek candidates who have been friendly to community issues?

Another unexpected development was the infusion of new Greek immigrants caused by the 1965 immigration law reform, which incidentally served as an early testing ground for Greek American lobbying. This new blood, comprised of essentially urban Greek immigrants, is much different from the early rural wave of immigration and includes many Greeks with professional and scientific training. One need only examine the telephone book of any major American city to see the large number of physicians and dentists with identifiably Greek names. The same is true at universities and research centers, where Greek-born and first and second-generation Greek Americans occupy positions of tenure and academic importance.

It is difficult, I believe, to predict the direction of the Greek American community. As mentioned earlier, it is a cohesive, homogeneous group, unlike so many of its ethnic counterparts —much smaller than the Italians, Poles, and Hispanics, but larger than the Russians, Arabs, Armenians, and smaller nationalities, and much more visible.

By any objective criterion the political progress of Greek Americans has been impressive, constructive, and in keeping with the best in American political tradition. Greek Americans who have volunteered to serve their fellow citizens have generally been individuals of good education, high personal standards, and with a commitment, regardless of party, to an open and progressive society. This latter point is particularly critical because without this concern for educational and economic opportunity, Greek American politicians, in effect, would be turning their backs on the very conditions that permitted their entry into the mainstream. Rarely have Greek American leaders advanced ideas or programs that were either purposely or unknowingly exclusivist or discriminatory. We should not forget that even Spiro Agnew was elected county executive on a platform of liberal change and racial equality.

I would trust and have every confidence that Greek Americans will continue to enter public life in increasing numbers. This involvement should continue to reflect the high personal standards of the Greek American community—hard work, love of family, respect for church, and a patriotism that refreshingly mirrors the immigrants' naive or romantic love for America. The success of people like Brademas, Christopher, Petris, Sarbanes, Tsongas, and their political colleagues, after all, represents the fulfillment of the vision which their fathers and grandfathers had when they entered Castle Garden and sailed past the Statue of Liberty. Greek American political involvement exemplifies the classical and modern Greek's love of political battle and the American tradition of public service. I believe on balance that this marriage of traditions has produced beneficial results for the nation and the Greek American community. It is with much anticipation that we await what the next twenty-five years will bring, and that will be another excellent topic for some enterprising scholar.

CHAPTER 5

THREE GENERATIONS OF
GREEK AMERICANS:
A STUDY IN ETHNICITY*

BY

ALICE SCOURBY

This study proposes to measure ethnic identity among three generations of Greek Americans living in the New York metropolitan area. New York City has the largest Greek community in the United States. Although the evidence reveals variation from generation to generation, the majority of Greeks still have a relatively strong attachment to their ethnic culture, in spite of identification with American society.

A cursory look at the literature dealing with Greek ethnicity only disappoints those looking for a clear and simple definition of what constitutes ethnicity for the Greek American. One reads, on the one hand, that the Church has been remiss in providing its parishioners with an understanding of Hellenism and, as a result, has led Greek Americans to view Hellenism in parochial and tenuous terms. Because of this, runs the argument, Americans of Greek descent have been so brainwashed as to regard ritualistic religion, along with Greek music, cuisine, and dance, as comprising the alpha and omega of Greekness. On the other hand, one also reads that the Church has provided the solidarity and inspiration without which a Greek American community would have been impossible.[1] Its supporters maintain that the Church has succeeded

*This article was originally published in the *International Migration Review* 14:1 (Spring 1980) 43-52. Used with permission.
[1]Theodore Saloutos, "The Greek Orthodox Church in the United States and Assimilation," *International Migration Review* 7:4 (Winter 1973) 395-408.

despite the inveterate factionalism that has plagued it through-out this century. In 1970, when the delegates to the Clergy-Laity Congress approved the substitution of English for Greek in the liturgy, it was viewed by many as the only realistic action that could be taken in light of the fact that a new gener-ation of Greek Americans was emerging without a competent knowledge of the Greek language. It was regarded as a genu-ine effort to reconcile Hellenism with the demands of Amer-ican society.

This seemingly innocuous attempt to salvage the younger generation by making the Church more relevant to them repre-sented a long delayed response to the grievances lodged by the second generation, who found the Church's role alien to their secular experience. The recent introduction of English in the Church was spurred by the belief that this alienation could be overcome by providing a basis for communication on a variety of social issues, including abortion, birth control, and mixed marriages. The underlying rationale was that the application of long held concepts such as the "logos" was no longer viable in a society dominated by scientific modes of thought.

Simultaneously, one also reads articles that report that the third generation of Greek Americans feels affinity neither for the Church nor for their Greek heritage, and does not identify strongly with folkloristic values. The authors suggest that the locus of identification for the younger generation has changed, that they have opted for "class" rather than religion or na-tionality as the locus of belonging. They have done this, runs this thesis, because they are far more psychologically secure in their Americanism than were prior generations. As a result, "class" and "status" have become the sine qua non of their identity.[2]

Some Greek Americans identify ethnically with a popular fair of music, dance, and food, only to have it demeaned as trivial by others who impose a hierarchy of values that alien-ates most of the population of Greek descent. Since a pecking order functions as the affirmation of one's worth in most socie-ties, this need to rank groups from Brahmins to untouchables should not strike us as too unusual. It is true that the cultural appurtenances that are deemed trivial are, in and by them-

[2]See George A. Kourvetaris, "Patterns of Generational Subculture and Intermarriage of the Greeks in the United States," *International Journal of Sociology of the Family* 1 (May 1971) 34-48.

selves, meaningless. Yet, in the collective act of sharing they are transformed from something profane to something sacred by providing the esprit de corps so essential to a collective sense of belonging and community.

Clearly, ethnic identity is extremely difficult to pinpoint. The concept is a fluid one and changes along a continuum of such variables as generation, education, occupation, and class. For example, the first generation of Greek immigrants who came to this country in the early part of this century viewed nationality and religion as part and parcel of their identity. For this reason, the Church became the major vehicle through which the immigrants' world was protected. Language, religion, old world customs, and endogamous marriages were the accepted indices of Greek identification.[3] Any deviation by their children constituted a threat to their security, self-image, traditional roles, and well-being.

Their children, the second generation, experienced their parents' definition of ethnicity as a liability. Despite this, the Greek Church, the Greek school, and the Greek language became integral parts of the self-image of these reluctant participants. They became "Greek Americans," whose very national appellation signified their bordering on two worlds. The collision of these two worlds reversed the natural order of things, so that the children became the culture bearers and the social arbiters for their parents. This paper is not the place to analyze the demeaning experiences and rejections suffered by the second generation in their efforts to adjust to American surroundings within the ideological framework of the "melting pot."[4] The English language, one of the most important indices used in measuring adjustment to American culture, was hampered by the fact that, for the second generation, Greek had to be spoken at home, albeit limited by a vocabulary dictated by the exigencies of day-to-day living. Nevertheless, ethnicity for this generation was still identified with language, tradition, and religion, but it was altered in conjunction with the American ethos of success and upward mobility.

By the 1950s, a third generation of Greek Americans was

[3]See Mayone J. Stycos, "The Spartan Greeks of Bridgetown: Community Cohesion," *Common Ground* 8 (Spring 1948) 24-34.
[4]For these experiences, see "The Forgotten Generation," *Athene* 10:4 (Winter 1950) 22-3, 41-2; and Theodore Saloutos, *The Greeks in the United States* (Cambridge, Mass.: Harvard University Press, 1964) 310-25.

emerging, and a new definition of ethnicity was in the wind. This new definition was articulated by social scientists who believed that ethnicity based upon nationality and language was gradually being replaced by religion in the lives of all Americans. They measured religiosity by a belief in God and attendance at religious services. Belonging to a religious institution was not only a new way of determining one's ethnicity, but was a legitimate way of being an American, because while one was expected to give up the ways of the "old world," one was never expected to give up one's religion. However, the three religions having institutional status were Protestantism, Catholicism, and Judaism.[5] Obviously, Greek Orthodoxy was excluded. What did this mean for the third generation of Greek Americans? Was being Greek different from being Greek Orthodox? Given the above thesis, it would seem not.

In the mid-1960s, we sampled seventy-one third-generation Greek Americans in the New York metropolitan area and found that religion continued to provide the context of self-identification for them. Indeed, while identification with language and customs and a preference for endogamous marriages persisted, it was with a marked ambivalence. For example, on the one hand they wanted the Church to substitute English in the sermon, but on the other they did not want all Orthodox churches to merge.[6]

In a recent study of first, second, and third-generation Greek Americans totaling 160 participants, it was found that there was less Greek school attendance with each succeeding group. Fewer of the third generation spoke Greek, and increased identification as being American was noted among the younger generation, as was a significant increase in the number who approved of marriages to non-Greeks as compared with those of the first and second generations.

The Study

The following data are derived from a sample of 160 individuals of Greek descent living in the New York metropolitan

[5]Will Herberg, *Protestant, Catholic, Jew* (New York: Anchor Books, 1950).

[6]See Alice Scourby, "Third Generation Greek Americans: A Study of Religious Attitudes," doctoral thesis, New School for Social Research, 1967 (published in 1980 by Arno Press, New York).

area. The sample was fixed by circumstance. The questionnaire used in this study was prepared both in English and in Greek. The first part was a personal data sheet on which the subjects were asked to designate their age, sex, education, and other census information. The second part of the questionnaire consisted of items measuring the rate of assimilation. Indices included language, church attendance, religious attitudes, identification with cultural values, and exogamy, which would permit the respondent to be placed in either of two categories: ethnoreligious or ethnocultural. The first reflects the ethnic identification associated with the first generation, i.e., religion, language, and nationalism, while the latter reflects a wider range of cultural values, i.e., Greek history, dance, music, cuisine, and social organizations.

The sample was drawn from several sources, including religious and secular organizations. Of the 160 individuals, 46 percent were males and 54 percent females. The age groups represented were 13-22 years (n = 76), 23-45 years (n=52), and 46-68 years (n=32). Of the total sample, approximately two-thirds were either in high school or had completed it. The remaining third had completed one to four years of college or postgraduate work.

Forty-two percent of the sample were students, 18 percent professionals, while 32 percent were equally divided between white-collar workers and housewives. Six percent were blue-collar workers and two percent were unemployed. Thirty-eight percent of the professional category were found in the first generation, 35 percent in the second generation, and 27 percent in the third generation.

Forty-two percent of the respondents' fathers were white-collar workers, 30 percent blue-collar, 16 percent professional, and 12 percent other than the above. The greatest concentration of blue-collar workers was found in the second and third generations. The white-collar group was equally divided between the second and third generations, while two-thirds of the professional group were found among fathers of the third generation.

Sixty-seven percent of the respondents' mothers were housewives, comprising the majority for all three generations. Eleven percent were white-collar, 10 percent professional, and 8 percent blue-collar. The remaining 4 percent were either unemployed or deceased.

These findings were consistent with the 1970 census,[7] which reports that 27,949 males of Greek ancestry who were 25 years old and older, from a total of 87,143, had completed high school. Of these, 22,115 or 82 percent had completed four years of college or more. In contrast, only 9,613 or 20 percent of native-born women of Greek background totaling 42,396 completed high school and went on to complete four or more years of college. Less than half of the women who entered college graduated, revealing the persistence of traditional attitudes regarding role expectations of males and females. It should be noted, however, that the 1970 census data indicated a significant rise of native-born females of Greek ancestry in the professional category: 8.3 percent in 1950 and 17 percent in 1970. As of 1970, the largest number of native-born women of Greek descent were in the category of clerical and kindred workers, whereas the largest number of native-born males of Greek ancestry were in the professional, technical, and kindred category, followed by the category of managers and administrators. This information is consistent with the occupational distribution found in our study. Of the 75 males and 85 females in our sample, 31 were of the first generation, 62 of the second, and 67 of the third generation. They responded to the questionnaire as follows:

The Greek Language. A significant index of assimilation is the declining use of the ethnic language. The answers were coded as follows: Do you speak Greek? (1) Yes; (2) No; and (3) No, but understand it. We found that erosion took place across the second and third generations. Of the second generation, 96.7 indicated that they spoke Greek, while 57.8 percent spoke Greek among the third generation. In the "No" category, the second generation comprised 3.3 percent of the total and the third generation 21.9 percent (chi-square = 35.119, 2 d.f., sig. @ .005).

Should English Replace Greek in Church? The individuals in the first generation unanimously responded in the negative. The second generation was divided and the third generation was unanimous in wanting the sermons delivered in English. Both the second and third generations, however, demonstrated

[7] US Bureau of the Census, *Census of the Population: 1970,* PC(2): 114..

a more traditional response when asked if English should replace Greek in the liturgy. Of the second generation, 58.3 percent preferred the liturgy in Greek, while the third generation was divided. One explanation for their split attitude toward the sermon and the liturgy may be that the latter represents the sacred, transcendental aspect of the religious experience and does not require knowledge of the language, while the sermon represents the Church's position on issues both religious and secular (chi-square = 16.7375, 4d.f., sig. @ .005).

Greek School. The Greek school has traditionally been a most important vehicle for transmitting ethnic identity. First-generation parents knew instinctively that their children would be quickly Americanized without supportive institutions to counteract it. Attendance in Greek school was significant between the second and third generations. Ninety percent of the second generation and 70.3 percent of the third generation had attended (chi-square = 15.715, 2d.f., sig. @ .005).

Intermarriage. The ethnic background of one's friends is an indicator of prospective mates from which one will choose. The respondents were asked if they would marry someone who was not of Greek extraction. Responses were coded as follows: (1) Yes; (2) No; and (3) Indifferent. With each successive generation there was an increased tendency toward marrying outside the group. Of the first generation, 51.6 percent reported that they would prefer to marry someone who was Greek, and 30 percent of the second generation compared to 25 percent of the third generation expressed similar sentiments (chi-square = 10.4402, 4 d.f., sig. @ .05).

Contact with Greek Mass Media. The question of involvement with Greek mass media indicated a decline from first to third generation. Of the third generation 55.2 percent expressed no contact, while only 7.4 percent of the first generation reported a similar response. Statistical significance was found between the first and third generations (chi-square = 12.4316, 2 d.f., sig. @ .005).

Church Attendance. Respondents were asked if they attend church: (1) Every Sunday; (2) Every other Sunday; (3)

Several times a year. Thirty-eight percent of the first generation, 61 percent of the second, and 65 percent of the third generation go to church at least every other Sunday. The second generation is inclined to attend church more often than the first generation. When education is kept constant, those in the first and second generations seem to attend church less frequently (chi-square = 18.342, 4 d.f., sig. @ .005).

Attitude toward the Church. The respondents were asked to indicate their attitude toward the Church, coded as follows: (1) Strongly favorable to the Church; (2) Neutral; and (3) Strongly against the Church.[8] All three generations were either strongly favorable or at least neutral. Of the first generation, 35.5 percent were strongly favorable, 51.6 percent were neutral, and only 3.2 percent were strongly against the Church. In the second generation, 78 percent were strongly favorable while 20 percent were neutral and none were strongly against. The third generation comprised 56.3 percent strongly favorable, 39.1 percent neutral, and 3.1 percent strongly against. Ten percent failed to respond. The second generation was significantly more favorably inclined toward the Church. Only three individuals in the sample were strongly against the Church—one from the first generation and two from the third.

First-generation college graduates tended to be more critical of the Church than their second-generation counterparts. They were opposed, however, to the use of English in church, did not support an American Orthodoxy, and chose friends of similar ethnic background. Sixty-one percent indicated that their friends were Greek, compared to 25.3 percent of the second generation and 14 percent of the third generation.

Ethnic Identity. The respondents were asked to identify themselves as either: (1) Greek; (2) American; (3) Greek Orthodox; (4) Greek American. The second and third generations tended to identify as either Greek American or Greek Orthodox, but a trend was discernible in the third generation to identify as American. The first generation identified as Greek or Greek Orthodox (multiple answers obviated chi-square). A further inquiry was made as to whether there was a difference between being Greek and being Greek Orthodox.

[8]L. K. Thurstone and E. J. Chave, *The Measurement of Attitude* (Chicago: University of Chicago Press, 1932).

Fifty-eight percent of the first generation, 55 percent of the second, and 64 percent of the third generation felt that there is a distinction. As for a merging of all Eastern Orthodox churches, the first generation was opposed, the second was divided, and the third was strongly opposed to such a merger.

The Greek People. A final question dealt with impressions held of Greek people. The responses were coded as follows: (1) Positive; (2) Negative; and (3) Indifferent. No generation had negative attitudes, although a hint of indifference was discerned in the responses of the third generation.

The findings of this study show that both American-born and foreign-born Greek Americans have retained a relatively strong attachment to their ethnic background. It also indicates that the attainment of higher occupational status among the second generation did not result, as might have been expected, in a denial of ethnic identity or an abandonment of the Greek community.

The results have demonstrated that there is an association between ethnoreligious identification and generation that is significantly different at the one percent level. (See the table appended at the end of this article.)

The first generation is still strongly identified with an ethnoreligious dimension, while the third generation showed greater identification with the broader cultural values of the Greek American community. Confusion as to precisely what constitutes Greek ethnicity was reflected in the younger generation, who, while expecting both the sermon and the liturgy to be in English, were negative in their responses to becoming part of an American Orthodox Church which would unify all Eastern Orthodox churches. A myriad of inconsistencies was revealed. Clearly, so much of ethnic identity is an unconscious experience as well as an ambivalent one. The individual reacts to judgments and responses of people within the group as well as those outside. Judgments, both positive and negative, can operate to pull the person toward or away from the group into which one was born. How these positive and negative forces are transmitted to the third generation vis-à-vis the second generation is something about which little is known. The one thing that is clear is that more studies, ones that will take us beyond the anecdotal and descriptive narrative, are essential for an understanding of the complex phenomenon of ethnicity.

Complicating the picture even further has been the influx of new immigrants since the Immigration Act of 1965. According to the Immigration and Naturalization Service, 125,924 Greeks came to the United States between 1966 and 1975.[9] In the year ending June 1975, a total of 1,864 males in the age category 20-29 emigrated to the US as compared to 1,170 females. It is interesting to note that during this same period, 5,719 Greeks were classified as housewives, children, and other, with no occupation reported. The other largest category, craftsmen and kindred workers, numbered 1,223, while only 421 Greeks were listed as professional, technical, and kindred workers. If it can be agreed upon that ethnicity is affected by generation, occupation, and education, then the figures would lead us to expect the persistence of traditional attitudes regarding ethnicity, the role of the Church, and family size. Since the new arrivals are mainly young, this may portend a high birthrate for the next decade, while the second and third generations continue to have low fertility rates following the population trend of Americans in general. The demographic imbalance between the old immigrants and the new will produce needs and demands from different vantage points. The Greek American community has been and will continue to be fractured by the different rates of adjustment each group makes to the surrounding environment. Therefore, Greek ethnicity can only be understood within a specific social context.

For the majority of the new immigrants, identification is rooted in nationality and the Church. If they do not find a Greek church, they build one. An unestimated number of Greek churches not affiliated with the Greek Archdiocese of North and South America have already been founded in the New York metropolitan area. It should not be surprising that the recent arrivals from Greece expect a Hellenized church, thus repeating the pattern of earlier immigrants who sought continuity of experience and solidarity within the Church. They view the introduction of English in the Church as part of a conspiracy to "de-Hellenize" it. If the Greek language and Greek values are not the focal points of the established Church, then other avenues for maintaining self-esteem and security will be sought, as indeed they are being sought. In time, the

[9]US Department of Justice, Immigration and Naturalization Service, *1975 Annual Report*, 65.

children of the new immigrants may react against the ethnic church their parents hold on to so tenaciously and, if so, a new ethnic identity will arise, in a form determined, in part, by the structure of the larger society.

VALUE ORIENTATION BY GENERATION

	ETHNORELIGIOUS number (%)	ETHNOCULTURAL number (%)	TOTAL
1st generation	24 (75.0)	8 (25.0)	32
2d generation	38 (57.5)	28 (42.4)	66
3d generation	26 (41.9)	36 (58.0)	62
TOTAL	88	72	160

chi-square = 9.62, 2 d.f., sig. @ .01

CHAPTER 6

THE ROLE OF THE CHURCH IN THE EVOLVING GREEK AMERICAN COMMUNITY

BY

NICON D. PATRINACOS

The role of the Church in the evolving Orthodox community in America can hardly be properly defined and evaluated without focusing back on the primitive community and its immigrant priest. Those two set the stage for the particular development that carried the community to its present well-being and to today's American-born priest. Indeed, some of the fundamentals conditioning our own self-understanding and place in American society can be traced back to them and their underlying philosophy of being in America.

The first priests who came to America with the first immigrants or shortly thereafter did not come here on behalf of the Church, i.e., with the mandate and authority to guide the experience of the newly transplanted and agonized seekers of a better future for themselves and their families. They came as immigrants themselves, and they had to cope with the same psychological turmoil of being uprooted and the same problem of language and adaptation. Sharing thus the same problems of the immigrants, they proved of invaluable help to them by offering the solace of worship and that inward fortification that derives from receiving the Orthodox sacraments.

However, being in most cases of an insignificantly higher level of education than that of their new parishioners, they failed to see the necessity of learning the language as soon as possible in order to enable themselves to serve their people much more effectively. Some actually died here after thirty or forty years still unable to carry on an intelligent conversation in English.

Unable to communicate with their environment, and thus finding themselves moving from one difficult and emotionally painful situation to another, the immigrants clung to the Greek language not only as a symbol of their traditions and ethnic identity, but as the sole instrument of retaining their Greek character and life. They hoped, as all immigrants did, and many still do, that their stay here would be only temporary, actually only as long as would be absolutely necessary to amass some personal fortune and then return to their mother country and native human environment. But these beforehand calculations did not work out either for the immigrant or for his priest, just as they do not work out even today. Scooping money from the streets proved to be an escapist's dream, grown out of the poverty that plagued him in his old country.

The real problems of the immigrant, however, did not prove monetary. Working hard and saving systematically, he quickly succeeded in managing his financial needs and those of his family here or in Greece. The problems that were destined to be with him for the rest of his life were problems of which he knew nothing before. In his native land he occupied a certain status and played a particular role under the umbrella of a culture that was indigenous to the country and native to him. There were a number of written and unwritten codes and modes of behavior, which demanded his loyalty and obedience but supplied him as well with protection and rights. In other words, he lived in an environment in which he could grow, protected against those potential enemies that might have attempted to destroy his inner order and the peace that derives from such an orderly coexistence between his thoughts, emotions, and will.

The tragedy, then, of the immigrant began with finding himself deprived of the inner security that a culture provides to the individual born in it and burdened with an inward confusion resulting from a conflict between credos, moral codes, and the emotional turmoil generated by a communication barrier.

Once the immigrant found himself in such a complex predicament, he had nowhere else to turn but to the inner world he brought with him to America. It was at this point in the development of the immigrant in his new world that the services of his priest proved invaluable, saving him from emotional deprivation and mental derangement. The immigrant priest was best equipped to bring the immigrant back to the old-world values he left behind and back to the culture he was born in, for he possessed the necessary material both in books and in his mind. Furthermore, his training gave him the know-how to build for the immigrant a vault in which he could not only safeguard the values of his heart and mind, but to which he himself could retreat in order to protect himself from the confusion and hostility of his new environment.

This mental ark gradually took flesh and bones in the structure of the first church building, which was usually a redecorated church of another ethnic group that had succeeded in elevating itself financially and socially and had moved out to a better neighborhood. The opening of the first Greek church in America set the nature and objectives of the Greek American community for all time to come. Even today, the church building is not only a place of worship, but the central point and center of community life in matters covering almost all of the facets of personal and communal experience. Envisioned by the first priests as an ark entrusted with the valuables of the phyletic heritage that condition personal experience, it really proved to be such an ark (notwithstanding the fact that with the passage of time and the change in group circumstances the parish became, in some instances, a ghetto—a status from which even today some of our communities are struggling to free themselves).

Thus, the role of the priest in safeguarding, often single-handedly, the sanity and progress of the immigrant during the infancy and adolescence of the community has proved invaluable. His goal, however, was not personal religion, but group religious expression and an adherence to the ideals of the ethnic heritage, which he was avowedly promulgating at all times. This neglect of establishing and nurturing the type of religion we call "personal," on the strength of which one succeeds or fails in the better part of his waking experience, still plagues our Church here, and we shall examine this more closely later on. However, the immigrant priest cannot be held responsible for neglecting his true call in the eyes of God, for he came from an environment in which personal religion was limited to emotional religious expression, while the moral character of the individual was expected to be shaped by group mores and group ideologies and, above all, by ethnic objectives and ideals.

While church and community were growing and going through their adolescence, however, their complete identification with ethnic objectives proved responsible for a deep political division, stemming from political conflicts in Greece, which almost destroyed not only what had been achieved, but threatened their future with deep and permanent scars. The most important characteristic of this civil war in our Greek American communities was the fact that the standard bearers, and in many cases the instigators, were the immigrant priests themselves, thus proving beyond doubt that the mission that mattered most to them, in their minds and hearts, concerned their ethnic heritage rather than Christ, whom they were preaching and who, according to some of them, spoke Greek during his epiphany on earth!

Still, after all the infighting and subsequent reconciliations, the communities survived and succeeded in obtaining in the process a national ecclesiastical leader in the person of Archbishop Athenagoras, who completed his life as the Ecumenical Patriarch.

The Greek American

We come now to the American-born. The second generation of Greek Americans had no deep problems within their immigrant family. They learned Greek rather effortlessly, primarily because their needs and wants could not be answered otherwise, which was due to the inability of their parents to speak English and their determination that their children should remain Greeks living in America. The community school, which began functioning as soon as the first American-born generation reached school age, was manned mostly by the immigrant priests. Besides the language, these priests imparted to the youngsters ideas and ideals, some of which were later to bring them in opposition to prevailing American standards and cause them pain and, in some cases, serious inner conflicts. But as a whole, the first American-born generation came through two cultures and two sets of ideas and ideals unharmed—due in part to the fact that the American culture of the time valued and required discipline, family coherence, and control.

This situation changed, however, with the coming of the third and fourth generations. The sacred ghetto, the ark of the immigrant's treasures, was let open, and ambient influences began to enter. The American-born, together with the more ambitious from among the immigrants, began to seek the approbation of American society. This marks the period of the building of imposing churches and community compounds, together with the passing of leadership of the parishes over to American-born priests educated in the United States.

In addition, two other very important events gradually came to pass: the appearance and constant rate of increase of mixed marriages, and the decrease in attendance of classes in the Greek language and Greek cultural history. At the same time, a new school appeared in the community, one originally established by the national leadership of the Church and unreservedly supported by priests and parents: the school commonly called Sunday school. The mission of the Sunday school proved highly important in safeguarding and teaching the cultural foundation on which Greek Orthodoxy stands and without which it remains a mere theology. Many children born today to Greek American parents attend Sunday schools, a fact that lays a tremendous burden on the conscience of our priests and bishops as regards what is taught there and by whom. And though Sunday school days are easily forgotten by the adolescent in search of self-emancipation, the imprint of a good Sunday school education can be used later—usually with the coming of the first child—as a sound foundation on which the newly married couple can build a religion all their own, but which still bears the marks of Greek Orthodoxy.

Our Church, however, even after its organizational maturity into an Archdiocese, failed to accompany the American-born through the pains of growing up, through his encounters with ideas and undercurrents demanding his soul, and did not adequately provide him with the direction and sure-footing that a mature personal religion affords the individual. Although chronologically our Church has entered adulthood, its inner growth proved to be on a different level than the one required for guiding and aiding the individual into the life in Christ and into a balanced and self-realizing personal experience. Our Church's vitality today consists of an organizational tightness and excellence that would really be a big plus for our survival here as an ethnic group, if only it were accompanied by an extensive and successful program of religious orientation and guidance conceived for and encompassing all ages and all walks of life.

Of course, it may not be entirely to the discredit of our Church that it remained attached to the image and needs of the immigrant Greek, whom it served and still serves exceedingly well. After all, apart from the Sunday schools, what systematic spiritual guidance and care our Church did provide for most segments of our American-born congregation was for the most part what could be gleaned from our liturgical services. And, although the spiritual value of the liturgical experience should not be minimized as a tutor for a personal religious experience, church ceremony and liturgical pageantry do not have the same impact on the American born as they do on the immigrant, and neither do they carry the same sense of sanctification for them as they do for our older people. Still, this is because we ourselves have failed to spell out intelligently and effectively the nature of our liturgical practices and life.

The recent division of our Church into independent bishoprics will certainly change our situation radically, perhaps sooner than most of us expect. In what direction remains to be seen, but with the decentralization of the national leadership, the coherence and unifying force it exercised on the Church up to now will certainly diminish. As with all organizations, the power lies with those who control the flow of money to the central treasury. Those are now the bishops and, ultimately, the community priests, whose power is rapidly rising to the point of holding the balance of power within the hierarchy and determining and formulating future policies, including religious programming and election of hierarchs.

The failure of our Church to offer effective spiritual aid, in terms of an all-embracing program, is reflected, in part, by the alarming rise in the number of mixed marriages. About 60 percent of the marriages performed in our Church are mixed, i.e., one party is Orthodox and the other non-Orthodox. And this figure does not even take into account Orthodox parties, especially young men, who marry in other churches or men and women who received Orthodox baptism—and in some cases Orthodox upbringing as well—who marry non-Christians.

One must naturally view a considerable number of these marriages as resulting from the steamroller of American culture. However, the majority of our mixed marriages are closely connected with the fact that our Church has done little to intelligently enlighten our young people about the dangers of mixed marriages before they become so deeply involved that they are unable to control their emotional attachment to the non-Orthodox party. Moreover, our Church has hardly encouraged marriages to Orthodox parties of different ethnic extraction. A number of older priests would actually prefer seeing a young Greek marry outside the Church rather than marry an Orthodox of non-Greek extraction—mostly because of national enmities and hatred in the Balkans, where most Orthodox populations are situated. Indeed, after fifty years of adult life, our Church is still very hesitant about having open relations with other Orthodox Churches beyond the common celebration of the Sunday of Orthodoxy and conclaves whose nature is usually more social than anything else. For years and years we have been preaching and hammering about the purity of the Greek Orthodox family and the preservation of our language as the *vehicle* of our faith and tradition. Now, it is all escaping our hold, as we confine ourselves to the status of an immigrant church whose avowed purpose is to preserve family and language as the very cornerstones of Greek Orthodoxy.

More importantly, however, we have failed to equip the Greek American with an organum for living, with a rational, detailed, and defensible charter of beliefs and practices, with a moral code that could be consulted and followed by anyone attempting to create his own Greek Orthodox experience. And by *organum* we do not mean simply literature but rather something more personal—a consultant that an Orthodox Christian could keep beside him for life for intimate and regulating guidance. This is what is called spirituality. It is the most vital aspect of living, far above and beyond mere religious emotionality responding to moving celebrations and traditional rhetoric, and our Church appears to be in dire need of it.

The ineffectiveness of our Church in the life of the Greek Orthodox becomes obvious whenever one tries to remember how many times in his life he has made decisions of importance in strict compliance with the prescriptions of the Church, even against his own theory of being and behaving. The result of this inquiry will in most cases be a sad one for the Church.

Up to now, a solution to the spiritual deprivation that has plagued our Church for so many years has proven elusive. In part, this can be attributed to two factors. First of all, our Church has become too concerned with organizational as opposed to spiritual issues and has lost—hopefully only for the present—the true spiritual element of religion. Secondly, the makeup of the Greek American community itself is becoming increasingly heterogeneous.

In summing up, then, we should state that the role the Church has played up to now in the developing Greek Orthodox community has been a complex and in many respects a self-effacing one. Our three leaderships have all earned excellent marks for their work in establishing and advancing the Church as an institution and thus providing the Greek American who is sensitive as regards his parental immigrant status with a footing of legitimacy and importance in American public life. The Church served the immigrant quite effectively in this manner, safeguarding our continued existence here as well as our determination to survive and prosper. But in so doing, our church leaders often assumed roles that were not appropriate for them, and as a result, laymen who could do an equally good if not better job in areas not strictly religious were excluded from our ethnic leadership. Our church leaders thought that they could provide the biblical "all things to all people," but in so doing they tended to forfeit their principal role of bringing Christ into the lives of the people they shepherded.

Furthermore, by devoting their ecclesiastical service almost exclusively to the institution—and by ultimately implying that they *are* the institution of the Church—our leaders prevented Greek American intellectuals and other professional people, who really reflect the success of the Greek immigrant in this country, from participating meaningfully in the life of the Church and applying their talents in its service. The result has been a segmented ecclesiastical life, with a sizable population spiritually floating about, seeking a spiritual moor to anchor to in this temporal environment.

Today's Greek Immigrant

Since the immigration laws were relaxed in the 1960s, a new influx of Greek immigrants has created new situations and new problems for the community and the Church. Their full impact on our established cultural and religious ways of life as well as on the lives of the immigrants themselves has not yet been fully recognized and appreciated. However, a tentative and brief discussion, limited only to indicating the underlying causes, could perhaps prove of some help at this time to churchmen as well as to sociologists in their endeavors to properly evaluate this new type of Greek American situation. The latest Greek immigrant is certainly different from the one whose descendants make up today's Greek American communities. His attitude toward life in general appears to be foreign to today's Greek American. His religious attitude and his political philosophy are indeed fundamentally different from those of the representative immigrant of the past, while his education is markedly different and academically superior. And although his coming to this country has been motivated in the main by the same perennial objective of seeking a better life and fortune in a strange country, his philosophy as to how to attain this goal is not exactly identical with the *hard work* attitude of the older immigrant. Besides, the emotional, religious, and ethnic bond that was primarily responsible for the founding and present well-being of the Greek American community seems to be absent from the hearts of the majority of these recent immigrants. Finally, in addition to all of these differences—in many cases irreconcilable—between the old and recent Greek immigrant, there is a certain negative attitude on the part of most of these newcomers toward America itself (the result, for the most part, of recent anti-American feelings generated by political ideologies and ethnic objectives in Greece).

Obviously, not all newcomers exhibit attitudes like those mentioned above, nor are they all motivated by philosophies which are negative toward community and country here. However, the fact that serious problems and unpleasant situations have arisen between many immigrants, on the one hand, and relatives, community, and Church, on the other, makes it imperative for both Church and community to recognize the problems and search for corrective measures that would spare the newcomers unnecessary pain and at the same time save the Greek American family and community from dissension and division (such as is already occurring in a number of communities in Canada).

In searching out the underlying causes of incongruous situations of this nature, one would do well to refer back to the old country and examine personal and group objectives there. Such objectives tend to generate forces that spur this type of immigrant to actions that often collide with accepted norms and mores here. In view of the fact that at the foundation of American life there lies, for better or worse, a personal and collective religious experience of considerable depth, the religious attitudes of these newcomers are extremely important in their psychological and cultural orientation. For reasons that could only briefly be touched upon here, personal religion—as a character-forming and regulating force and an experience that produces harmony both inside oneself and with others— is practically nonexistent among the new immigrants. In its place one can detect a kind of religious fear mixed with a tendency to take refuge in religious forms and objects of worship in times of personal desperation. Although these people will turn to the Church for the sacraments and other religious services that answer to their religious fear and the need for a form of pseudo-piety which they have retained from childhood, their conscious attitude toward the Church is anticlerical and antiecclesiastical. This is the obvious result of the failure of the Church in modern Greece to win over the educated class, whose members by personal philosophy consider themselves superior to clergymen and who still bear an intellectual allegiance to the credos of the French revolution. No doubt, the low level of education among the parish clergy, together with the scandalous lives of a number of higher clergymen, tends to foster and sustain this attitude and, needless to say, in turn undermines both family and national foundations.

Those among the latest immigrants who are personally ambitious and motivated by leftist political philosophies take the community with its church as their golden opportunity for quick social advancement without first having to prove themselves to the membership. This has happened in ghetto communities where these types of immigrants tend to congregate and can consequently muster enough voting strength to secure for themselves not only entry into community executive boards but, in time, domination over the community.

In communities where the newcomers do not have sufficient numerical strength for concerted exhibitions of dissatisfaction and disdain for the ways of their relatives and the established order of the community, the disharmony remains muted but explosive. But what separates the more articulate and unreserved newcomers from the Greek American community is not just envy for the wealth of America and the well-being of the Greek American. Feelings of this kind, together with the more definite enmity toward the governing order of both family and society in America, should have been expected, and the Church in particular should have taken measures to deal with these problems.

However, there is a much deeper gap between the Greek American and the recent Greek immigrant. Today's Greek immigrant is not an uneducated peasant who comes to America prepared to suffer all kinds of adversities, from personal humiliation to an inward crushing at the hands of either the people or the system of life and work in this country. He comes here with a formal and social education sufficient enough to enable him to observe and absorb situations and relationships and, consequently, to draw his own conclusions about people. things, and the country. The immigrant of the past lacked this kind of equipment, unless he was a professional expatriate such as a teacher, lawyer, or merchant of overseas experience.

Thus, today's Greek immigrant comes here with a theory and even with a cosmotheory of his own—including his own type of religion, which may be agnostic or atheistic, his own theory of society and the morals that should govern it, and his own political theory and brand of activism. His cosmotheory is limited to the powers of this earth and their struggle for supremacy, which is taken to be the meaning of living. If this sounds like a page from a philosophical and political essay against the western world, especially the United States, indeed it is. It is a resumé of life experience in a small and poor country where most young people grow up in a blind alley of inactivity and the expectation of a bleak personal future, and where there is little room for economic movement and personal advancement. The wits of the young are sharpened by harsh reality and political propaganda to an edge that can cut to pieces not only their real or imagined adversaries, but the young people themselves as well.

This smartness as a weapon for survival in a world of many with so little has become "the way and the truth," equated with morality and loaded with characteristics that can hardly contribute to the building up of a moral personality. Cheating, lying, outwitting and outdoing others in everything appears to be the prism through which the world is viewed. However, this type of personal morality negates the very traits and personal characteristics on the strength of which America has become what it is; it negates honest personal work within the protective framework of self-respect for others. Even the best of today's Greek immigrants bear traces of this type of mentality and exhibit obvious tendencies toward applying it in building up their personal lives here. If left unaided in their struggle for change, they are destined to a painful beginning and a doubtful future, neither of which they really deserve, being merely the innocent victims of their native environment.

Although not all newcomers to this country bring with them such an undesirable dowry of personality dispositions, personal philosophy, and habitual behavior, the fact still remains that undesirable situations exist and require the undivided attention and systematic help of those who are considered to be the guardians of the moral, cultural, and religious fiber of the Greek American community. These authorities include the Church, professional people from our academic and scientific worlds, and others who have distinguished themselves in business and in other endeavors in life. Unfortunately, the Church, with which initiatives of this kind rest by tradition, has done little to correctly recognize the situation and to consequently plan effective aid not only for the new immigrants but also for a great number of its own members who are involved in the newcomers' difficulties. A number of feeble attempts on the part of the Church in some of the communities that found themselves in serious difficulties on account of the immigrant influx were quickly dispelled by the pugnacity and determination of antireligious immigrants. They even succeeded, in some cases, in winning over members of the communities to their conviction that the Church had no business involving itself in the government of the community, its only function being to provide religious services for a fee.

The religious and intellectual leaders of the Greek American community should conduct an in-depth investigation of the situation and then draw up a far-reaching and permanent program of orientation that would enable the immigrants to earn a hopeful entry into the Greek American community and American society at large. It should be recognized by all that a smooth entry of Greek immigrants into American society by way of the Greek American community is not a matter of choice either for the immigrant or for the community—it is a must. Life in America is to a great extent culturally segmented and in many respects regulated by laws similar to those of survival in the wilderness. And although a few of us may be able to escape without punishment from subcultural territorial boundaries, the status of the rest will depend almost exclusively upon the degree of personal success they can attain, in the first place, within their group of cultural and ethnic origin.

Naturally, when inner growth and external circumstances improve to the degree where one feels constrained by subcultural territorial limitations, he may transcend his cultural territory. However, a cultural residue will remain with him for the rest of his life in the form of religious affiliation, family morals, or the particular angle he was taught to view life from in his childhood.

Once the existence and power of situations of this kind as molding forces supplying both essence and form to American culture itself are recognized, Church and community authorities should consider it their obligation to guide the immigrant into their midst and into American society by way of their community life. Helping the immigrant to find the right job is a serious undertaking and presupposes his being prepared to offer his best in a positive and unreserved manner. But this in turn presupposes that his political and social philosophy can be amended to such a degree that it becomes congruous with prevailing American attitudes and personal and national objectives. This, however, cannot happen before he is given a fair chance to objectively and intimately encounter the life of the community and the life of the nation. Church and community authorities must present him with opportunities to view and evaluate all aspects of American life and thought—both those that are desirable and those that non-Americans consider objectionable and rejectable.

Today's Greek immigrant is on the average in a position to evaluate conditions and circumstances which the older immigrant, because of the limits of his previous personal experience and exposure to world affairs, could not. He should not, therefore, be hammered with the assertion that everything American is good and the best in the world. His ethnic and cultural hang-ups should be allowed to run their course and, wherever possible, to revise themselves rather than be destroyed by force. His apparent or hidden nostalgia, which manifests itself particularly in times of personal difficulty, should be sympathetically viewed and even shared, instead of being ridiculed as a sign of personal weakness. All in all, he should be given the same opportunities and the same chances that would be given an individual in a stage of recovery from a severe shock and from the pain of parting with people and things he lived with and loved dearly. Without intending to sermonize, one can truthfully say that the interests of both the community and the immigrant require that he be treated "with love and understanding."

A matter of equal importance to a genuinely sympathetic attitude toward the new immigrant on the part of Greek Americans is affording him the opportunity and the means for learning the English language. Despite the fact that almost every immigrant has had painful experiences connected with his inability or difficulty in speaking the langauge of his adopted country, neither the Church nor the secular authorities of the community has ever fully realized the importance of language for the emotional and spiritual well-being of the immigrant and the role it is bound to play in his business or professional future. Seldom has formal instruction in the English language ever been offered to immigrants as part of the community program of guiding them into American life. And although every community in America commendably offers systematic and competent instruction in the Greek language for children born here, little instruction in the English language and American culture is offered the immigrant.

Every immigrant could learn English quickly and painlessly if courses were offered within the community by Greek American teachers. And again, the importance of knowing and acquiring a feeling for the English language on the part of the immigrant cannot be overemphasized. Haphazard knowledge of English has generated deep pains for otherwise successful immigrants in their relations with their children and their friends. The notion held by some of the older clergymen—which had actually become a kind of formal though tacit policy with the Church—to the effect that the less English immigrants learn the closer they will stay to the Church cannot be sustained by any criteria. Unfortunately, the Church has failed the immigrant in his first and most important steps in America.

The role of the Church, then, in the developing Greek Orthodox American community is far from over. If the Church can prove able to shed the vestiges of its immigrant approach to the problems of its American-born generations, it can perform a saving task for its people and for itself—and without losing its Greek Orthodox tradition, its cultural personality, or its liturgical language. For these, the American society provides ample room and a nourishing atmosphere.

CHAPTER 7

ETHNIC LANGUAGE AS A VARIABLE IN SUBCULTURAL CONTINUITY

BY

CHRYSIE M. COSTANTAKOS

This paper examines the issue of ethnic language as it relates to subcultural continuity. Although the United States is a multilingual society, there has been in this country a long tradition of abandonment among linguistic minorities of the mother tongue, a situation which has led to the basic attitude that language shift is a natural step expected from a psychologically mature minority population. "There is some prima facie evidence . . . that, while large scale language shift is usually considered indicative of a progressive attitude in the Americas and in Africa, in both Europe and Asia language loyalty is considered to be natural as well as wholesome."[1]

In his farewell comments after three years of service as the editor of the International Department of the *Journal of Marriage and the Family*, Dr. Gerrit A. Kooy described the phenomenon of ethnic language nonmaintenance in the United States as follows:

America, the country with an enviable sociology in the eyes of the non-American sociologist, is at the same time extremely insular. The grandchildren and great-grandchildren of those who spoke German, Dutch, Swedish, French, Italian, or another non-Anglo-Saxon language seldom possess such reading ability in a language other

[1]Heinz Kloss, "Types of Multilingual Communities: A Discussion of Ten Variables," *Sociological Inquiry* 36:2 (Spring 1966) 145.

than English that they really read contributions written in a foreign language.[2]

In such a milieu, as a result, the question of language and ethnic continuity takes a distinct significance. To those who find linguistic survival indispensable in ethnic continuity, disappearance of language may be tantamount to ethnic extinction.

Ethnicity in itself has had widely varying definitions, many of which assume linguistic distinctiveness as an essential component. An ethnic group, according to Melvin M. Tumin, denotes:

> . . . a social group which within a large cultural and social system, claims or is accorded a special status in terms of a complex of traits (ethnic traits) which it exhibits or is believed to exhibit. Such traits are diverse, and there is much variety in the complexes that they form. Prominent among them are those drawn from the religious and linguistic characteristics of the social group, the distinctive skin-pigmentation of its members, their national or geographic origins or those of their forebears.[3]

Tumin further notes that: "Ethnic as an adjective is often used interchangeably with religious, racial, national, cultural and subcultural."[4] In Joshua A. Fishman's words:

> Ethnicity designates a constellation of primordial awareness, sentiments, and attachments by means of which man has traditionally recognized the descriminada that relate him to some other men while distinguishing him from others. . . . Foreign ethnicity has normally been taboo only because it has been considered irrelevant to the higher mission and the greater opportunity envisioned by American nationalism. . . . We know very little about the anomalous half-life of ethnicity in pres-

[2]Gerrit A. Kooy, "Le Roi Est Mort; Vive Le Roi," *Journal of Marriage and the Family* 31 (August 1969) 427.

[3]Melvin M. Tumin, "Ethnic Group," in *A Dictionary of the Social Sciences*, eds. F. Gould and W. L. Kolb (New York: Free Press, 1964) 243.

[4]Ibid.

ent-day America. We know even less about which (if any) current expressions of ethnicity are conducive to language maintenance.[5]

William Beer, in an article entitled "Language and Ethnicity in France," discusses the relationship of language to ethnicity, pointing to both its importance and complexity. "Ethnic identities among others," he concludes, "satisfy the quest, part of which requires learning the language that serves as a repository of the ethnic culture."[6]

Talcott Parsons refers to the language-ethnicity relationship as he discusses the various components which have figured historically in the ethnic complex:

> In spite of the difficulty of being specific about criterial features and components, what social scientists have called ethnic groups do belong to a relatively distinctive sociological type. This is a group the members of which have, both with respect to their own sentiments and those of nonmembers, a distinctive identity which is rooted in some kind of a distinctive sense of history.... A particularly prominent aspect of cultural identity ... has been language ... Language ... has been closely associated with a relatively diffuse conception of a common cultural tradition.[7]

Language reflects social order. It facilitates the interpretation of shifts relative to social structure and cultural norms. The users and uses of language varieties represent aspects of more encompassing social patterns and processes.[8] Or, as Joyce Hertzler put it:

> A language is a culturally contrived and socially established system of standardized and conventionalized sym-

[5]Joshua A. Fishman, *Language Loyalty in the United States* (The Hague: Mouton, 1966) 402, 29, 31.

[6]William R. Beer, "Language and Ethnicity in France," *Plural Societies* 7:2 (Summer 1976) 91-3.

[7]Talcott Parsons, "Some Theoretical Considerations on the Nature and Trends of Change of Ethnicity," in *Ethnicity: Theory and Experience*, eds. Nathan Glazer and Daniel P. Moynihan (Cambridge, Mass.: Harvard University Press, 1975) 56, 54.

[8]Joshua A. Fishman, ed., *Advances in the Sociology of Language* (The Hague: Mouton, 1971) 9.

bols. As a system it is a body of self-consistent, rule-governed, interfunctioning parts. The constituent symbols have specific and arbitrarily imposed meaning and common usages for purposes of socially-meaningful expression and for communication in the given society (or technically in the given "language community"). . . . Language is the primary and fundamental out-growth of the life of the people of the language community; for in a very real sense it itself embodies and reveals the entire human socio-cultural heritage in all its past and present aspects more generally and comprehensively than any other block or sector of institutions.[9]

Joseph H. Greenberg suggests that "linguistic and extra-linguistic segments of culture are intimately connected in a number of different ways."[10] In any language, there are terms with several connotations, and every element of speech acquires its secondary meaning derived from the context or the social environment within which it is used, taking a special tinge from the actual occasion in which it is employed. Every social group has its own private code, and all the features mentioned are only accessible to the members of the in-group. They all pertain to the scheme of expression; they are not teachable or able to be learned in the same way as vocabulary would be.

National characteristics, traits, manners of thought, action, and speech are transmitted from generation to generation through the medium of language. Stephan George Chaconas, in his work *Adamantios Korais: A Study in Greek Nationalism* (based on the life of Korais, the outstanding Greek philologist of the eighteenth century), analyzes Korais' work based on the concept that language made and preserved nationality. Language possessed a distinctive quality that was interwoven with national character and was thus a badge for nationality. Korais, according to Chaconas, enlarged his ideas to include the thesis that blood affinity of the ancient and modern Greeks was substantiated by the linguistic continuity of the Greeks, which could be easily traced back to the Greeks of the ancient classics in a kind of unbroken succession. A language that had endured and survived foreign domination many times through-

---

[9]Joyce O. Hertzler, "Social Uniformation and Language," *Sociological Inquiry* 36:2 (Spring 1966) 301-2.
[10]Joseph H. Greenberg, *Language, Culture, and Communication* (Stanford, Calif.: Stanford University Press, 1971) 9.

out the centuries constituted historical evidence that "Greek was an indigenous tongue with its roots going back to the early centuries before Christ."[11]

The speech had evolved from the mother tongue, from the inner soul of the national group and was the product and heritage of the Greek people. To Korais, as to many other philologists of the romantic era, nationality was only limited by language and, therefore, all persons who spoke Greek were Greek nationals. Chaconas further elaborates on Korais' conceptualization of nationality, pointing to the three uniting factors of language, belongingness to the same country, and religion, as the existing relationship and the bonds which held together the Greek nation.[12] "Although Korais placed language first in importance among the three irreducible factors comprising nationality, he nevertheless thought that other peculiarities, such as ethnic customs and habits, were also of marked significance."[13]

The linguistic component, however, is not included in the conceptual scheme of all social scientists whose work has focused on the manifestation, meaning, and significance of ethnicity. In their broad definition of ethnicity, Glazer and Moynihan place the emphasis of ethnicity on the label of an ethnic group which serves a boundary-maintaining function and not on substantive cultural differences such as language, religion, etc.[14] Fredrik Barth supports the same notion of ethnic groups and boundaries when he stresses that "the critical focus . . . becomes the ethnic boundary that defines the group, not the cultural stuff it encloses."[15] Thus, such a definition of ethnicity emphasizes social processes of exclusion and incorporation, which contribute to the boundary-maintaining and identity-defining functions of ethnicity which in a sense point to the position that the actual content of ethnic groups may in effect not be all that different. Milton Gordon is one of the proponents of cultural differences of ethnic groups, but without the consideration of ethnic language as a prime component

[11]Stephen George Chaconas, *Adamantios Korais: A Study in Greek Nationalism* (New York: Columbia University Press, 1942) 50.

[12]Ibid., 48-75.

[13]Ibid., 75.

[14]Glazer and Moynihan, *Ethnicity: Theory and Experience*, 1-25.

[15]Fredrik Barth, *Ethnic Groups and Boundaries* (Boston: Little, Brown and Company, 1969) 11-5.

of distinctiveness.[16] Trudgill sees no link in language and race, but accepts that:

> ... in many cases language may be an important and even essential concomitant of ethnic-group membership. This is a social fact ... and it is important to be clear about what sort of processes may be involved. In some cases, for example, and particularly where languages rather than varieties of a language are involved, linguistic characteristics may be the most important defining criteria for ethnic group membership. For instance, it is less accurate to say, that Greeks speak Greek than to state that people who are native speakers of Greek (i.e., who have Greek as their mother tongue) are generally considered to be Greek (at least by other Greeks) whatever their actual nationality. ... In any case, ethnic group differentiation in a mixed community is a particular type of social differentiation and, as such, will often have linguistic differentiation associated with it.[17]

This paper is presented with the underlying assumption that ethnic language may well be a significant factor to be considered with regard to the definition of Greek American ethnicity. Elements of the significance attached to language became evident in this exploratory study, attempting as it were to elicit attitudes toward the Greek language and its maintenance and to assess its importance as a factor in subcultural continuity.

Methodological Considerations

There are two approaches to the present study, which is based on data collected for an earlier study on Greek American subcultural continuity. One approach to the study probes into attitudes toward ethnic language. Attitudes toward ethnic language are analyzed in relation to generational status, such status used as a dimension in subcultural continuity. The Greek

[16]Milton Gordon, *Assimilation in American Life: The Role of Race, Religion and National Origin* (New York: Oxford University Press, 1964) 19-59.

[17]Peter Trudgill, *Sociolinguistic* (New York: Penguin Books, 1974) 60.

language is taught to the Greek American child at home and at the parish Greek school, much weight being placed on the latter in cases of third and fourth-generation Greek American children whose parents are native born and English speaking. The Greek school is an integral part of the subcommunity. Instruction in Greek begins late in the afternoon, following the day in public or private school. There are, of course, today several day Greek schools where language instruction is part of the regular school curriculum.

The second approach to the study examines ethnic language proficiency as a variable in subcultural continuity, manifested as identification with ethnicity in its various dimensions. It focuses on the relationship of such variables to a set of statements reflecting traditional ethnic values and continuity processes. It includes sources of ethnic identification as tradition in both its classic and modern forms, church, language, music, food, kin relations, and processes such as patterns of interaction, contact with the mother country, homogamy, community involvement, and family and kin contact.

Thus, for the first part, the data analyzed hypothesizes that attitudes toward ethnic language remain positive, although maintenance is losing ground as one moves along the generational continuum. Secondly, the study assesses ethnic language proficiency as a variable in subcultural continuity, hypothesizing that such a variable is an important factor for the ethnic identification of the group under consideration—such identification assumed to be strongest among those whose language proficiency is greater. The study is exploratory, stressing "hypothesis generation" rather than "hypothesis testing," and draws upon the resources of a metropolitan Greek American subcommunity.[18]

The Sample

Two hundred and eleven Greek Americans responded to a prepared sociocultural questionnaire, and forty of these respondents were interviewed in depth on the basis of an open-ended, semi-structured interview schedule. Twelve of these forty respondents (three from each group of old immigrants,

[18]See Barney G. Glaser and Anselm L. Strauss, *The Discovery of Grounded Theory: Strategies for Qualitative Research* (Chicago: Aldine, 1967) 21.

recent immigrants, second and third-generation native-born Greek Americans) were interviewed for a second time, prior to the writing of this paper, in order to validate congruence of data collected in earlier interviews.

The sample of the 211 questionnaire respondents consisted of 44.5 percent males and 55.5 percent females, 66.5 percent of whom were born in the United States, 28.6 percent in Greece, and 4.9 percent in areas occupied by Greece in the past and still maintaining large Greek populations. Approximately three-fourths (74.5 percent) of them were of urban origin, as contrasted to 24.5 percent of rural origin. Of the total number of respondents, 34.1 percent were first-generation Greek Americans with years of residence ranging from one to forty-four. Those who arrived in the United States before 1940 ("old migrants") comprised 15.6 percent of the total sample, and those arriving after 1940 ("new migrants") accounted for 18.7 percent. Second-generation Greek Americans made up 42.5 percent of the sample and third-generation Greek Americans comprised 19 percent. The remaining 4.3 percent were children of intermarriages, categorized as "other." The Greek areal affiliation included the Ionian Islands, the Aegean Islands, the islands of Crete and Cyprus, the Peloponessus, central and northern Greece, as well as regions designated as "other Greece," such as Asia Minor and Egypt. With regard to formal socialization experiences, 69.7 percent of them were educated only in the United States, 14.9 percent only in Greece, and 15.4 percent in both countries. The respective educational levels reached include 65.4 percent no education in Greece, 10.4 percent some or grammar school, 8.1 percent some high school, 9.5 percent high school graduates, 4.7 percent had some college, and 1.9 percent college graduates or beyond. The educational level in the USA was reported as none by 15.9 percent, some or grammar school by 2.4 percent, some high school by 18.5 percent, high school graduates 19.0 percent, 21.8 percent some college, and 23.2 percent college graduates or more.

With regard to language proficiency, which was self-evaluated, 3.8 percent reported no proficiency in the Greek language, 8.1 percent assessed their proficiency as poor, 21.3 percent as fair, 37 percent good, and 29.9 percent fluent. It is significant that almost two-thirds of the group assessed their proficiency as good or fluent, and only one-third as poor or nonexistent. The group is English speaking, with fluency on a 66.5 percent level and with 19.1 percent evaluating their proficiency as good,

10 percent as fair, 3.8 percent as poor, and one respondent (.5 percent) spoke no English.

The demographic characteristics on the marital status of the group reveals 35.1 percent of the group to be single, 50.2 percent married, and 1.9 percent separated. The group reflects a high degree of endogamy, with only 9.3 percent having married people from other nationalities. Most of the married respondents had children, the majority reporting two children. Most respondents (67 percent) lived in a nuclear family, with the remaining third living in some type of an extended family, including grandparents and other relatives. Finally, while the majority (70.5 percent) of the respondents were Greek Orthodox, less than half (47.0 percent) reported being active in church attendance.

The subsample of forty Greek Americans, men and women who were interviewed in depth, is considerably representative of the overall sample. Striking differences were: a higher percentage of them (42.5 instead of 35.1 in the larger sample) was single, and fewer of them were active in the Church (37.5 versus 47 percent). Both of these differences indicate that the subsample consisting of volunteers reflects overrepresentation of the least traditional subjects from the entire sample.

Instruments

The research instruments consisted of (1) a sociocultural questionnaire, consisting of statements covering broad topics—such as self-image with regard to ethnicity and the dominant culture, attitudes toward language, church, Greek community involvement, views on mate selection, attitudes toward marriage, family and kin interaction as well as general attitudes—which was responded to by all 211 subjects; and (2) semi-structured, open-ended, in-depth interviews of the subsamples of 40 and 12 respondents chosen from the large sample of 211. The interview guide probed into the definition of ethnicity, the meaning of Greek tradition, attitudes toward the Greek language and Hellenic institutions, deethnization of the Greek Orthodox Church manifested in language shift, and actual behavior reflected in frequency and occasions of ethnic language use, reliance and preference for the Greek press, other media, and literature and cultural activities. Complementarity in instrument use was emphasized, with interviews substantiating those trends indicated in the statistical analysis of the questionnaire responses. Chi-square was used as the statistical test of significance, with the null hypothesis rejected at the 0.5 level of probability.

Limitations

Since the bulk of the data was obtained through the use of the questionnaire, the strengths and weaknesses of this technique will have to be borne in mind. The sampling technique may constitute a limitation, since one can never be certain that the sample chosen represents the whole, and is never able to say with any degree of accuracy whether information supplied by the sample is true of the universe from which the sample is drawn. At no point is randomness claimed in the selection process, and the data, therefore, is considered only as applicable to the group under consideration, the findings to be regarded as suggestive and tentative. A major bias may well be the self-evaluation of language proficiency by the respondents, as perceptions differ as to what such proficiency represents. Additionally, the unevenness of the groups in terms of the numbers of respondents would have to be reckoned with in the analysis of findings. In the case of the interview, the involvement and bias of the interviewer may add to the limitations. It is hoped that the complementarity of the instruments, together with the duality of approaches to the treatment of data, will counterbalance strengths and weaknesses, thus in no way discounting the validity of the results within the existing limitations.

Discussion and Analysis of Findings

The first part of the discussion focuses on the attitudes toward ethnic language as exhibited in the responses of the generations of the sample of respondents. Table 1 depicts such attitudes, suggesting in an overall way that language holds symbolic meaning in ethnic identification.[19] In response to the statement "Knowledge of Greek is a must for every Greek

[19]The five tables referred to are appended at the end of this article, pp. 160-70.

American family," there was more agreement than disagreement to this statement. Generational differences are reflected on a descending order, with the old migrant group projecting the highest agreement (75.8 percent), followed by the recent migrants (64.1 percent), second generation (58.4 percent), third generation (42.5 percent), and the "other" group (11.1 percent). The lower level of agreement by the recent migrant group and the substantial ambivalence are possibly suggestive of a degree of conflict resulting from attempts to adjust, efforts to be accepted, desire to learn the English language, and a tendency to reject obvious elements of foreignism. On the other hand, knowledge of Greek is not an issue with this group presently. There is high disagreement by the group in toto to the statement that "Any attempt to preserve the Greek language is a lost cause," reinforcing the previous suggestion of the symbolic meaning language holds in ethnic identification. It is significant to observe the generational breakdown and the strongest disagreement revealed by the native groups, including the offspring of mixed parentage. The overall ambivalence is of low magnitude, and the strongest agreement is projected by the migrant generation. Intergenerationally there is a low level of disagreement. It was indeed of extreme interest to find the same sentiments expressed in the interviews. Even though there were intergenerational differences as to how intense the feeling was, the desire to know the language was unquestionably there, intensified in some cases after travel to Greece. How the language can be preserved was more the issue, not the knowledge of the language. There seems to be more of an objection to the structure of the Greek school rather than the imposition of learning the Greek language. Those, of course, may represent responses on the ideal level now that the stigma of foreignism is somewhat more removed from the reality of the past. Everyone seems to disagree with another statement testing attitude toward ethnic language, that "As a rule, migrant Greeks make no attempt to learn the English language." Disagreement on the part of the recent migrants may well be a function of the recency of their migration, a fact which tests this issue presently.

The old migrants and the third generation disagree less (60.6 and 60.0 percent, respectively), both groups being perhaps more objective and less emotional with regard to this question. Checking age as a contributory variable, one finds it statistically significant (chi-square $= 33.9217$, 14 d.f., sig.

@ .01). The statement "The educated migrant often foregoes use of the Greek language in an attempt to identify closer with the dominant American culture" evidenced ambivalence, with the migrant groups disagreeing more and the strongest disagreement coming from the recent migrants, the group that this question might presently concern most. The second generation followed very closely in its disagreement, but showed higher ambivalence, undoubtedly the function of age and generational status. In fact, both those variables emerge in statistical significance (age: chi-square = 25.6042, 14 d.f., sig. @ .05; generational status: chi-square = 18.1094, 8 d.f., sig. @ .05).

It is rather surprising to find the level of agreement projected in response to the statement that "Recommendations should be made for day Greek parochial schools," the agreement of the group in toto reflecting on the level of 55.5 percent. The migrant generations, as one might expect, agreed the strongest (old migrants 75.8 percent, and recent migrants 81.1 percent). The agreement on the part of the native-born generations on levels ranging from 48.9 to 32.5 percent together with a considerably high degree of ambivalence (35.0 percent for the third generation) may well be suggestive of a desire for continuity, the means of partaking with as little conflict as possible in two worlds. Reinforcing the positive sentiments toward ethnic language is also the response to the statement that "When in the company of other Greek Americans, we use mixed language." Although the statement is not statistically significant, the distribution of responses is of interest as it points to a direction supported by feelings expressed in the interviews. Such feelings were verbalized as a sense of belongingness, peoplehood, "the little things that no one else understands," the sheer satisfaction of facilitation in communication, a symbolic value and attachment to meanings best expressed through this medium.

A case can be also made for the ethnic language as a force in subcultural continuity on the basis of response distribution to the statement "Most native Greek Americans would like to correspond with their relatives in Greece using the Greek language." With a 56.5 percent of the total group agreeing and an over 50 percent agreement for the native-born generations coupled with a considerable degree of ambivalence, it appears that, at least on the ideal level, ethnic identification and desire for continuity is unquestionably reflected. When allegiance to institutions is called for, there is a splitting of loyalties favoring nativity status and suggestive of intergroup resentments. The results of the testing of ethnic language proficiency, self-evaluated by the respondents between the polarities of "no knowledge" to "fluency," in relation to subcultural continuity are reflected in the responses of the group to statements expressing dimensions of ethnic identification. They are summarized in tables 2, 3, 4, and 5 and are grouped as "Self-Image with Regard to Ethnicity and the Dominant Culture," "Attitudes toward Language, Church, and Greek Community Involvement," "Mate Selection, Marriage, and Kin Relations," and "General Attitudes," respectively.

Table 2 highlights the relationship of language proficiency to ethnic identification. In general, testing self-image with regard to ethnicity projects a close relationship to language proficiency. Agreement and/or disagreement, depending on the content of the statement, progressively relate to language proficiency as one moves along the proficiency continuum. There is considerable disagreement, for example, to the statement that "Efforts of Greek Americans to establish institutions of their own are in vain." Out of a group of 210 respondents including native-born Greek Americans of the second and third generations as well as children of intermarriages, 160 respondents disagreed, and 24 had "no opinion." Disagreement stands on the ascending order as one moves along the continuum of language proficiency. The group with the greatest fluency disagrees the strongest, such group most likely including a substantial percentage of migrants. It is of interest to note, however, that even the groups reporting "none" or "poor" knowledge of the ethnic language disagreed on levels ranging between 62.5 and 76.5 percent.

There are deviations from linear relations in statements of high statistical significance, specifically statements tied to ethnic identification in historical perspective, statements testing allegiance to the country of origin vis-à-vis the host country and/or the country of birth, and statements probing into intergroup perceptions, relations, and attitudes. Distributions of responses to such statements as "There was no pride in being of Greek descent before World War II," "Identification with Greece is stronger now than ever before," "Migrant Greeks saw and see their stay in the USA as a transitory period," "Native-born Greek Americans and Greeks who have lived in the USA for a long time never get along with recently migrated Greeks," "It would be nice if one could travel more often to Greece to revitalize the culture," and the strong statement of allegiance expressed in "A Greek is a brother no matter what his status and mode of living," reveal deviations and high degrees of ambivalence attributable to the operation of intervening variables. Indeed, cross-tabulations of relevant demographic variables reflected statistical significance of intervening variables such as age, place of birth, location (urban or rural), number of years in the US, generational status, educational level and background (US, Greece), English-language proficiency, marital status, number of children in family of procreation, intermarriage, occupation, ethnic church activity, and organizational membership. As an example, place of birth and age were significant intervening variables in the distribution of responses to the statements "Identification with Greece is stronger now than ever before" (age: chi-equare = 19.53233, 10 d.f., sig. @ .0340; place of birth—US, Greece, other: chi-square = 9.32383, 4 d.f., sig. @ .0535; marital status: chi-square = 24.25293, 8 d.f., sig @ .0021; number of children—family of procreation: chi-square = 18.15279, 10 d.f., sig. @ .0524; educational level—Greece: chi-square = 21.39534, 10 d.f., sig. @ .0185) and "Migrant Greeks saw and see their stay in the USA as a transitory period" (place of birth—US, Greece, other: chi-square = 10.38344, 4 d.f., sig. @ .0344; age: chi-square – 30.68660, 10 d.f., sig. @ .0007; educational level—US: chi-square = 22.24188, 10 d.f., sig. @ .0139; occupation: chi-square = 36.40257, 18 d.f., sig. @ .0063; marital status: chi-square = 16.77246, 8 d.f., sig. @ .0326; generational status: chi-square = 42.70670, 14 d.f., sig. @ .001; community organizational membership: chi-square = 6.44373, 2 d.f., sig. @ .0399).

Of extreme interest is the high level of agreement to statements pointing to specific sources of ethnic identification such as food, music, and traditional dances, the strongest agreement and identification revealed by the groups whose language proficiency is reported as "good" or "fluent." Intervening variables are suggested as contributory to the fluctuations of the response distributions. Indeed, generational status emerged as one intervening variable of significance in the cross-tabulation of the statement "Greek music is very much a part of every gathering in Greek American homes" (chi-square = 27.97881, 14 d.f., sig. @ .0143). Marital status (chi-square = 26.10826, 8 d.f., sig. @ .0010), age (chi-square = 36.85716,

10 d.f., sig @ .0010), occupation (chi-square = 47.05043, 18 d.f., sig. @ .0002), intermarriage (chi-square = 11.46462, 2 d.f., sig. @ .0032); church activity (chi-square = 34.36240, 14 d.f., sig. @ .0018), generational status (chi-square = 34.36240, 14 d.f., sig. @ .0018), and educational level–USA (chi-square = 26.70529, 10 d.f., sig. @ .0029) emerged in statistical significance as intervening variables in the distribution of responses to the statement "Greek Americans enjoy Greek dances more than Greeks from Greece." The overall high levels of agreement, however, unmistakably direct attention to an existing relationship of language proficiency and identification with certain aspects of ethnicity, most especially music and dance.

In summary, the findings summarized in table 2 point to the significance of ethnic language proficiency in ethnic identification. Such a relationship, however, is not a simple relationship, but one emerging in complexity and in need of further study and evaluation.

Table 3 provides interesting answers to statements probing into language proficiency and attitudes toward language maintenance and ethnic church and community organizational involvement. Responses to the statements included in the table take a distinct significance as ethnic language preservation is a major issue today for the Greek American subcommunity in the United States, a subcommunity of diverse constituency encompassing at least four generations of Greek Americans and a segment of children of mixed parentage. The official position of the Greek Orthodox Church, the superstructure of Hellenism in America, is one progressively accepting the language shift in church and parish organizations based on the alleged inevitability of change and the search for an indigenous church relevant to the American setting. The responses of the group reflect progressive agreement with the statement "Knowledge of Greek is a must for every Greek American family," with a deviation projected by the "fluent" group, which agrees on the 63.5 percent level while the group of "good" proficiency exceeds this agreement (71.8 percent). The high levels of ambivalence and disagreement by the "none," "poor," and "fair" groups are reflective of the significance of such intervening variables as generational status (chi-square = 31.77087, 14 d.f., sig. @ .0043), age (chi-square = 31.22375, 10 d.f., sig. @ .005), place of birth (chi-square = 16.01180, 4 d.f., sig. @ .0030), intermarriage (chi-square = 7.56659,

2 d.f., sig. @ .0227), church activity (chi-square = 15.28210, 4 d.f., sig. @ .0042). The level of agreement reflected in response to the statement "Most native Greek Americans would like to correspond with their relatives in Greece using the Greek language" is somewhat surprising, as one would consider such a statement a weak variable. At least on the ideal level, the desire for continuity is present in this group of respondents from a metropolitan area Greek American community, and support for community organizations of any means that would preserve Greek heritage is projected in their responses to the statement "One should support the Greek community organizations as the best means of preserving Greek heritage." Interview material both from previously and recently conducted interviews points to positive attitudes toward language, church, and community organizations, albeit with an emphasized desire to see meaningful and substantive changes of quality and ideological commitment. A realistic view of the emerging Greek American ethos in all its breadth and dimensions is indicated as there is a need for understanding and dialogue among the diverse constituency of Hellenism in America. Interview data is strongly at variance to the tendency to believe that language shift in church will unify and strengthen the Greek American community. A young third-generation interviewee who had traveled through Europe and visited Greece for the first time last year had this to say:

Why is it that many Europeans speak several languages fluently and we seem to have such problems with language in this country? I came back from my trip with a completely different attitude toward knowledge of Greek. I felt so inadequate, and in a way sad for speaking Greek so poorly. As a matter of fact, I am now considering taking courses to improve. There must be a way, easier way, of inspiring children to study and speak at least the language of their forefathers. It is so much easier when one is young. I am now convinced, more than ever, that it is not change to English in church but revamping of Greek and Sunday schools that is in order —family, church, and community working together.

Table 4 probes into views on mate selection, marriage, and relations to kin. Views and procedures for the selection of partners distinguish family systems, and Greeks traditionally held definite ideas on the mate-selection process. Such selection was to take place with strict definitions as to how the choice was to be made and who were socially and religiously permitted to marry. Historically, the Greek family was patriarchal in form, the husband being the powerful figure and the decision-maker. Masculinity was preferred, and males of the family were the desired sex to assure continuity of the line of descent and were privileged in rights and rewards. Family was revered, and functions were carried out within a network of kin relationships. Obligations toward parents—aged parents in particular—were paramount, and such obligations extended beyond the nuclear family.

As one delves into the responses to statements on mate selection, one is impressed with the strength of values governing dating and social behavior. There is a progressively higher disagreement to the statement that "Girls should be allowed to ask boys for dates," disagreement being highest among those whose language proficiency is greatest. Deviations can be traced to the influence of intervening variables. It is of interest to note that the disagreement by the "fluent" group drops to a lower level than that of the "good" group (70.5 to 73.7 percent respectively), the fluent group most likely including some modern and upwardly mobile Greek Americans. Examining intervening variables, life-cycle patterns emerge in significance (marital status: chi-square $= 16.04967$, 8 d.f., sig. @ .0417; age: chi-square $= 22.97890$, 10 d.f., sig. @ .0108). Life-cycle patterns are of basic consideration for many native-born Greek Americans; a quest for cultural anchorage when marriage and children come reaffirms their allegiance to ethnic values. Sex is an intervening variable which emerged in statistical significance a few times, but only in cases where an issue was unquestionably sex-linked (chi-square $= 14.30905$, 2 d.f., sig. @ .008). Occupation (chi-square $= 36.67445$, 18 d.f., sig. @ .0058) is significant with this and many other statements because of its effect on the assimilative process through the economic opportunities and the social mobility it affords.

Loyalty to family and respect for parents are signified by the distribution of responses to the statement "A boy does not have to account to his parents about his whereabouts." There is considerable disagreement in an ascending order as one moves along the language proficiency continuum. The disagreement of those who spoke "no Greek" is of a much smaller magnitude, consistent with previous findings and the result of life-cycle patterns (marital status: chi-square = 19.25581, 8 d.f., sig. @ .0038; age: chi-square = 28.41867, 10 d.f., sig. @ .0015). Marriage within the group and relations to kin are values in change, with conflicting elements in their acceptance and rejection. Responses to the statements that "Most Greek Americans marrying outside their group find it essential to be accepted by the Greek community" and "Greek people should not marry outside their faith" give us a picture of the change, the progressively greater acceptance of social inter-action out of the group and marriage. Although there is a discernible agreement with the statements testing traditional values and patterns of behavior among the ethnic language proficiency groups, the levels of disagreement, ambivalence, and fluctuation point to values in change. It is to be noted, however, that such changes are simultaneously occurring in Greece, and we are in effect witnessing changes that will have to be evaluated within the larger context.

As we move to the analysis of data in areas of kin rela-tions, mobility, kin and nonkin interaction, obligations for in-teraction, differentiation of the nuclear family from kin, and obligations to aging parents, we are struck with the inevitabil-ity of change, but also with the indication of kin orientation and desirability for interaction. Intergroup differences are consistently in evidence, ethnically identifiable values being favored by the groups of ethnic language proficiency. There appears to be a lessening of kin relations beyond the confines of the nuclear family, but there are strong suggestions for extensiveness in kin orientation, strongest among the proficient groups, which include a number of recent migrants. The strongest kin orientation is in the context of filial responsibili-ties. Indeed, responses to the statements "For the sake of fam-ily happiness, one should help aging parents who are physic-ally able to maintain themselves independently, if this is finan-cially possible" and "It is considered a stigma for American children of Greek descent to place their parents in a home for the aged; parents belong with their children" project agree-ment on an ascending order along the language proficiency continuum, strongest among the "fluent" groups. Notable is the difference in agreement to the second statement between the "good" and "fluent" groups (41.2 and 63.8 percent respec-tively). Place of birth and location (urban or rural) are the intervening variables of significance (chi-square = 14.70723,

4 d.f., sig @ .0053; and chi-square = 6.38911. 2 d.f., sig. @ .0410, respectively).

In short, traditional values relative to marriage and kin have undergone change, although the family emerges with considerable strength in subcultural continuity. Attitudes and kinship behavior are not consistent from one area to another and among the different groups, as intervening variables of significance result in fluctuations of causative relationships. There is, nonetheless, a relationship between language proficiency and identification with ethnic values. Thus, the issue of ethnic language maintenance in subcultural continuity merits special attention and consideration.

Table 5 depicts the response distribution of the group to statements reflecting general attitudes and values that have been noted by students of Greek ethnicity as characterizing the Greek, both as a person and as a member of his group. The results summarized in this table, however, do not point to a clear-cut relationship of such values and attitudes to ethnic language proficiency among the group of respondents.

Philotimo, the "sense of honor," is something that gives meaning to every Greek's life as an individual or family or group member.[20] The distribution of responses indicates a positive relationship between this variable and ethnic language fluency. The respondents agree progressively that "Greeks will go to any expense to safeguard their sense of *philotimo*, their respect for honor." However, the levels of ambivalence, ranging between 14.3 and 23.3 percent, and the levels of disagreement, ranging from 42.9 to 18.6 percent among the respondents reporting their knowledge of the ethnic language as "none," "poor," or "fair," reinforces previous indications that the relationship is far from a simple linear one but indeed the product of a multiplicity of intervening variables in operation. Interview information revealed that even the meaning of the word was unfamiliar to many of the native-born groups, and that change of values has occurred in succeeding generations in areas considered of almost sacred meaning to the Greek personality. Such change nonetheless has happened and is happening in the motherland, as disagreement to the level of 16.7 percent by the fluent group, undoubtedly including a considerable representation of migrants, would indicate.

[20]Dorothy D. Lee, "Greece," in *Cultural Patterns and Technical Change*, ed. Margaret Mead (New York: a publication of UNESCO, 1953) 80.

In an authoritarian Greek family the roles were clearly defined, and household activities were in the domain of the female. Attempting to elicit tendencies toward egalitarianism in family roles, one finds deviations from agreement with the statement, such agreement not following ascending order along the language proficiency continuum. In addition, the overall agreement is weak, with almost a split between agreement and disagreement, in addition to considerable ambivalence. As one examines intervening variables of significance, the multiplicity of factors in effect becomes evident, as variables such as marital status (chi-square = 40.45105, 8 d.f., sig. @ .0010), children in family of procreation (chi-square = 29.58966, sig. @ .0010), English language proficiency (chi-square = 13.15045, 6 d.f., sig. @ .0407), occupation (chi-square = 37.89252, 16 d.f., sig. @ .0016), church membership (chi-square = 12.12405, 2 d.f., sig. @ .0023), and community organizational membership (chi-square = 11.02706, 2 d.f., sig. @ .0040) emerge in high statistical significance.

Students of Greek society and culture invariably mention that Greeks love to talk, and the responses of the group sustain this value, albeit with some variation exhibited by the fairly proficient in ethnic language group.[21] The overall agreement of the group stands at the level of 64.5 percent, with indecision on the 18.7 percent level. Generational status and length of stay in the United States will have to be considered for groups removed by the necessities of life of the New World, which do not allow for the flexibilities of life and conditions of the village society in Greece.

The value placed on educational pursuits is maintained on a high level of acceptance, with no discernible differentiation in terms of ethnic language proficiency.

It would appear from the responses to the statements of general attitudes and values attributable to Greek ethnicity that Greek language proficiency is a factor at work affecting segments of the group and individuals within a group differently. There are several variables in operation, and a distinctly direct relationship is not present. There are indications of dualism in loyalties suggestive of the unmistakable effect of the assimilative process. The Greeks of yesterday, whether in the United States or the country of origin, are not the same as

[21]Ernestine Friedl, *Vassilika: A Village in Modern Greece* (New York: Holt, Rinehart and Winston, 1962) 81.

the Greeks of today, and will not be the same as the Greeks of tomorrow.

Summary and Conclusions

The generalizations which can be drawn from the study of ethnic language and its relation to subcultural continuity, after analysis of both attitudes toward the language and the relationship of ethnic language proficiency to ethnic identity, point to the significance of ethnic language as a variable in subcultural continuity. The findings suggest that the Greek language holds symbolic meaning in ethnic identification, such meaning often exemplified in the emergence of a "mixed language" form, used especially by the native-born generations and to a lesser extent by the migrant groups. Such a linguistic form provides the group with solidarity and cohesiveness, a common bond of special sentimental attachment and value. Both hypotheses were supported—that is, attitudes toward ethnic language remain positive despite considerable erosion, generationally, in language maintenance; and, secondly, ethnic identification is strongest among those whose language proficiency is greatest.

There was a strong intergenerational disagreement to any statement alluding to nonmaintenance of this dimension of ethnic identification, and, in general, ethnic identification statements, stressing both values and social processes of continuity, tended to reflect greater agreement as one moved along the self-evaluation continuum of ethnic language proficiency, which ranged between the polarities of "no knowledge" to "fluency." The emerging themes were strongly supported by raw interview material, and the issue for many of the interviewees was more the question of "how" to preserve the language, rather than "why." Although many of the interviewees related horrifying experiences of Greek school days, a number of them expressed regrets for having resisted the efforts of home and afternoon schools. A repeated theme dealt with relevancy of teaching materials, instructional content, educational methodology, and conflicting feelings toward foreign-born mother language teachers.

Generationally, it is beyond question that the dynamic aspects of language preservation have suffered, not only among the native-born generations but with migrants as well, and erosion is observed even within one generation. Language maintenance presents to the Greek Americans a weakening process of subcultural continuity, as indeed to other ethnic groups. Such weakness, however, does not seem to be based on linguistic prejudice but rather lack of effective coordination of efforts on the part of the family and the afternoon Greek school, compounded by the monolinguistic orientation of the dominant culture.

Shift of ethnic language to English in church is not overwhelmingly favored by the group of this investigation, both in terms of liturgy and sermons. There is, however, greater agreement for the change to English sermons. A number of respondents, although not Greek speaking or comprehending the language of the liturgy, expressed enjoyment in the mysticism of the ritual and did not wish it to be changed. Taking Hofman's assertion that "use of the mother tongue in church sermons seems to be the most meaningful index of language maintenance because the sermon is probably most sensitive to the linguistic needs and preference of the congregation as a whole,"[22] such expressed acceptance of change may well point to erosion and deethnization, with serious implications for language maintenance. If the "ethnic parish has no special ideological or traditional link to the linguistic status quo, Anglification of its services is bound to occur in time."[23]

It becomes evident from the analysis of the data exploring the relationship of language proficiency and ethnicity that this is not a simple relationship, but rather a multiple causation of intervening and simultaneously operative variables. Distributions of responses often revealed deviations from linear relations and there emerged certain consistent trends suggestive of the complexity of the relationship. Intervening variables such as generational status, age, place, and location of birth, recency of migration, educational background—where received, educational level attained both in Greece and in the US, occupation, family life-style patterns, parish membership and activity, as well as outside dominant culture influence, have compounded the picture.

In summary, as Greek Americans become progressively heterogeneous in composition—generationally, ethnically, and

[22]John E. Hofman, "Mother Tongue Retentiveness in Ethnic Parishes," in Fishman, *Language Loyalty*, 133.
[23]Ibid., 136.

in terms of social class membership—traditional links to the linguistic status quo impose the test of inexorable deethnization on the Hellenes of the diaspora. The findings support the significance of the Greek language in the ethnic identification of this group, at least on the ideal symbolic level, and the desire for maintenance and continuity. It would appear that ethnicity for this group serves more than a boundary-maintenance function, and there is strength reflected in identification of specific sources of ethnicity, one of them being language. Yet, unequivocably, ethnic language maintenance is a progressively weakened process of subcultural continuity. Is the process reversible? It is often as difficult to escape from the gratification of doom prediction as it is from the pleasure of wishful thinking. But realism dictates understanding that the results of this study, as gratifying as they may be for the expression of desire for language continuity, point to the need for further study and for serious assessment of the desirability and climate provided in opportunities for bilingual education as a vehicle of ethnic language maintenance.

Ethnic language maintenance may indeed be accomplished only with the support of public policy, change of attitudes of the dominant culture, and minority groups' achievement of security and acceptance. It is doubtful that the trend for deethnization can be reversed and the clock turned back, but it is perhaps not too late to put a new clock in motion. It is certainly worth trying, for the benefit and enrichment of all.

TABLE 1
Attitudes toward Language

Statement	Respondent	Agree	No Opinion	Dis-agree	Total No.
			Percentages		
"Knowledge of Greek	old migrants	75.8	3.0	21.2	33
is a must for every	recent migrants	64.1	10.3	25.6	39
Greek American	second generation	58.4	7.9	33.7	89
family."	third generation	42.5	12.5	45.0	40
	"other"	11.1	22.2	66.7	9
$\chi^2 = 17.6445$, 8 d.f., sig. @ .05		57.1	9.0	33.8	210
"Any attempt to	old migrants	20.0	6.7	73.3	30
preserve the Greek	recent migrants	26.3	2.6	71.1	38
language is a lost	second generation	8.9	5.6	85.6	90
cause."	third generation	7.5	2.5	90.0	40
	"other"	22.2	0	77.8	9
not significant		14.0	4.3	81.6	207
"As a rule, migrant	old migrants	24.2	15.2	60.6	33
Greeks make no	recent migrants	20.5	5.1	74.4	39
attempt to learn the	second generation	13.3	2.2	84.4	90
English language."	third generation	22.5	17.5	60.0	40
	"other"	11.1	0	88.9	9
$\chi^2 = 18.1427$, 8 d.f., sig. @ .05		18.0	7.6	74.4	211
"The educated migrant	old migrants	36.4	15.2	48.5	33
often foregoes use	recent migrants	43.6	5.1	51.3	39
of the Greek language	second generation	37.1	16.9	46.1	89
in an attempt to	third generation	40.0	35.0	25.0	40
identify closer with	"other"	22.2	44.4	33.3	9
the dominant American					
culture."					
$\chi^2 = 18.1004$, 8 d.f., sig. @ .05		38.1	19.0	42.9	210
"Recommendations	old migrants	75.8	12.1	12.1	33
should be made for	recent migrants	81.1	5.4	13.5	37
day Greek parochial	second generation	48.9	16.7	34.4	90
schools."	third generation	32.5	35.0	32.5	40
	"other"	44.4	11.1	44.4	9
$\chi^2 = 30.9876$, 8 d.f., sig. @ .001		55.5	17.2	27.3	209

TABLE 1 (Continued)

Statement	Respondent	Agree	No Opinion	Dis- agree	Total No.
			Percentages		
"When in the company	old migrants	82.1	10.7	7.1	28
of other Greek	recent migrants	74.4	10.3	15.4	39
Americans, we use	second generation	86.7	3.3	10.0	90
mixed language."	third generation	77.5	0	22.5	40
	"other"	66.7	0	33.3	9
not significant		81.1	4.9	14.1	206
"Most native Greek	old migrants	66.7	23.3	10.0	30
Americans would like	recent migrants	55.3	18.4	26.3	38
to correspond with	second generation	56.7	16.7	26.7	90
their relatives in	third generation	52.5	25.0	22.5	40
Greece using the	"other"	44.4	22.2	33.3	9
Greek language."					
not significant		56.5	19.8	23.7	206
"Most native Greek	old migrants	36.4	15.2	48.5	33
Americans will give	recent migrants	63.2	10.5	26.3	38
their help to Greek	second generation	47.8	21.1	31.1	90
institutions in the	third generation	47.5	35.0	17.5	40
USA, but are not	"other"	66.7	11.1	22.2	9
sensitive to the					
needs of Greece."					
$\chi^2 = 16.2534$, 8 d.f., sig. @ .05		49.5	20.5	30.0	210
"Migrant Greeks	old migrants	31.3	12.5	56.3	32
think of Greece	recent migrants	43.6	17.9	38.5	39
first and then of	second generation	52.2	17.8	30.0	90
the Greek institu-	third generation	55.0	32.5	12.5	40
tions in the USA."	"other"	55.6	22.2	22.2	9
$\chi^2 = 18.7812$, 8 d.f., sig. @ .02		48.1	20.0	31.9	210

TABLE 2
Self-Image with Regard to Ethnicity and the Dominant Culture

Statement	Respondent	Agree	No Opinion Percentages	Dis-agree	Total No.
"Efforts of Greek	none	0.0	37.5	62.5	8
Americans to establish	poor	11.8	11.8	76.5	17
institutions of their	fair	15.9	20.5	63.6	44
own are in vain."	good	15.4	3.8	80.8	78
	fluent	7.9	11.1	81.0	63
$\chi^2 = 16.3465$, 8 d.f., sig. @ .05	TOTAL	12.4	11.4	76.2	210
"There was no pride in	none	0.0	62.5	37.5	8
being of Greek descent	poor	11.8	29.4	58.8	17
before World War II."	fair	6.8	18.2	75.0	44
	good	21.8	25.6	52.6	78
	fluent	27.0	6.3	66.7	63
$\chi^2 = 26.5443$, 8 d.f., sig. @ .001	TOTAL	18.6	20.0	61.4	210
"Identification with	none	12.5	75.0	12.5	8
Greece is stronger now	poor	29.4	17.6	52.9	17
than ever before."	fair	57.8	22.2	20.0	45
	good	57.7	15.4	26.9	78
	fluent	65.1	17.5	17.5	63
$\chi^2 = 27.2186$, 8 d.f., sig. @ .001	TOTAL	55.9	19.9	24.2	211
"Migrant Greeks saw and	none	0.0	50.0	50.0	8
see their stay in the USA	poor	17.6	35.3	47.1	17
as a transitory period."	fair	38.6	29.5	31.8	44
	good	49.4	18.2	32.5	77
	fluent	55.6	4.8	39.7	63
$\chi^2 = 26.1286$, 8 d.f., sig. @ .001	TOTAL	44.5	19.1	36.4	209
"Money and financial	none	25.0	50.0	25.0	8
assistance has never	poor	35.3	47.1	17.6	17
stopped flowing to	fair	64.6	24.4	11.1	45
Greece."	good	70.5	14.1	15.4	78
	fluent	76.2	9.5	14.3	63
$\chi^2 = 22.5753$, 8 d.f., sig. @ .001	TOTAL	66.4	19.0	14.7	211

TABLE 2 (Continued)

Statement	Respondent	Agree	No Opinion	Dis-agree	Total No.
			Percentages		
"Native-born Greek	none	0.0	62.5	37.5	8
Americans and Greeks	poor	17.6	23.5	58.8	17
who have lived in the	fair	28.9	15.6	55.6	45
USA for a long time	good	35.9	19.2	44.9	78
never get along with	fluent	27.0	4.8	68.3	63
recently migrated					
Greeks."					
$\chi^2 = 25.1986$, 8 d.f., sig. @ .01	TOTAL	28.9	16.1	55.0	211
"Migrant Greeks do not	none	0.0	62.5	37.5	8
think of native American-	poor	5.9	76.5	17.6	17
born Greeks as Greeks."	fair	11.1	31.1	57.8	45
	good	30.8	25.6	43.6	78
	fluent	21.0	21.0	58.1	62
$\chi^2 = 31.9201$, 8 d.f., sig. @ .001	TOTAL	20.5	31.0	48.6	210
"Native Greek Americans	none	50.0	37.5	12.5	8
do not as a rule want to	poor	47.1	35.3	17.6	17
identify with the unedu-	fair	40.0	17.8	42.2	45
cated Greek migrant	good	57.7	11.5	30.8	78
element."	fluent	46.0	7.9	46.0	63
$\chi^2 = 18.2320$, 8 d.f., sig. @ .02	TOTAL	49.3	14.7	36.0	211
"Native Greek Americans	none	37.5	62.5	0.0	8
are proud of the	poor	47.1	35.3	17.6	17
educated migrant	fair	75.6	15.6	8.9	45
Greek."	good	74.4	14.1	11.5	78
	fluent	77.8	14.3	7.9	63
$\chi^2 = 18.4434$, 8 d.f., sig. @ .02	TOTAL	72.0	18.0	10.0	211
"A Greek is a brother no	none	12.5	25.0	62.5	8
matter what his status	poor	23.5	5.9	70.6	17
and mode of living."	fair	37.8	11.1	51.1	45
	good	48.7	17.9	33.3	78
	fluent	54.0	7.9	38.1	63
$\chi^2 = 16.4985$, 8 d.f., sig. @ .05	TOTAL	44.5	12.8	42.7	211

TABLE 2 (Continued)

Statement	Respondent	Agree	No Opinion	Dis-agree	Total No.
			Percentages		
"It would be nice if one	none	62.5	37.5	0.0	8
could travel more often	poor	64.7	29.4	5.9	17
to Greece to revitalize	fair	75.6	8.9	15.6	45
the culture."	good	88.5	6.4	5.1	78
	fluent	85.5	6.5	8.1	62
$\chi^2 = 20.6994$, 8 d.f., sig. @ .01	TOTAL	81.9	10.0	8.1	210
"A Greek name in any kind	none	37.5	50.0	12.5	8
of successful endeavor	poor	76.5	17.6	5.9	17
fills one with pride."	fair	73.3	8.9	17.8	45
	good	79.5	11.5	9.0	78
	fluent	82.5	3.2	14.3	63
$\chi^2 = 20.8098$, 8 d.f., sig. @ .01	TOTAL	77.3	10.4	12.3	211
"Any person of Greek	none	0.0	75.0	25.0	8
descent who Americanizes	poor	11.8	23.5	64.7	17
his name is looked upon	fair	13.3	17.8	68.9	45
with contempt from his	good	28.2	19.2	52.6	78
fellow Greeks."	fluent	38.1	14.3	47.6	63
$\chi^2 = 27.3601$, 8 d.f., sig. @ .001	TOTAL	25.6	19.9	54.5	211
"Greek food is very much	none	37.5	25.0	37.5	8
a part of the cuisine of	poor	82.4	0.0	17.6	17
the Greek American	fair	88.9	2.2	8.9	45
families."	good	88.5	5.1	6.4	78
	fluent	86.7	6.3	7.0	63
$\chi^2 = 18.9171$, 8 d.f., sig. @ .02	TOTAL	85.3	5.2	9.5	211
"Greek music is very much	none	50.0	12.5	37.5	8
a part of every gathering	poor	70.6	0.0	29.4	17
in Greek American homes."	fair	82.2	4.4	13.3	45
	good	94.9	1.3	3.8	78
	fluent	93.7	0.0	6.3	63
$\chi^2 = 27.4986$, 8 d.f., sig. @ .001	TOTAL	88.2	1.9	10.0	211
"Greek Americans enjoy	none	12.5	75.0	12.5	8
Greek dances more than	poor	41.2	52.9	5.9	17
Greeks from Greece."	fair	45.5	9.1	45.5	44
$\chi^2 = 63.8292$, 8 d.f., sig. @ .001	good	70.5	9.0	20.5	78
	fluent	73.0	6.3	20.6	63
	TOTAL	61.4	14.3	24.3	210

TABLE 3
Attitudes toward Language, Church, and Greek Community Involvement

Statement	Respondent	Agree	No Opinion	Dis-agree	Total No.
			Percentages		
"Knowledge of Greek is a	none	0.0	25.0	75.0	8
must for every Greek	poor	23.5	11.8	64.7	17
American family."	fair	45.5	13.6	40.9	44
	good	71.8	5.1	23.1	78
	fluent	63.5	7.9	28.6	63
$\chi^2 = 29.8218$, 8 d.f., sig. @ .001	TOTAL	57.1	9.0	33.8	210
"The educated migrant often	none	37.5	62.5	0.0	8
foregoes use of the Greek	poor	35.3	29.4	35.3	17
language in an attempt to	fair	42.2	22.2	35.6	45
identify closer with the	good	42.9	19.5	37.7	77
dominant culture."	fluent	30.2	7.9	61.9	63
$\chi^2 = 24.9881$, 8 d.f., sig. @ .01	TOTAL	38.1	19.0	42.9	210
"Most native Greek Americans	none	12.5	75.0	12.5	8
would like to correspond with	poor	35.3	17.6	47.1	17
their relatives in Greece	fair	62.2	17.8	20.0	45
using the Greek language."	good	57.9	19.7	22.4	76
	fluent	62.3	14.8	23.0	61
$\chi^2 = 22.6400$, 8 d.f., sig. @ .01	TOTAL	56.5	19.8	23.7	207
"Most native Greek Americans	none	50.0	37.5	12.5	8
will give their help to Greek	poor	58.8	29.4	11.8	17
institutions in USA, but are	fair	37.8	15.6	46.7	45
not sensitive to the needs of	good	39.0	26.0	35.1	77
Greece."	fluent	68.3	12.7	19.0	63
$\chi^2 = 23.1187$, 8 d.f., sig. @ .01	TOTAL	49.5	20.5	30.0	210
"It is absurd to insist on	none	62.5	0.0	37.5	8
using the Greek language in	poor	76.5	5.9	17.6	17
Church, we run the risk of	fair	29.5	13.6	56.8	44
losing our youth."	good	42.1	9.2	48.7	76
	fluent	28.6	6.3	65.1	63
$\chi^2 = 19.2943$, 8 d.f., sig. @ .02	TOTAL	38.9	8.7	52.4	208
"One should support the Greek	none	75.0	25.0	0.0	8
community organizations as	poor	52.9	17.6	29.4	17
the best means of preserving	fair	68.9	17.8	13.3	45
Greek heritage."	good	76.6	3.9	19.5	77
	fluent	77.8	15.9	6.3	63
$\chi^2 = 17.0643$, 8 d.f., sig. @ .05	TOTAL	73.3	12.4	14.3	210

TABLE 4
Mate Selection, Marriage, and Kin Relations

Statement	Respondent	Agree	No Opinion	Dis-agree	Total No.
			Percentages		
"Most Greek Americans	none	0.0	62.5	37.5	8
marrying outside their group	poor	23.5	17.6	58.8	17
find it essential to be	fair	28.9	35.6	35.6	45
accepted by the Greek	good	41.6	23.4	35.0	77
community."	fluent	42.6	11.5	45.9	61
$\chi^2 = 20.2810$, 8 d.f., sig. @ .01	TOTAL	36.1	23.6	40.4	208
"Girls should be allowed	none	75.0	12.5	12.5	8
to ask boys for dates."	poor	29.4	11.8	58.8	17
	fair	9.1	25.0	65.9	44
	good	17.1	9.2	73.7	76
	fluent	16.4	13.1	70.5	61
$\chi^2 = 26.7106$, 8 d.f., sig. @ .001	TOTAL	18.4	14.1	67.5	206
"A boy does not have to	none	50.0	12.5	37.5	8
account to his parents	poor	35.3	5.9	58.8	17
about his whereabouts."	fair	20.5	10.3	69.2	39
	good	11.4	1.4	87.1	70
	fluent	5.3	7.0	87.7	57
$\chi^2 = 24.6510$, 8 d.f., sig. @ .01	TOTAL	15.2	5.8	79.1	191
"If our child would have to	none	37.5	25.0	37.5	8
marry a non-Greek, they	poor	41.2	5.9	52.9	17
should at least marry in	fair	48.9	17.8	33.3	45
the Greek Orthodox Church."	good	72.4	9.2	18.4	76
	fluent	66.7	12.7	20.6	63
$\chi^2 = 16.5534$, 8 d.f., sig. @ .05	TOTAL	61.7	12.4	25.8	209
"Greek people should not	none	25.0	0.0	75.0	8
marry outside their faith."	poor	5.9	5.9	88.2	17
	fair	37.8	13.3	48.9	45
	good	44.7	9.2	46.1	76
	fluent	57.1	6.3	36.5	63
$\chi^2 = 20.3979$, 8 d.f., sig. @ .01	TOTAL	43.1	8.6	48.3	209

TABLE 4 (Continued)

Statement	Respondent	Agree	No Opinion	Dis-agree	Total No.
			Percentages		
"Children should not leave	none	37.5	0.0	62.5	8
home before they get	poor	11.8	5.9	82.4	17
married."	fair	41.9	11.6	46.5	43
	good	57.1	7.8	35.1	77
	fluent	61.9	4.8	33.3	63
$\chi^2 = 20.3979$, 8 d.f., sig. @ .01	TOTAL	51.0	7.2	41.8	208
"The place for sons is the	none	37.5	0.0	62.5	8
parental home until they	poor	11.8	5.9	82.4	17
marry."	fair	26.7	17.8	55.6	45
	good	46.8	9.1	44.2	77
	fluent	49.2	6.3	44.4	63
$\chi^2 = 17.4578$, 8 d.f., sig. @ .05	TOTAL	40.0	9.5	50.5	210
"It is unthinkable for girls	none	25.0	0.0	75.0	8
to leave their parental home	poor	11.8	5.9	82.4	17
before marriage."	fair	46.7	6.7	46.7	45
	good	59.7	2.6	37.7	77
	fluent	63.5	6.3	30.2	63
$\chi^2 = 22.0670$, 8 d.f., sig. @ .01	TOTAL	52.9	4.8	42.4	210
"It is expected in a Greek	none	0.0	60.0	40.0	5
family that brothers would	poor	6.3	0.0	93.8	16
see their sisters married	fair	18.6	7.0	74.4	43
first."	good	19.4	11.1	69.4	72
	fluent	27.1	3.4	69.5	59
$\chi^2 = 26.1268$, 8 d.f., sig. @ .001	TOTAL	20.0	8.2	71.8	195
"Dowry and financial arrange-	none	0.0	75.0	25.0	8
ments are for the benefit of	poor	0.0	17.6	82.4	17
children and the Greek family	fair	20.0	26.7	53.3	45
stands by this concept."	good	35.9	19.2	44.9	78
	fluent	28.6	11.1	60.3	63
$\chi^2 = 31.0356$, 8 d.f., sig. @ .001	TOTAL	26.1	20.4	53.6	211

TABLE 4 (Continued)

Statement	Respondent	Agree	No Opinion	Dis-agree	Total No.
			Percentages		
"If a mother and married	none	37.5	62.5	0.0	8
daughter live in the same	poor	47.1	29.4	23.5	17
household, there is always	fair	53.3	11.1	35.6	45
trouble."	good	65.4	11.5	23.1	78
	fluent	60.3	15.9	23.8	63
$\chi^2 = 20.2584$, 8 d.f., sig. @ .01	TOTAL	58.8	16.1	25.1	211
"When a person marries, it	none	12.5	75.0	12.5	8
is the marriage relatives	poor	11.8	23.5	64.7	17
he associates with most	fair	30.8	25.6	43.6	39
often."	good	26.8	26.8	46.5	71
	fluent	34.5	13.8	51.7	58
$\chi^2 = 18.0566$, 8 d.f., sig. @ .05	TOTAL	28.0	24.4	47.7	193
"Protection and financial	none	37.5	50.0	12.5	8
help is a moral obligation	poor	11.8	35.3	52.9	17
towards relatives who have	fair	34.2	26.3	39.5	38
migrated recently."	good	53.5	8.5	38.0	71
	fluent	58.6	15.5	25.9	58
$\chi^2 = 25.2844$, 8 d.f., sig. @ .01	TOTAL	46.9	18.2	34.9	192
"Helping the mother country in	none	0.0	37.5	62.5	8
any way, and by helping	poor	5.9	29.4	64.7	17
relatives, is the duty of	fair	23.7	26.3	50.0	38
every Greek even if he	good	39.4	12.7	47.9	71
has never visited Greece."	fluent	43.1	15.5	41.4	58
$\chi^2 = 17.4554$, 8 d.f., sig. @ .075	TOTAL	32.8	18.8	48.4	192
"It is better to take a good	none	0.0	37.5	62.5	8
job near your parents and	poor	5.9	23.5	70.6	17
relatives than to take a	fair	7.9	13.2	78.9	38
better job and you will have	good	26.8	9.9	63.4	71
to move away from them."	fluent	22.4	5.2	72.4	58
$\chi^2 = 18.3797$, 8 d.f., sig. @ .02	TOTAL	18.8	11.5	69.8	192

TABLE 4 (Continued)

Statement	Respondent	Agree	No Opinion	Dis-agree	Total No.
			Percentages		
"When relatives go into	none	0.0	75.0	25.0	8
business together, they	poor	12.5	50.0	37.5	16
are likely to end up	fair	38.5	28.2	33.3	39
enemies."	good	47.1	21.4	31.4	70
	fluent	47.3	16.4	36.4	55
$\chi^2 = 21.7491$, 8 d.f., sig. @ .01	TOTAL	40.4	26.1	33.5	188
"A woman should take her	none	42.9	57.1	0.0	7
husband's side even if her	poor	43.8	25.0	31.3	16
mother does not think he	fair	53.8	30.8	15.4	39
is right."	good	70.0	18.6	11.4	70
	fluent	70.7	12.1	17.2	58
$\chi^2 = 16.1507$, 8 d.f., sig. @ .05	TOTAL	63.7	21.1	15.3	190
"For the sake of the family	none	62.5	37.5	0.0	8
happiness, one should help	poor	56.3	6.3	37.5	16
aging parents who are	fair	79.5	7.7	12.8	39
physically able to maintain	good	79.4	7.4	13.2	68
themselves independently,	fluent	82.8	6.9	10.3	58
if this is financially possible."					
$\chi^2 = 17.9576$, 8 d.f., sig. @ .05	TOTAL	77.8	8.5	13.8	189
"It is considered a stigma	none	25.0	50.0	25.0	8
for American children of	poor	37.5	25.0	37.5	16
Greek descent to place their	fair	39.5	18.4	42.1	38
parents in a home for the	good	41.2	26.5	32.4	68
aged; parents belong with	fluent	63.8	8.6	27.6	58
their children."					
$\chi^2 = 16.2408$, 8 d.f., sig. @ .05	TOTAL	46.8	20.2	33.0	188

TABLE 5
General Attitudes

Statement	Respondent	Agree	No Opinion	Dis-agree	Total No.
			Percentages		
"Greeks will go to any	none	42.9	14.3	42.9	7
expense to safeguard their	poor	52.9	17.6	29.4	17
sense of *philotimo*, their	fair	58.1	23.3	18.6	43
respect for honor."	good	74.3	5.4	20.3	74
	fluent	79.6	3.7	16.7	54
$\chi^2 = 18.1270$, 8 d.f., sig. @ .05	TOTAL	69.2	10.3	20.5	195
"Greek culture places	none	37.5	50.0	12.5	8
greatest value on male	poor	64.7	11.8	23.5	17
sex."	fair	41.0	33.3	25.6	39
	good	64.3	10.0	25.7	70
	fluent	69.1	9.1	21.8	55
$\chi^2 = 20.8327$, 8 d.f., sig. @ .01	TOTAL	59.8	16.4	23.8	189
"It is said that Greek men	none	12.5	62.5	25.0	8
are vigorously opposed to	poor	31.3	12.5	56.3	16
household work of any kind."	fair	54.5	15.9	29.5	44
	good	46.8	15.6	37.7	77
	fluent	38.3	13.3	48.3	60
$\chi^2 = 18.7430$, 8 d.f., sig. @ .02	TOTAL	43.4	16.6	40.0	205
"Long and animated conversa-	none	37.5	50.0	12.5	8
tion before any decisions	poor	56.3	6.3	37.5	16
are made form a part of	fair	48.9	24.4	26.7	45
Greek life at all levels."	good	72.4	14.5	13.2	76
	fluent	72.4	19.0	8.6	58
$\chi^2 = 20.8119$, 8 d.f., sig. @ .01	TOTAL	64.5	18.7	16.7	203
"Greeks consider visiting	none	37.5	50.0	12.5	8
between relatives a highly	poor	100.0	0.0	0.0	17
favored form of recreation."	fair	84.4	8.9	6.7	45
	good	82.1	5.1	12.8	78
	fluent	79.7	1.7	18.6	59
$\chi^2 = 36.0155$, 8 d.f., sig. @ .001	TOTAL	81.6	6.3	12.1	207
"Greeks place high value	none	50.0	25.0	25.0	8
in educational advances."	poor	100.0	0.0	0.0	17
	fair	90.0	10.0	0.0	40
	good	88.6	5.7	5.7	70
	fluent	96.3	0.0	3.7	54
$\chi^2 = 24.1428$, 8 d.f., sig. @ .01	TOTAL	90.5	5.3	4.2	189

CHAPTER 8

GREEK BILINGUAL EDUCATION IN HISTORICAL PERSPECTIVE

BY

VIVIAN ANEMOYANIS

Eleven years have passed since Congress enacted the Bilingual Education Act. However, it is important to remember that the concept of bilingual education is not new in this country, and did not begin with Title VII. Bilingual schools formed part of the initial education movement in the US and were instrumental in formulating the early educational philosophy of the public school system.

The history of public bilingual schooling in the United States divides itself into two main parts: pre-World War I and post-1963.[1]

From the period of 1839 to the 1880s, German was the only non-English tongue admitted as a medium of teaching, except for French in Louisiana and from 1848 Spanish in New Mexico. The heyday for the public bilingual schools was before the Civil War.

During the period of 1880-1917 there were German-English bilingual schools in Cincinnati, Indianapolis, Baltimore, New Ulm, Minnesota, and in an unknown number of rural places. In other schools, German was taught as a subject but not used as a medium of instruction. Norwegian, Czech, Italian, Polish, and Dutch were also occasionally taught but not used as teaching mediums.

[1]See T. Andersson and M. Boyer, *Bilingual Schooling in the United States*, 2 vols. (Austin, Texas: Southwest Educational Development Laboratory, 1970).

By the time that the United States had entered World War I, there was a new wave of nationalism and these schools disappeared, despite their success. Even the learning of foreign languages in public schools received an extremely low priority during the subsequent decades. In addition, Congress enacted a restrictive policy of immigration aimed at keeping out Eastern and Southeastern Europeans. The word "minority" was used with a negative connotation, as Italians, Poles, and other groups were viewed as problems because of their foreign languages and strange customs.[2]

During this period, the public schools were effectively used to assimilate all foreigners. Laws were established in many states which prevented the use of foreign languages for instructional purposes.[3] This was the period in which the Israel Zangwill metaphor of America as a "melting pot" was greeted with enthusiasm.[4]

In order to advance, it was necessary for the recently settled as well as the newly arrived Eastern European to conform and assimilate into the larger society. The price of membership prescribed by the society at large "was the acceptance of the dominant culture and the loss of one's identity."[5] The result of assimilation was the maladjustment of the immigrants. As a result of this, Congress established an Immigration Commission, which expressed a preference for the earlier immigrants from Northern and Western Europe. The Commission viewed the new immigration from Eastern and Southeastern Europe with a great deal of contempt.[6]

By 1930, the US census revealed that the languages brought by the immigrants were rapidly vanishing as mediums of daily conversation, even among most older foreign-born individuals. Additionally, at this time, few native-born had resource to foreign-language newspapers and periodicals. The forced assimilation and Americanization of the foreign-born and their

[2]See Mary Jenkins, *Bilingual Education in New York City* (New York: NYC Board of Education, 1971).

[3]Ibid.

[4]Israel Zangwill, *The Melting Pot* (New York: Jewish Publication Society of America, 1909).

[5]Albert D. Ullman, *Socio-Cultural Foundation of Personality* (Boston: Houghton Mifflin, 1965).

[6]US Congress, Sixty-first Congress, third session, Senate document no. 747, *Report of the Immigration Commission* (Washington, D.C.: US Government Printing Office, 1921).

children were almost complete, in spite of the fact that they constituted 11.3 percent of a population of 123,202,660.[7]

The rebirth of bilingual education dates back to 1963 in Miami, Florida, forced by the large wave of children of Cuban refugees who came into the country and whose educational needs had to be met. The bilingual schooling experiment was so successful in the Coral Way School in Dade County, Florida, that educators throughout the country took note and even began to consider this approach as a viable alternative in meeting the educational needs of millions of children in the nation.[8] It was not until the enactment of the Bilingual Education Act, however, that this movement received much greater impetus.

In 1967, bills were introduced in Congress to amend the Elementary and Secondary Education Act of 1965 to provide for bilingual education programs. Hearings were held in the summer of 1967 in the Southwest by Senator Ralph Yarborough of Texas and in the East by Senators Robert Kennedy and Jacob Javits of New York. At these hearings, the Mexican American and Puerto Rican representatives spoke of the great need for bilingual and bicultural programs. Their testimony reflected both the increasing demand for large-scale bilingual programs and the strong united support for federal subsidies for bilingual education. The amendment was known as the Bilingual American Education Act of 1965, effective as of July 1, 1968, and was administered by the United States Office of Education.

The Bilingual Education Act has had tremendous effect on state and local educational policies. Prior to its enactment, the majority of the states had legislation making English the sole medium of instruction. By 1971, thirty of the fifty states permitted or required some form of bilingual instruction in local classrooms. However, twenty states prohibited such instruction. But by 1975, only ten of these states outlawed bilingual education.

Over the last ten years there has been a marked increase in state support for bilingual education. Of the original twenty states in 1971 that actually prohibited the use of any language other than English as the language of instruction, only seven

[7]Edward C. Kirkland, *A History of American Economic Life* (New York: F. S. Crafts and Company, 1947).

[8]Albar A. Peña, "Bilingual Education: The What, the Why and the How," *NABE* 1:1 (May 1976) 27.

continue to do so today. However, in most states the statute is not enforced, as is the case in Delaware, Idaho, Nebraska, and North Carolina, which receive Title VII funds. Their acceptance of these funds constitutes a tacit endorsement of the value of bilingual education.

The most significant state legislation has been from Massachusetts and Texas, both of which mandated bilingual education and appropriated funds for its implementation.[9] In addition, Illinois, California, Colorado, Louisiana, Michigan, Alaska, New Mexico, and New York have appropriated state funds for the support of bilingual-bicultural education. Legislation permitting schools in New York to utilize a vernacular other than English in the classroom was passed by the New York State Legislature in 1967.

In the opening statement of the New York State Position Paper on Bilingual Education of August 1972, State Commissioner Ewald Nyquist said that differences in language and culture effectively excluded approximately 300,000 children from meaningfully participating in our educational system. Failure of schools to respond to the educational needs of these children resulted in academic failure, demonstrated sequentially by low reading scores, high dropout rate, and barriers of entry into meaningful employment. This was the plight of many of our non-English speaking pupils. The position paper called for the total involvement of our educational system to help the non-English speakers become, along with all other pupils, all that they were capable of becoming.

The *Lau v. Nichols* decision (1974) was a landmark decision for non-English speaking children. In this decision, the US Supreme Court unanimously held that the failure of the San Francisco school district to provide for the special needs of nearly 1,800 non-English speaking students of Chinese descent was in violation of Title VI of the Civil Rights Act of 1964. The Court ruled that San Francisco must either overcome language barriers for students not receiving compensatory help or face the loss of its federal financial assistance. It based its determination on the provisions of the 1964 Civil Rights Act, which bars discrimination because of color, race, or national origin in any activity receiving federal funds, as well as on regulations promulgated by HEW, the agency au-

[9]Idem, "Bilingual Education: An Overview," *Today's Education* (January-February 1975) 72.

thorized to conduct compliance reviews of federally aided school systems. In 1970, the HEW Office for Civil Rights also found that students from other cultures who have English language deficiencies were often denied equal access to educational programs.[10]

The Lau decision, however, did not mandate a specific program or plan. The Court remanded the question of how barriers were to be overcome to the federal court and to the San Francisco school system. Possible plans might have included programs in English as a second language and holding classes in Chinese, Spanish, and Tagalog (the national language of some Filipinos).

In August of 1974, in the case of *ASPIRA of New York Inc. v. the Board of Education of the City of New York,* the Board of Education signed a consent decree with ASPIRA in federal court. This consent decree, over which Judge Frankel presided, established certain citywide elements in the education of children whose functional language was Spanish. The consent decree resulted from an agreement with ASPIRA and averted protracted litigation. ASPIRA of New York, a Puerto Rican organization, had brought a class action suit charging that the city school system failed to meet the needs of Spanish-speaking children, thus causing high truancy and dropout rates among the youngsters.

The elements of the program—which were to be provided in full by September 1975 to all children in the "class," i.e., those children whose English-language deficiency prevented them from participating in the learning process and who could more effectively participate in Spanish—were (a) intensive instruction in English; (b) instruction in subject areas in Spanish; and (c) the reinforcement of the pupil's use of Spanish and reading comprehension in Spanish, where a need is indicated. Additionally, and not at the expense of these three elements, these students would spend maximum time with other children so as to avoid isolation and segregation from their peers.[11]

In addition to this, the consent decree called for the Board of Education of the City of New York to develop an improved method of identifying and classifying children who were Span-

[10]Betty E. Sinowitz, "The Court Speaks Out," *Today's Education* (January-February 1975) 83.

[11]*Consent Decree in ASPIRA et al. v. Board of Education et al.,* August 29, 1974, p. 23.

ish speaking and Spanish surnamed. The Language Assessment Battery was developed and used throughout New York City by March 1975.

Both the Lau and the ASPIRA decisions stated that their respective city school systems were not meeting the educational needs of non-English speaking pupils. The ASPIRA decision, however, went further and mandated that a certain program be provided to meet the educational needs of children identified as needing the program.

The ASPIRA Consent Decree mandated the special program only for Hispanic pupils in New York City. The other language groups in the city, such as the Italians, the Greeks, and the Chinese, met with Chancellor Irving Anker and demanded that the consent decree be extended to all children whose dominant language was other than English. On June 26, 1975, Chancellor Anker issued Special Circular 114, extending the consent decree to the other language groups. However, Special Circular 114 was ignored throughout New York City, and the central Board of Education did not monitor its implementation.

In the summer of 1977, the Office for Civil Rights (HEW) found the New York City Board of Education to be in violation of Title VI, and charged that an equal educational opportunity was not being provided to New York City's non-Hispanic, non-English speaking minority children.

In the fall of 1977, the Board of Education of the City of New York submitted to the US Office for Civil Rights a plan which was accepted by OCR.[12] This plan was part of an application for a waiver of ineligibility in seeking federal funds under the Emergency School Aid Act. The plan also satisfied federal regulations related to Title VI. The Lau plan, as it was called, provided for appropriate instructional programs for children who could not participate effectively in the English-language programs. Since the consent decree had focused on students of Spanish-language background, the Lau plan specifically addressed students with similar needs whose home language was other than Spanish. The Lau plan mandated a program of instruction for non-Hispanic, non-English speaking pupils and contained all the elements of the ASPIRA Consent Decree program.

The federal, state, and local mandates have had their impact on Greek bilingual programs in New York City. Greek

[12]Board of Education Memorandum, November 1, 1977.

bilingual instructional programs currently exist in New York City public schools in the Astoria and Long Island City sections of Queens, the Washington Heights section of Manhattan, and the Bayridge section of Brooklyn.

Community School District 30, Queens, encompasses Astoria, Long Island City, Jackson Heights, and parts of Woodside, Corona, and East Elmhurst. The district has a student population representing more than forty different language groups.

The largest Greek-speaking community in the United States is found within the boundaries of this school district. Currently there are 2,500 pupils in the district's schools who come from Greek-speaking homes. Six hundred of these pupils are classified as limited English proficiency. Of this group of pupils, four hundred are currently being serviced in the district's Greek bilingual programs, while the other two hundred are receiving instruction in English as a second language. Greek bilingual programs are found in four elementary and two junior high "magnet schools" in Long Island City and Astoria, where there are large concentrations of Greek-speaking students. Parents of students from other schools in the district have the option of sending their children to these magnet schools. The Greek bilingual instructional components are funded through city tax levy funds, ESEA Title VII, and in some schools, New York State funds.

When the Greek bilingual program was first founded in 1974, it served about 150 students, primarily recent arrivals from Greece. At first, there was very little parental support for the bilingual programs. Parents were afraid that if their children matriculated in a bilingual program they would not learn English. Thanks to the persistence of the bilingual staff, parents have become better informed as to the benefits of bilingual education. Some parents can now compare the progress their younger children are making academically with that of their older children who did not attend a bilingual program, and are very much pleased with the results.

This current school year, the Greek bilingual component is in its fifth year of a five-year ESEA Title VII grant. In addition to supportive services, Title VII provides funds for teacher training and curriculum development for Greek bilingual materials. District 30 is one of the few Greek curriculum development centers in the United States affiliated with a public school program. In addition to District 30's curriculum development project, the Northeast Center for Curriculum Development in the Bronx has been funded by Title VII to produce curriculum materials in Greek.

District 30's curriculum project first began in 1974 with Title VII funding. The need for curriculum development arose from the lack of appropriate material in Greek which followed the prescribed curriculum of the Board of Education of the City of New York.

All of District 30's bilingual instructional programs are transitional in nature. The pupils remain in the bilingual programs until they are deemed proficient enough in English to be mainstreamed into a monolingual English program. Pupils must remain in the bilingual program for at least a year. At the end of each year they are given the Language Assessment Battery, an instrument which measures English language proficiency. If they score above the 20th percentile on this test, they are deemed eligible for the mainstream program.

Several organizational models are used in the district's bilingual programs, depending on the number of eligible pupils per school and per grade. Where there are enough pupils per grade to form self-contained classes, they are formed. In other cases, nongraded semi-self-contained classes are formed. In the self-contained classes, pupils spend the entire school day with a bilingual teacher, while in the nongraded semi-self-contained classes, pupils spend half a day with a bilingual teacher and the other half with a monolingual teacher.

Regardless which organizational model is used, however, all pupils in bilingual classes receive intensive instruction in English and substantive area instruction in the dominant language. That is, they receive mathematics, science, and social studies in Greek as well as instruction in Greek language arts.

The self-contained Greek bilingual classes are usually formed in the lower grades, K and 1, where the children come from homes where English is not spoken. These self-contained classes have been tremendously successful. Children are first taught in the language they've learned in their homes. They learn to read in Greek and then in English, and they are highly motivated due to their successful school experiences. Parents have been so pleased with the results that in some schools they are now asking for maintenance bilingual classes. That is, they want their children to continue in bilingual programs and receive bilingual instruction even after the children are deemed eligible to be mainstreamed and the school district is no longer legally bound to provide such instruction.

In conclusion, I would like to reiterate that bilingual education has provided children with positive school experiences, both academically and socially. It has preserved and strengthened their self-image and has provided them with a sense of self-worth for themselves and their families.

CHAPTER 9

HELLENIC ORTHODOX EDUCATION IN AMERICA

BY

EMMANUEL HATZIEMMANUEL

In 1932, the late Patriarch Athenagoras, then Archbishop of America, addressed an encyclical letter "To All Congregations of the Greek Orthodox Archdiocese of North and South America," in which he called the founding of "Greek Orthodox communities" on American soil "one of those admirable expressions and achievements of the Greek spirit and Greek vitality that heralds their strength and undying presence through the centuries." He also called the communities "centers of religious, ethnic, educational and social life, and means of moral reformation and sanctification."

Indeed, the historical development and progress of Greek Americans, mainly from the last decade of the past century—when a significant impetus for Greek immigration to the New World began—to this day, testifies to the truth of the by now classic definition of Athenagoras of the Greek community. It is by now an indisputable historical fact that the intellectual, religious, ethnic, and social survival and further development of Greek Americans within the American multi-ethnic society took place within the perimeter of the Greek Orthodox ecclesiastical community.

This type of community at times set effective barriers against the assimilating forces of the American environment and afforded the Greek immigrant the opportunity, climate, and spiritual means he was in need of in order to preserve, cultivate, and develop his spiritual profile and identity, which

Athenagoras in another one of his famous encyclical letters (July 31, 1935) designated to be "our great pride, the fact that we are Greeks."

In return for his hard work, America provided the Greek immigrant with the possibilities of securing a relative financial and material affluence. It gave him the means to raise and educate his children in a manner in which he himself wished. It respected and protected his human rights. It presented him with democratic freedom and social opportunity and respect. It adopted him and made him its citizen and allowed him to manage his own soul. And it was here, by exercising his given rights to manage the affairs of his own inner world, that the Greek immigrant showed vision, spiritual strength, and vitality. He founded the community, a fortress by which to protect and within which to cultivate and further develop his spiritual profile and identity.

By properly and methodically using his ingenuity, his capabilities, and his time, the Greek immigrant acquired needed material goods within the free American society of today. But material goods do not necessarily secure for us spiritual well-being as well. The known anthropologist, Margaret Mead, said, "we call spiritual health the seeking of a new kind of life that does not so much stress care for the body as it does cultivation of mind and soul."

Within the perimeter of the community one can find a number of conditions and powers that tend to preserve for us our "well-being," "spiritual health," or "our spiritual profile and identity." This is because, first of all, it is through the community that we preserve our spiritual bonds with one another deriving from our common ethnic ancestry, which, in a way, constitutes an extension of our families and our binding link with race and nation where the ark of our spiritual civilization is preserved. The individual can hardly survive and spiritually progress if he is severed from his indigenous group. Contemporary anthropology takes isolation and severance from the phyletic group to mean, in most cases, spiritual withering. The spiritual growth of the individual begins with the family and, in our case, may reach its potential within the perimeter of our community life, where the flame of our spiritual civilization is kept alive. This is not crude patriotism, even if it may sound so to some, nor does it imply hatred for the beliefs and practices of others, or disapproval of other ethnic groups here. And neither does it seek to lessen in any way our love for our adopted country, America.

Secondly, the community offers the needed physical facilities for a many-faceted group expression, the constituent parts of which are the following: religious worship, social and cultural expressions, religious education of the young, the teaching of the Greek language and cultural history, and physical education and athletics. We have today functioning, as a result of hard work and sizable financial obligations on the part of our people, 530 building complexes all over the country. These represent an investment of at least $500 million, and their maintenance and proper functioning costs, in personnel and projects, in the vicinity of $120 million a year.

Finally, it is within the community and under the spiritual guidance of the Archdiocese of North and South America that the content and extent of our spiritual heritage, our Hellenic Orthodox learning, has been studied, analyzed, and crystalized into a charter of AIMS AND PURPOSES, that is, into the philosophy and program of a continuous education of Greek Americans. Our Hellenic Orthodox learning constitutes an admirable mosaic, the component parts of which are the products of the genius and of the historical, family, social, political, artistic, and religious experience of our people. As such, it should be identified with Greek Orthodoxy and its finest hours, but also with its trials and tribulations. They both bear the seal of endurance against the corruption that changes in time have imposed upon lesser religious and spiritual institutions.

As Orthodoxy, then, we understand and we teach by way of our community programs relating to religious and Greek education the art, language, literature, and religion of our people, which in the course of the three thousand years of our history have matured into a tested personal and group experiential continuum. It is in the light of this kind of interpretation of Orthodoxy that our concepts of the purpose and meaning of man's life are clearly sketched out, and enlightening and positive answers to the neediest wants of our souls are offered together with all those powers that lead the will to a moral and creative life. In brief, the mystery of the being of man, of his life and his destiny are, to our understanding, correctly interpreted in the light of a spiritual experience of three thousand years. This, without the help that may be derived from all kinds of philosophical thinking, from secular political theories to contemporary technology and the advances of the physical sciences.

All the above has been crystalized in the form of educational objectives and are reflected as a system all through the educational program of the Archdiocese and its implementation on the level of community schools. Every year, during the Greek Letters Week, the primate of the Greek Orthodox Church of America, Archbishop Iakovos, repeats the promise he made in an encyclical letter (January 4, 1967) to the effect that "the Archdiocese has supported and cultivated and will continue to support and cultivate, for as long as it does exist, the Greek Letters as an educational preparation and introduction to the spirit, tradition, and handing down of Greek Orthodoxy." Also, the Archbishop says that Greek fine arts, such as sculpture, architecture, drama, or music, will continue to remain an expression of beauty and perfection and, in their essence, as a revelation in form and content of the spiritual dynamics of the human soul and as the domain where perfection may be sought out.

The Greek press, TV, and radio, in their turn, as also our priests, teachers, community leaders, parents, and other notable Greek Americans, each in his own capacity and in his own way have likewise understood and interpreted Greek Orthodoxy and have helped and are helping every endeavor aimed at securing the necessary conditions—material and spiritual— for successfully pursuing the noble task of giving experiential form to what we call the Hellenic Orthodox ethos by the means of an educational system we call Greek Orthodox education.

It is fortunate, in this respect, that during the various stages of the Greek communal development in America, discussion and even dispute were allowed to make valuable contributions. And though there has been no doubt or dispute regarding the nature and fundamental objectives of our Hellenic Orthodox education, appraisal of the role played by organizations, including the Archdiocese, in implementing these fundamentals in terms of schools and other educational means has to vary. Lay organizations and brotherhoods have had their say and have advanced their criticism whenever they felt that the policies of those responsible for this type of education fell short of their expectations. Naturally, in instances in which this dialogue was kept on a high level, it produced beneficial results. However, it created dissension and unnecessary bitterness whenever it was lowered to a level or irrational emotionality and pursuit of unrealistic situations.

A creative dialogue relating to our Hellenic Orthodox education should begin on the basis of the following:

1. According to the patriarchal tomos of May 17, 1922, "Orthodox parishes within North and South America, up to now functioning singularly and irregularly, and in some instances outside the orderly perimeter defined of old by the Fathers, are judged to be in need of ecclesiastical legal care so that everything may be done in grace and according to decreed order. These parishes are hereafter embodied into one ecclesiastical province, with the title of Archdiocese, in canonical dependence upon the Patriarchal and Apostolic Throne as being one of its own Metropoleis."

2. Our Archdiocese covers today the United States, Canada, and South America, and includes 530 community establishments for the purpose of serving the religious, social, educational, cultural, and charitable needs of their members.

3. The community organizations of our Archdiocese are under the supervision and guidance of the central authority (Archdiocese) but are governed locally by democratically elected officers. This means that the quality of community educational programs is relative to the guidance, local economic status of membership, demographic considerations, and the quality and personal education of the elected members of the executive board of each community.

4. On the community premises a continuous kind of Greek Orthodox education should be offered to cover all ages and all educational levels. This education includes worship, catechetical education, the teaching of the Greek language and civilization, cultural orientation, and the discharge of the charitable obligations inherent in our system of beliefs and practices.

More specifically:

—For the purpose of divine worship we have church buildings that have been built originally or changed into the Orthodox ecclesiastical architectural style and have been decorated inside with frescos and icons of our Byzantine ecclesiastical tradition.

—For the purpose of teaching the Greek language and Greek cultural history we have proper school buildings which provide shelter for afternoon schools, Greek American day schools, kindergarten schools, classes for adults, etc. These types were established in response to particular needs in each community. Thus, a particular type functioning in a commuity reflects the latter's size, the geographical distribution of its membership, and the American educational environment in that particular locality. It is obvious, then, that these school types can hardly correspond to the school types prevalent in Greece.

—The Department of Education of our Archdiocese has issued curricula for all of these school types together with readers for teaching the Greek language and civilization based on current educational approaches and methods and specifically designed for children born in America.

—For the religious education of the young we have complete curricula and a complete series of books.

—For equipping our clergy with the necessary education for the purpose of successfully pursuing their many-faceted mission within the American society we have a theological school, equal in all respects with corresponding schools of other religions here and with the university theological schools in Greece.

—In answer to the need of having teachers who would be aware of our educational system here and of the psychology and experiential patterns of our children in America, the Teachers Training Department of St. Basil's Academy provided for many years excellent teachers. Beginning this year, teachers from Greece are taking graduate courses at our Hellenic College which will enable them to successfully serve our educational objectives here.

—Seminars are held in each of our dioceses at regular intervals aimed at acquainting our teachers with the latest methods and new materials pertaining to the teaching of Greek. Also, a seminar of three weeks' duration is held every year in Greece with the cooperation of the Greek Ministry of Education.

—In cooperation with the educational authorities of both the State and the City of New York, we have succeeded in securing the recognition of the Greek language as being of equal status with other foreign languages taught in American schools (Spanish, French, German). Thus, our children have the opportunity to take the annual academic exam (Regents) and can attend Greek classes in high schools in which Greek is offered.

—The Greek Ministry of Education has recognized the service of those who have been and are teaching in our schools for a prescribed number of weeks as meriting a pension.

—With the recent appointment of a Counselor on Education at the Greek Consulate General in New York and three others in Canada, the Greek Ministry of Education is now in a position to have a clear and correct picture of our educational situation here.

—For protecting children from broken homes, St. Basil's Academy offers an invaluable service, as also does St. Michael's Home for our aged who need shelter and other care.

—The Ladies Philoptochos Society, with branches in every one of our communities, discharges the charitable obligations of our Church as they occur all over North and South America.

The above enumeration of projects, which have proved responsible for a more effective educational endeavor on our part, naturally lead to areas in which our efforts remain wanting.

We need, first of all, the extensive and wholehearted cooperation of the intellectual class of our people in support of the spiritual mission that is carried on within the community. Most of our professional people seem to avoid, for many reasons, offering their talents and abilities to serving the spiritual objectives of our Church. Needless to say, there are ample exceptions, but the fact remains that the spiritual objectives of the Greek Americans have received no effective support on the part of our intelligentsia. Consequently, in most communities the pursuing of the spiritual objectives of our ethnic and religious entity has been left to well-meaning people whose abilities do not in most cases match the needs of the communities mainly because of lack of proper education and other needed preparation which is necessary for correctly understanding and successfully pursuing aims and goals on which our very survival in this country depends. Often, a great deal of time and effort is consumed in collecting moneys and in building structures while the quality of education is completely neglected.

In the domain of ethnic capital, those who could help the most, specifically the shipowners, save for a number of notable and very generous exceptions, hardly participate in our common endeavors on both the community and national levels. Most of whatever has been done in terms of churches, schools, and other places of gathering for the purpose of deliberating or socializing has been paid for by the working class of our ethnic group, by those who did well by hard work for many years and those who work hard now to do well in the future. Finally, the government of Greece has shown an interest in our educational problems, but only recently. Our communities, meanwhile, under the guidance of our Church, grew into a power of considerable spiritual, cultural, and even political import within the multi-ethnic society of America with no help whatsoever from the Greek state. Our people acquired as an ethnic group an entity with a purpose and a destiny all of its own. Our educational system is not an extension of the educational system of Greece and it cannot be understood correctly if it is weighed by the standards by which the educational system of Greece can be evaluated.

STATISTICAL NOTES

Greek American Day Schools

In the school year of 1978-1979, twenty-two Greek American day schools functioned under the supervision of the Office of Education of the Greek Orthodox Archdiocese of North and South America. Of these, twelve were located in the Greater New York area, three were in Chicago, and one each functioned in Northridge, Calif.; Washington, D.C.; Tampa, Fla.; Lowell, Mass.; Houston, Texas; Canada; and South America (Sao Paulo, Brazil).

The total number of enrolled students was 6,533. There was a total number of 322 teachers, 254 for the English program and 68 for the Greek program.

The schools listed above include:

    4 pre-school centers
    21 kindergarten schools
    22 elementary schools
    15 junior high schools
    4 with high school grades (9 or 10)
    2 high schools (one private)

Greek Language and Culture Afternoon Schools

In the school year 1978-1979, 403 Greek language and culture afternoon schools had a total enrolment of 28,849 students, with 838 teachers. The following table reflects the increase in students and teachers from the 1970-1971 to the 1978-1979 school years:

SCHOOL YEAR	SCHOOLS	STUDENTS	TEACHERS
1970-1971	340	24,200	550
1971-1972	350	25,100	660
1972-1973	355	25,700	680
1973-1974	360	26,050	702
1974-1975	375	26,500	735
1975-1976	382	28,036	796
1976-1977	393	28,622	819
1977-1978	398	28,681	831
1978-1979	403	28,849	838

The numbers of different types of schools, along with the total student enrolment in each, for the 1978-1979 school year was as follows:

SCHOOL TYPE	NUMBER	ENROLMENT
pre-school	45	763
kindergarten	21	377
elementary	270	25,571
junior high	37	639
adult education	56	648
other	35	851
TOTAL		28,849

Of these schools, 94 functioned on a five-day-a-week program; 71 functioned on a four-day-a-week program; 66 functioned three days per week; 86 functioned two days per week; and 84 functioned on a once-a-week program.

The approximate annual cost per student is $1,000 in the day schools and $250 in the afternoon schools.

The approximate annual cost for the entire operation of the school system is $6,533,000 for the day schools and $7,212,250 for the afternoon schools. The combined approximate annual cost for both school systems is $13,745,250.

At the end of the 1978-1979 school year, the total number of enrolled students in all types of schools was 35,382, and the total number of full-time and part-time teachers was 1,160.

Apart from the teachers in the day schools who teach full-time, approximately 20 percent of the remaining served full-time in the combined capacity of either teacher-secretary or teacher-cantor.

A number of communities used the services of qualified volunteer teachers.

CHAPTER 10

THE GREEK ORTHODOX LADIES PHILOPTOCHOS SOCIETY AND THE GREEK AMERICAN COMMUNITY

BY

STELLA COUMANTAROS

In 1902, at the Holy Trinity Church in New York, a small group of Greek Orthodox women met to form the first official Greek Orthodox Ladies Philoptochos Society under the guidance of Rev. Methodios Kourkoulis of Smyrna (Turkey). Modeling their society on the Ladies Philoptochos Society of Smyrna, the women enlisted the help of the well-to-do in order to assist needy Greek immigrants and their families. As a result of the efforts of these pioneers of Philoptochos (Friends of the Poor) and the social services they provided, the passage of many Greek immigrants through Castle Garden on Ellis Island was made easier, and the trauma of separation from their native land and assimilation into a new culture became less painful.[1]

The leadership of the Church-affiliated philanthropic societies was generally drawn from among the Greek Orthodox women refugees from Constantinople and Asia Minor, fleeing from the Turkish holocaust of the early twentieth century. Because of the persecution of the Greek minority in Turkey, they

[1] All facts concerning the organization and membership of the Philoptochos Society are from the public records of the Society. The Philoptochos chapter files, convention records, Director's reports, and minutes of National Board meetings are available for study at the Philoptochos National Office at 8 East 79th St., New York, N.Y.

left a comfortable and in many instances an affluent life to seek refuge in America. For the most part they were the only educated women in the early Greek American communities and the only women who came from cities, such as Constantinople and Smyrna, where Greek educational and philanthropic societies had flourished.[2] On the other hand, the majority of the new immigrants came from the mainland of Greece and some of the Greek islands to escape the dire poverty of the Greek state. They were essentially a rural population with a bare minimum of education, if any at all.[3]

Most women who emigrated to the United States in appreciable numbers in the early part of this century were home oriented. Their lives centered around family, home, and church. Very few women left home to work, and fewer learned the English language or communicated with their non-Greek neighbors. The loneliness of the new life, the separation from familiar surroundings, friends, and family left behind in Greece, brought them closer to their Church. The Greek Orthodox Church, with age-old traditions and rituals, gave the women a sense of being safe in a world that was so different from that which they had left. Banding together in a common activity of homemaking, friendship, and worshiping in church imparted to these immigrant women a sense of sisterhood. Invariably, a ladies auxiliary, devoted to the immediate philanthropic needs of their fellow parishioners, was created.

The first of these groups was established in New York City in 1894.[4] The women worked unselfishly in the churches, preparing the *prosfora*—the bread used in the liturgy—and the ceremonial foods for funerals. They helped the priests deal with families beset by financial difficulties, illness, and death; they serviced the altar cloth and the priestly robes; they decorated the *epitaphion*—the funeral bier used on Good Friday. They cooked and baked for community festivals and traditional Christmas and Easter celebrations. They provided many of the first Greek teachers in homes, stores, and existing churches, and also taught Sunday school.

[2]For the legacy of Byzantine philanthropy, see Demetrios J. Constantelos, *Byzantine Philanthropy and Social Welfare* (New Brunswick, N.J.: Rutgers University Press, 1968) 3-16.

[3]See Thomas Burgess, *Greeks in America* (New York: Arno Press, 1970).

[4]See the national records and files of the Holy Trinity Cathedral chapter of Philoptochos in New York City.

The Greek Orthodox Ladies Philoptochos Society, through its independent chapters, continued to meet the expanding needs of the community until 1931, when its President, Mrs. Eriphili Vrachnos, turned its charter over to the late Patriarch, the then-Archbishop, Athenagoras. Thus began the new National Philoptochos Society, which today has a chapter in every parish of the Greek Orthodox Archdiocese of North and South America. Thus began the transition from a parochial organization to one of national stature.

At the present time, the National Greek Orthodox Ladies Philoptochos Society has over 50,000 members and 575 chapters, compared with 14,000 members and 375 chapters in 1960. The purpose and mission of the society has remained constant: preserving the faith, educating the young, and helping those who are less fortunate. To accomplish these goals, Philoptochos has a variety of fundraising methods. They include solicitation of donations, bazaars, social functions, fashions shows, rummage sales, the publication of ethnic cookbooks, and other innovative activities which might appeal to the community.

During life's crises of illness or death in a family, the Philoptochos women are there to offer comfort, support and compassion. They volunteer in hospitals, nursing homes, and the Peace Corps. They earmark funds for community services, national research drives such as Cooley's Anemia Research, and the Arthritis and Easter Seals Telethons, as well as scholarship programs. From a parochial philanthropic organization established to assist the early Greek immigrant, the Society has become more sensitive to other issues and problems over the past five decades.[5] For example, in 1937 the Philoptochos Society assisted in establishing the Holy Cross Seminary in Pomfret, Connecticut—a turning point in providing the Greek Orthodox Church with a native-born clergy educated in America. In 1944, the Society contributed the proceeds collected from a Vasilopita celebration to help purchase the Ruppert Estate "Eagle's Nest" in Garrison, New York, which was to serve as a children's home. The estate was renamed St. Basil's Academy and is now a chartered tax-exempt philanthropic in-

[5]D. J. Constantelos, ed., *Encyclicals and Documents of the Greek Orthodox Archdiocese of North and South America: The First Fifty Years, 1922-1972* (Thessaloniki: Patriarchal Institute for Patristic Studies, 1976) 134, 213, 296, 297.

stitution of the Greek Orthodox Archdiocese of North and South America.

In the wake of World War II, the Philoptochos mobilized its resources to feed and comfort those suffering in strife-torn Greece. The first ambulance sent to Greece at the end of the war bore the name of the Philoptochos Society. In 1953, the Philoptochos sent clothing and funds to the victims of the earthquake that devastated the Ionian Islands. In 1958, its contributions helped found St. Michael's Home for the Aged, under the leadership of the late Archbishop Michael, and in 1960, Philoptochos set up the Foster Parent Plan for Greece. Under this plan, numerous needy and orphaned children in Greece were assisted. In cooperation with the Patriotic Institute of Athens, the women undertook "spiritual adoptions" of children in homes, camps, and orphanages. They also secured dowries for poor young women.

A "second wave" of Greek immigrants to the United States in the 1960s created new needs. Refugees of politics and poverty, the new immigrants had to surmount the language barrier, which blocked their access to public services. Addressing the complex problems created by the influx of these immigrants, His Eminence, Archbishop Iakovos, in October 1971, established the Archdiocesan Social Health and Welfare Center in Astoria. His Grace, Bishop Philotheos, was appointed Program Director, and this writer was named Director of Social Services.

We set out to study the needs of the new immigrant and to: (a) assist those who were handicapped by language difficulties in obtaining help through existing channels; (b) facilitate communication between non-English speaking Greek immigrants and social agencies, the police, schools, and hospitals; (c) offer emergency financial assistance to those who, cut off from family and friends, were unable to help themselves; (d) contact hospitals for medical assistance and special surgery for those who needed it in this country and in Greece; (e) visit, counsel, and console Greek Orthodox aliens at the Immigration Detention Home; (f) help Greek foreign students with immigration and related problems; and (g) tend to the problems of the aged and their families, who are torn in deciding how to best care for their loved ones.

Our efforts in all these areas culminated in a dynamic program, recognized by city, state, and federal agencies. The pilot project instituted in 1971 in Astoria was terminated after

one year, and the work was transferred to the National Philoptochos Office in the Archdiocese, where the services continue
to be available to those in need.

In 1972, the Society established the Philoptochos Women
for Hellenic College to help support the Hellenic College and
Holy Cross School of Theology in Brookline, Massachusetts.
The following year, the Canton Hellenic Nursing Home in
the state of Massachusetts was completed, the culmination
of nearly twenty years of efforts by the local Philoptochos
chapter. Philoptochos women continue to volunteer their services to patients at the nursing home, which has a capacity of
120 beds and is in the process of adding 40 more. In 1974,
Philoptochos instituted support for the Greek Children's Cardiac Program at New York Hospital as a national project. In
the face of a total lack of pediatric cardiac facilities in Greece,
children suffering from heart ailments are flown to the United
States where vital surgery is performed. The Society also contributes regularly to all hospitals that provide cardiac medical
services to Greek children free of charge.

It was not until the Cyprus tragedy in 1974, however, that
the organizational efficacy and political clout of the Philoptochos Society emerged. Under the Philoptochos Foster Parent
Project "Caress," more than five thousand displaced Cypriot
children have received approximately $1.2 million in monthly
payments. Philoptochos contributed more than $107,000 to the
Archdiocesan Cyprus Relief Fund, in addition to a $20,000
special collection for shipments of medicine, food, and clothing
in excess of 300,000 tons. In addition, the Society spearheaded
a letter-writing campaign aimed at President Ford, Secretary
of State Kissinger, Congressmen, and Senators in protest of
the Turkish invasion and illegal occupation of Cyprus.

In 1977, in response to appeals from Orthodox missionaries
in Africa, Asia, Alaska, and Latin America, the Philoptochos
Society took up the Archdiocesan Missions Project as a national project. Under the Archdiocesan Mission Project, Philoptochos contributes to the building of churches, education of
the young, needs of the poor, and supports the training of
Orthodox clergy to serve in the developing countries. That
Philoptochos does not feel itself confined to parochial concerns
is reflected in the position papers presented at our biennial
conventions, which seek to examine a variety of social problems ranging from battered women, child abuse, and abortion
to sex education and pornography. To be sure, this is part of

an acculturation process taking place both within the Greek community and the Church. His Eminence Archbishop Iakovos announced "a new period of Church life," counseling that "Orthodoxy loses nothing by conversing with heretics and ecumenists. Orthodoxy in the Americas must study itself. Our principle task is to rid ourselves of all self-righteousness, prejudices, and denominational complexes." Philoptochos has heeded the message and has reached beyond the boundaries of the parish church.

Given this broader perspective, Philoptochos has made significant contributions to the Cambodia Relief Fund, has participated in the International Year of the Child, and has helped draft resolutions as a member of the United Nations Advisory Committee, condemning all forms of religious intolerance and discrimination against women, and supporting the principle of human rights.

Recognition of the Society's activities was expressed by the late Archbishop Makarios of Cyprus in 1975 when he blessed the Society for "meritoriously responding to the anguish and needs of the refugee children of Cyprus." In 1977 His Eminence, Archbishop Iakovos dedicated the "Philoptochos Room" at St. Basil's Academy in memory of the Society's founding pioneer women. Having purchased the Academy's estate in 1944, Philoptochos has not ceased contributing to its operating expenses and has recently pledged to build the Archbishop Iakovos Athletic Center.

As we approach the end of the twentieth century and reflect on the fifty years of community involvement by the Philoptochos Society, we see that it has evolved from a small group of women whose primary concern was with the immigrants and the disadvantaged members of the Greek community to a national body with concerns of a much broader scope. Given the increased education of the new Philoptochos women, the complexity of contemporary problems, the interdependence of the modern world, and the ecumenical movement, as well as the need for understanding between diverse groups for human survival, it was inevitable that our philanthropic society broaden its focus to include issues of a national and international scope.

CHAPTER 11

MENTAL HEALTH SERVICES TO THE GREEK AMERICAN COMMUNITY OF NEW YORK CITY: A THREE-YEAR EXPERIENCE

BY

THEONI VELLI-SPYROPOULOS*

In recent years, epidemiological studies have increasingly come to consider the experience of *stress* to be one of the determining factors in the manifestation of disease in general and mental illness in particular. Change in the life of the individual is a major factor in his experience of stress, which is the organism's automatic and dynamic sequence of reactions to the new situation until adjustment can be achieved. The change-stress-reorganization-continuity experience is fundamental to human growth and constitutes a basic and continuous process in life.

Thus, stress as a variable in the manifestation of disease refers to life experiences in which, for a variety of reasons, the organism has not been able to achieve reorganization and adjust to the new situation. The intensity and duration of the experience of stress is related to the quantitative and qualitative aspects of the new situation and reflects the organism's ability to reorganize, restructure, and redefine itself and its environment in order to achieve a satisfactory level of adjustment and sustain its equilibrium and continuity while changing.

*I would like to thank Dimitris A. Spyropoulos, M.D., for his assistance in the preparation of this paper.

Change in the life of the individual can be viewed as being of two broad types, each of which has a different stress-effect both in intensity and duration. One of these types is "other-imposed" change—one finds oneself in a new situation that one had no control over either in terms of preventing it or creating it. The death of a family member, natural disasters, war, and aging are examples of this type of change. The other type of change is "self-imposed," in the sense that one plays an active role in creating the new situation and has varying degrees of control over it. Geographic and social mobility can be examples of this type of change. Timing, among other factors, in the sense of degree of anticipation of or planning for the new situation, has a different stress-effect in both types of changes.

Although there is a substantial body of knowledge about the former type of change, the "other-imposed," there is only limited knowledge about the experience of adjustment to the latter, the "self-imposed" change, and the correlation of this experience to the mental health status of the individual.

Immigration falls within the general category of mobility, which is considered a "self-imposed" type of change. Immigration provides the conditions for major changes in the life of the individual and the inevitable experience of varying degrees and levels of stress. Yet, immigrant populations have rarely been studied from the point of view of epidemiology of disease in general and mental illness in particular. On the other hand, the sociopolitical and economic characteristics of these groups have been by and large examined by different disciplines. Even in the field of the behavioral sciences, however, the phenomenon of immigration has primarily been studied in terms of group dynamics and intergroup relations[1] or in terms of comparative patterns of child development and socialization processes.[2]

In 1965, M. B. Kantor edited and published *Mobility and Mental Health*,[3] which included an article by H. Murphy on

[1]A. Hollingshead and F. Redlich, *Social Class and Mental Illness: A Community Study* (New York: John Wiley & Sons, 1958); E. Streuning, J. Rabkin, and H. Peck, "Migration and Ethnic Membership in Relation to Social Problems," in *Behavior in New Environments*, ed. E. Brody (Beverly Hills, Calif., 1969).

[2]P. Graham, "Environmental Influences on Psychosocial Development," *International Journal of Mental Health* 6:3 (1977) 7-31.

[3]M. B. Kantor, ed., *Mobility and Mental Health* (Springfield, Ill.: Charles C. Thomas, 1965).

"Migration and the Major Mental Disorders."[4] On the basis of his review of a series of studies on the issue of immigration and mental health, Murphy demonstrated that the high rate of first psychiatric hospital admissions among members of immigrant groups all over the world can be only partly explained by factors such as occupation, education, marital status, or ethnic origin, suggesting that the stress experience of immigration itself has to be included as a variable in the study of immigration and mental disorders. Some other publications on this issue worth noting are Odegaard's 1932 article on "Immigration and Insanity,"[5] a census-type of study which established an association between immigration and the rate of psychiatric disorders; and the studies on acculturation and mental illness by Hallowell in 1950 and Sauna in 1959,[6] which showed a positive correlation between scores on an acculturation scale and scores on a maladjustment scale among first, second, and third-generation immigrants. These authors suggest that the high degree of maladjustment among those who also scored high on the measure of acculturation may be related to the simultaneous experience of weak identification with one's ethnic group and rejection by the dominant group of the host country.

Also worth noting is Margaret Mead's 1960 article on "Cultural Change and Character Structure,"[7] in which she presents a series of accounts of conflict situations in families in which the immigrant parents' value system is different from that of their children, who are more able and more willing to accept and incorporate the value system of the culture of the host country. Related to Mead's account is Mann's 1966 article on "Family Values in Overlapping Cultures,"[8] which provides data showing that adult immigrants are unwilling and also

[4] Ibid.

[5] O. Odegaard, "Immigration and Insanity," *Acta Psychiatrica et Neurologica*, supplement 4 (1932).

[6] A. Hallowell, "Values Acculturation and Mental Health," *American Journal of Orthopsychiatry* 20 (1950) 732-43; V. Sauna, "Differences in Personality Adjustment among Different Generations of American Jews and Non-Jews," in *Culture and Mental Health*, ed. H. Opler (New York: Macmillan, 1959) 50-93.

[7] Margaret Mead, "Cultural Change and Character Structure," in *Identity and Anxiety*, eds. M. R. Stein, A. J. Vidick, and D. N. White (Glencoa, Ill.: Free Press, 1960) 88-98.

[8] J. Mann, "Family Values in Overlapping Cultures," *Journal of Social Psychology* 69 (1966) 209-95.

find it very difficult to abandon their customs and value systems. In the fall of 1977, the *International Journal of Mental Health* dedicated a full issue to "Children's Mental Health and Psychosocial Development," with Dr. Norman Sartorius, Director of the Division of Mental Health of the World Health Organization, serving as editor. The issue included an article by P. Graham on the subject of the "Environmental Influences on Psychosocial Development,"[9] which reported that comparative studies of rates of disorder among immigrant children and children of the indigenous population reveal that immigrant children have higher rates of disorder and as a group are considered to be at a high risk of developing cognitive and emotional disorders. Finally, a 1976 article by John Cassel on the "Contributions of the Social Environment to Host Resistance"[10] alerted the health-related academic community to the neglected fact that marginal status in society has been found to be common among people who develop schizophrenia, become alcoholics, are victims of multiple accidents, or commit suicide. Marginality was viewed by Cassel as a state of deprivation of meaningful contact with the larger society and other groups. This state of deprivation was also found among members of ethnic minorities who were rejected by the dominant host group and among individuals with high rates of occupational and residential mobility.

Before proceeding with a summary of selected studies on the issue of immigration and mental health as regards members of Greek immigrant groups, it should be emphasized that, at present, the available information on the relationship between immigrant status and mental disorders is far from being conclusive or holding predictive validity. A fundamental methodological shortcoming of the studies on this issue is that immigrant groups are usually compared with the populations of the host countries but not with the populations of the countries of origin, which share similarities in demographic and socioeconomic characteristics with the immigrant group but have not migrated. Furthermore, the factors contributing to the development, severity, and duration of the dysfunctioning of the individual immigrant or the immigrant family are multiple and to a large extent idiosyncratic and unique to the particular case.

[9]See note 2.
[10]John Cassel, "The Contributions of the Social Environment to Host Resistance," *American Journal of Epidemiology* 104:2 (1976) 107-23.

Although the hardships of the process of adjustment among Greek immigrants have been the theme of many literary accounts, the systematic study of Greek immigrant groups in terms of issues related to mental health has only recently begun. In July 1978, the Institute for Child Care in Athens sponsored an international symposium on "The Child in the World of Tomorrow" and included a special session with five panelists on the issue of "Greek Migration—Internal and External." A. Amira presented a paper dealing with the issue of the degree of fulfillment of the expectations of Greek immigrant parents in Australia regarding upward socioeconomic mobility of their children through education: "A Longitudinal Study of Greek Immigrants in Australia." In this unique study, measurements of expectations and level of fulfillment were taken at three points in time, the first just before immigration, the second about two years after immigration, and the third about fourteen years after immigration. The data revealed that for the great majority expectations had not been met primarily because of lack of appropriate programs in the host country to service the needs of immigrant children. V. Filias, in his presentation "Specific Aspects of the Migrant Child Abroad," gave data on Greek immigrant families in Germany, emphasizing the negative effects that de facto ghetto-like life, isolation, and marginality have on the socialization and general development of immigrant children. D. Madianou reported on the effect that family separation had on the psychosocial development of children. His study, "The Socio-Psychological Impact of Out-Migration to West Germany on Greek Family Members Left Behind," also identified variables such as consensus among family members regarding the decision to migrate and the effect that the father's absence had on the development of children. I. Manganara presented "Selective Problems of Migrant Children in Sending and Receiving Countries," a comparative study of developmental patterns and levels of dysfunctioning among children who remained in the country of origin when one or both parents emigrated and children who returned to the country of origin alone or with one or both parents after a period of migration. M. Nikolinakos, in his paper "Some Issues about Migrant Children and the Future of the Labor Market in Immigration and Emigration Countries," emphasized that the problems of Greek immigrant children appear to be independent of country of immigration and developed a thesis from the point of view of political economy regarding the future of the labor market in the sending and receiving countries.

In the fall of 1978, at the National Conference of Neurology and Psychiatry in Thessaloniki, M. Madianos presented "Acculturation and Mental Health among Immigrants in New York City: A Pilot Study." This paper included data regarding the relationship between measurements of degree of acculturation and measurements of manifestation of psychopathological symptoms.

A year later, in the fall of 1979, the Center for Mental Health in Athens sponsored a conference on preventive psychiatry, which included two sessions on the issue of immigration and mental health. At one session, M. Madianos presented data on "A Comparative Study of the Mental Health Status of Greek Immigrants and Immigrants of Other Ethnic Groups." M. Markidis and M. Madianos reported their "Observations on Psychiatric Disorders among Cypriot Immigrants in London," whose level of dysfunctioning necessitated psychiatric hospitalization. D. Nikolaidis and G. Georgoulas reported on their observations of psychopathology among Greek immigrant teenagers in Switzerland: "Psychiatric Disorders among Children and Adolescents of Greek Immigrant Families." This writer presented "Preventive Mental Health Services to Greek Immigrant Families in New York City: A Community Multiservice-Agency Model," a summary of findings regarding characteristics of Greek immigrant families serviced at the HANAC Child and Family Counseling Service in New York City, which discussed prevention in terms of a community-based multiservice setting.

In a round table discussion at the same conference, T. Evdokas, who presented a paper on "The Process of Adjustment among Refugees and Immigrants," took up the issue of the psychological differences between refugees and immigrants as well as the different stress-effects that the individual experiences in the process of integration into the larger society as compared to the stress-effects experienced in the process of assimilation. Finally, G. Lykestos, in his report on "Psychological Stress for Families of Immigrants Who Remained in Greece," emphasized the seriousness of psychological dysfunctioning among families in which the father has migrated and has been absent from home for long periods of time. Lykestos also pointed to the urgent need for research in this neglected area.

In general, the studies of the relationship between immigrant status and mental health among Greek immigrant groups parallel those regarding other ethnic groups both in terms of areas of concern and methodology. Up to now, the main contribution of these studies has been the identification and definition of variables (factors, characteristics) related to the stress-effect of the experience of change following immigration. These variables or indicators either maximize the probability of the occurrence of dysfunctioning or contribute to its intensity once it has occurred. To summarize, among these indicators, *prolonged* periods of limited contact with the larger community (marginal status) reflect the individual's (family's) difficulty in achieving the reorganization and restructuring necessary for adjustment to the realities of the new environment. Some of the psychological consequences of this status are feelings of transiency, resistance to learning the language of the host country, exaggerated forms of ethnic identity with the country of origin, and perception of the new environment as hostile and rejecting. Among the antecedent factors are degree of similarity between expectations prior to immigration and realities following immigration, separation of family members because of immigration, consensus among family members regarding the decision to emigrate, and prior experience with migration (internal or external).

We now turn to a summary of general observations and specific characteristics of the Greek immigrant families serviced at the HANAC Child and Family Counseling Service in New York City. The service was established in the spring of 1977 with funds from the New York State Department of Social Services, Special Services to Children. The need for such a service was based on HANAC's experience in servicing the immigrant community since 1972 and on the experiences of mental health professionals in the community. The concern for the unmet mental health needs of the Greek immigrant community of New York City was formulated and presented at a one-day symposium on the "Psychosocial Perspectives of the Greek American Community of New York City," held in March 1977 under the cosponsorship of the Greek American Behavioral Sciences Institute, the Hellenic American Neighborhood Action Committee (HANAC), and the American Hellenic Educational Progressive Association (AHEPA).

The client families seen at the counseling service number

about one hundred annually, primarily referred by schools, HANAC's Department of Social Services, and family courts. As specified by contract, they are all families with children eighteen years of age or under. The psychopathological characteristics of the clients are social withdrawal, "learning disabilities," sexual activity among teenagers (including pregnancies), antisocial behavior, alcohol and drug abuse, and family violence, with an increasing incidence of child abuse and neglect and battered women's syndrome cases. Among children of six to eighteen years of age, 20 percent were not in school, and of those who were in school, more than half were below grade level. The average household size was 3.7 members. The majority of the parents had not completed elementary school and were in the occupational category of unskilled labor. The families reported a per capita annual gross income of $3,300, with both parents working full or part time in the majority of cases. In addition, most lived in crowded housing conditions (2.4 persons per room). As regards their "marginal" status (as this status has been defined above), about 90 percent lived in buildings where the majority of residents were Greek, worked for Greek employers, conducted all their business at Greek-owned establishments, and received all services from Greeks. The majority of families did not own a car and spent their leisure time within the boundaries of their local communities. Only 30 percent belonged to a church (mostly churches that were under the Greek Archdiocese of North and South America), and only 6 percent were members of Greek fraternal organizations. Of those who were American citizens, only 15 percent were registered to vote.

Feelings of transiency, expressed as intentions to return to Greece, were verbalized in the manner of wishful thinking or frustration and were qualified by statements implying that returning to Greece without fulfilling the expectations before immigration would create a deep sense of failure. The knowledge of the English language possessed by the adults and the majority of the children was very limited. Recommendations to register in English as a second language (ESL) programs were followed in only 2 percent of the cases. References to "life" in Greece ranged from exaggerated forms of idealization to exaggerated forms of rejection, while references to "life" in the US were for the most part negative and at best ambivalent. Included in these statements were references to disappointing experiences with relatives in the US, who were viewed as rejecting "because they have become Americanized and have lost their Greek *philotimo.*"

In 63 percent of the cases some form of family separation related to immigration had occurred, and in about 25 percent of these cases at least one child (an infant or toddler) had remained in Greece, usually with grandparents, for at least two years before joining the parents. In addition, the majority of these families came from rural areas of Greece and had lived in some form of extended family situation prior to immigration. Thus, one of the changes related to immigration was the new experience of nuclear family living. In most cases, it seemed that the decision to emigrate was made by one of the spouses, usually the husband, although it can be argued that statements made in retrospect regarding the decision were affected by present realities.

The above characteristics of the client families serviced at the Child and Family Counseling Service can be viewed as specific to these families, who are in a state of crisis and threatened by disruption. However, since these characteristics have been identified as indicators which maximize the probability of the occurrence of dysfunctioning, their presence in the larger population, in this case the Greek immigrant population, can be interpreted to mean that members of this group are at a risk of developing different levels of dysfunctioning.

With this cautious interpretation of these indicators in mind, HANAC conducted a large-scale survey of demographic/ socioeconomic characteristics and needs of the Greek American community of New York City in 1978-1979, under the direction of the present author. Based on a weighted, stratified random sample of census tracts, the door-to-door survey yielded a total of 507 completed questionnaires. Of the 507 respondents, 102 were Greek Americans born in the United States, and 405 were born outside the United States. The following is a first-level descriptive analysis of characteristics of and responses given by the Greek immigrant respondents to selective items.

Forty percent of the members of immigrant households had come to the US after 1965. The average household size was 3.5 members. Thirty-five percent of adult males and 53 percent of adult females had less than six years of formal schooling. On the basis of a 50 precent sample of protocols, 15 percent of the children between the ages of six and eighteen were not in school, and 24 percent of those in school were one or more years behind grade level. Fifty-eight percent of the males and 88 percent of the females who were working fit the category of unskilled labor. Among the adult population, 79 percent were working either full or part time, and the per capita annual gross income was $4,450. Ninety-six percent lived in buildings other than one-family houses, and 69 percent rented their place of residence, with a ratio of two persons per room.

As regards geographic mobility, 12 percent reported that they had lived in countries other than Greece for more than one year prior to coming to the US. Although only 6 percent reported that they had moved to New York from another state, 32 percent had moved from one borough of New York City to another, and of those, 45 percent had moved more than once.

As regards "marginality," 60 percent of the respondents reported that they relied on friends and relatives for employment and other services. Only 50 percent reported that they either owned or had access to a car. Forty-eight percent reported being members of a church, and 26 percent of those who were members belonged to a church outside the Greek Orthodox Archdiocese of North and South America. Only 6 percent of those who were church members belonged to a church-affiliated organization. Membership in Greek fraternal organizations were reported by about 10 percent, with recreation the most common reason given for participating in the activities of the organization. About half of those who were eligible to vote reported that they actually did so.

As regards transiency, of those who had entered the US as permanent residents and had lived here for more than five years, about 50 percent became citizens, and 80 percent of the remainder reported that they did not intend to apply for citizenship. Sixty-four percent reported that they either planned to return to Greece or Cyprus (40 percent) or that they were uncertain (24 percent). Over 60 percent identified themselves as "Greek," as opposed to "Greek American," "American Greek," or "American."

Sixty-nine percent reported that one or more members of their household had difficulty communicating in English, and 32 percent reported that at least one child of school age had language difficulties. In about 30 percent of the cases, immigration had created a family separation. Sixty-one percent reported that the reason for immigration was economic, and 24 percent, mostly women, reported that they immigrated for "family" reasons. This last item may possibly imply that the decision to migrate was not taken jointly.

In terms of needs, more than 50 percent of the possible responses were expressive of the opinion that the Greek or Greek American youth had been quite or seriously affected by problems such as school dropout and drug and alcohol abuse. Congruent with the above was the finding that counseling service programs were viewed as of top priority, along with programs for improving employment skills.

The summary of indicators given above places the members of the Greek immigrant community of New York City at rather high levels of risk of developing different levels of dysfunctioning. Counseling services are obviously needed, but they cannot provide the solution to the problem, as these services are individual and family oriented and are only sought when the dysfunctioning has already reached high levels. It seems, therefore, that the problem of adjustment among recent immigrants must be viewed not as a problem pertaining only to certain individuals and families, but as a community concern. And, if viewed in this way, the various institutions of the community could begin to actively participate in the total effort of prevention.

CHAPTER 12

GREEK AMERICANS AND THE LAW

BY
MANOS M. LAMPIDIS

The exposure of the Greek American community to the legal system and the contrast between the experiences of the older immigrants and their children and those of the newer arrivals cannot be assessed with the accuracy demanded by the social scientist. The sources for this essay are primarily the experiences and impressions of the author, the opinions of people in the law enforcement field, and the opinions of the author's colleagues in the legal profession who have worked extensively over the years with Greek American clients. A further caveat should be added; namely, that the study is confined to the situation of the Greek community in the New York metropolitan area. Any conclusions do not necessarily obtain as to communities elsewhere.

The area of law that probably attracts the greatest public interest is criminal justice. From all accounts, the crime rate in the Greek American community prior to the liberalization of the US immigration laws in 1965 was extremely low.[1] This was attributable to the traditional work ethic and strong family ties. Crime among Greeks was indeed so low that the issue was considered not worth discussing. The rare instances of criminal acts by Greek Americans would literally cause shock waves and extreme embarrassment throughout the community. Any Greek implicated in antisocial conduct was declared to have brought dishonor upon thousands of law-abiding Greek Americans.[2]

[1]See Charles C. Moskos, Jr., *Greek Americans: Struggle and Success* (Englewood Cliffs, N.J.: Prentice-Hall, 1980) 43.
[2]Ibid., 44.

209

The 1965 Immigration Act resulted in a tremendous influx of immigrants, which gave new lifeblood to the Greek American community. Attracted by the tremendous prosperity of the United States of the sixties and perhaps seeing little hope in a homeland ruled by the colonels, these people came for much the same reasons as their predecessors. But as the Greek population grew, an increase in crime also became more and more apparent.

This trend does not appear to be attributable merely to the greater number. The consensus is that there is an actual and substantial increase in the rate. It is difficult to gauge that rate, however. Some of my colleagues and people in the law enforcement field contend that it is at the approximate level of the general populace. Most, however, hold that the greater probability is that it is still relatively low compared to the general populace and specifically to most other ethnic groups. My own random sampling of the criminal court calendar of Queens County seems to support the latter view.

Most of the offenses involving Greek American defendants are petty in nature and are usually property crimes rather than crimes against the person. However, burglaries, thefts, robberies, and drug dealing have been reported with greater frequency than in the past. Many white-collar crimes, such as theft of airline tickets, possession of forged documents, con games, and frauds of all kinds are no longer unusual. Other incidents are related to gambling, a problem in Greek American society that deserves serious attention. Homicide is rare, but it has occurred. Most violence is involved with matters of honor and passion or is a consequence of a property crime. However, hardly ever do we see the gratuitous violence that is endemic in the greater American society.[3]

Stories abound about the formation of a Greek "syndicate." There have long been Greek Americans affiliated with organized crime, but they were usually involved in the legitimate front businesses of the mobsters or in gambling operations rather than in the more sinister activities. These people worked on an individual basis for established organized crime rather than as members of distinctly Greek gangs.

Among the recent arrivals there have been reports of extortion and protection rackets from time to time, but there is little evidence that these involved more than a handful of indi-

[3]Ibid., 43-4.

viduals. Certainly it has not reached the proportions of the youth gangs in Chinatown, another once docile community undergoing even more drastic change.

Usually the group crime involves a specific action—a single large drug smuggling deal,[4] a major robbery, a fraudulent scheme—designed to make some fast money. The small gang may dissolve when the purpose is accomplished or when one or more members are apprehended. The groups tend to be transitory in nature, not ongoing permanent entities. No evidence can be found of godfathers, families, or national commissions.

Perhaps some Greek American criminals have visions of organizing themselves on a grand scale, but I personally doubt they would have much success. In his recent fictionalized account of the life of the famous gambler, Nick the Greek, Harry Mark Petrakis has a Sicilian mobster saying to the protagonist: "You Greeks . . . you fuss about being refined, civilized, all that stuff about culture . . . but scratch your skin and you got blood as hot as any Sicilian. You'd kill just as fast for vengeance and honor. One thing you never learned . . . you never learned to work together, to accept your vows of brotherhood and blood."[5] Thus, we see one salutary effect of the generally deplorable inability of the Greek Americans to properly organize and unite for any purpose.

The role of Greek Americans in organized crime is greatly exaggerated, not only in the perception of Greek Americans hearing of isolated incidents, but, unfortunately, also by the altogether too frequent stereotypes of Greek Americans in TV crime shows. The distortions portrayed by the media are tantamount to group defamation and should be met with the strongest protestations by the Greek American community.

Often we encounter among the new immigrants offenses not of moral turpitude, but of moral, social, and financial irresponsibility. Many retain the driving habits prevalent in Athens.[6] Some drive with expired licenses or registrations or without current insurance. Parking violation scofflaws owing

[4]*New York Times* (April 2, 1979).

[5]Harry Mark Petrakis, *Nick the Greek* (Garden City, N.Y.: Doubleday, 1979) 123.

[6]The image of Greek drivers as among the most reckless in the world has been confirmed by statistics that show them causing twice as many traffic deaths as drivers in any Western European country. See the *Hellenic Times* (September 18-24, 1980).

fines in the thousands of dollars are quite common. Businesses are frequently operated without the proper permits. The perpetrators of such minor infractions do not grasp that in America, laws relying for the most part on voluntary compliance, as opposed to more severe sanctions, exist for the common good. The violations are deemed victimless, and compliance is often regarded as a mere annoyance. When apprehended, the defendant makes vehement protestations of persecution and demonstrates his righteous indignation.

It is difficult to pinpoint the reasons for this increased crime rate among recent arrivals. We might ask whether it can be attributed to changed conditions in Greece over the past few years. Yet, looking for changed conditions in Greece over the past few years we find, to the contrary, the lowest crime rate in Europe, with no discernible increase since at least 1968, despite an almost astronomical trend toward urbanization. Rapes, murders, and robberies rarely occur.[7] Two-thirds of the homicides are crimes of honor, occurring mainly in underdeveloped rural areas.[8] Organized crime is insignificant. Youth gangs are nonexistent.[9] White-collar crimes, which do not incite great public outrages, are the most common offenses.[10]

The reasons given for this low crime rate are similar to those attributed to the earlier generation of Greek Americans. According to one prominent criminal lawyer in Athens, most felons are more concerned about the reaction of their families than that of the courts. The usual family response is: "How could you bring such shame on the family?"—not "Why did you do it?" or "How have we failed you?" He concluded that such a family response was the most effective deterrent to crime.[11]

One would ask how people recently coming from a society with such family constraints on personal conduct could change so easily in a new environment? Perhaps we should look to the America these people are seeing today. However distorted the picture may be, they are bombarded by the media with thefts that go unsolved and murderers going free because of strange

[7]*New York Times* (August 19, 1979).

[8]*New York Times* (February 10, 1980).

[9]*1977 Area Handbook for Greece* (Washington, D.C.: published under the auspices of the US Government by American University, 1977) 231-2.

[10]*New York Times* (August 19, 1977).

[11]Ibid.

laws, an inefficient court system, and an overworked, underpaid police force. Unrealistic hopes and expectations on arrival are replaced with frustration and disappointment when working at menial jobs in a sagging economy. These frustrations also lead to tensions within the family. Most persevere, but some, with few personal acquaintances and thus no family honor to protect, yield to temptation. The result is adapting to the new social environment far too easily and quickly. The rationale is: The smart ones are wearing spiffy clothes and driving Cadillacs, while the fool uncle is sweating every day working in the restaurant; the odds appear overwhelmingly in your favor—you aren't likely to be caught, if caught you'll probably get off, and if convicted you won't have to serve much time. This illusion is finally shattered by the clanging of the steel door in a Riker's Island or in an Attica.

On the civil side of the law, many recent immigrants have difficulty adapting and adjusting to the new environment. By and large, like their predecessors, they are an upwardly mobile group. Their goal is to own their own homes and businesses and become respected members of the community.[12] Recently, Greek Americans have shifted away from the traditional occupations, such as restaurants and florist shops, to other fields where market entry is accessible through competence and hard work. They are now getting involved, in increasing numbers, in contracting, painting, supermarkets, garment manufacturing, real estate holdings, and in an expanding fur trade. As their business interests grow and diversify, their legal problems become more complicated. The lawyers serving these people may have to shift from simple buy/sell agreements and partnership agreements to areas such as antitrust, estate planning, trademarks, securities issues, complicated real estate financing techniques, and tax shelters.

But many of these people will have to undergo a rather thorough change in attitude and adjust to ways of doing business that are different from those they left behind. For example, the belief in the role of influence in getting a desired legal result is a common misconception carried over from Greece. This reliance on *meson*, or having an *in*, can be ex-

[12]On Greeks in business in general see Moskos, *Greek Americans;* Stephanos Zotos, *Hellenic Presence in America* (Wheaton, Ill.: Pilgrimage Press, 1976); and Theodore Saloutos, *The Greeks in the United States* (Cambridge, Mass.: Harvard University Press, 1964).

tremely dangerous. Moreover, in a business transaction there is often an almost pathological desire to put one over on the party on the other side of the negotiating table. We also frequently encounter the view that Americans are naive and are fair game for exploitation. A premium is placed on *poneria*—the greatest business virtue. This Levantine way of doing business is characterized by a jealous assertion of one's own rights and a disregard for one's obligations, together with an indifference to the rights of others. Added to this is a tendency to evade compliance with administrative regulations.

A Greek American may choose a lawyer of some other ethnic background rather than a Greek-speaking lawyer despite the language barrier because he may have heard that this particular attorney has the right contacts with the right people. Thinking that the endemic practice of *rousfeti* obtains here as it does in Greece,[13] the client may be convinced that part of his attorney's fee actually goes to bribing some public official. The choice of such a lawyer can be disastrous. At best, if he is honest and competent, by reason of the failure to communicate he may not garner all the essential information and may prove unable to advise his client properly. At worst, the client may be the victim of slipshod work, excessive fees, and other exploitation.

In all societies lawyers suffer, whether deservedly or not, from skepticism and distrust by some segment of the public. This attitude is particularly strong among Greeks. The lawyer may be viewed as a person who by the very nature of his calling must be dishonest. The good lawyer is viewed as the one who will tell the most effective and convincing lies on behalf of the client. Several Greek immigrants are amused by the similarity in sound upon learning the new English words "liar" and "lawyer." I do not know what experiences some people may have had with lawyers in Greece or the standards of ethics of the Greek Bar, but this mistrust can be to the client's detriment. Some people fail to speak candidly and openly to a lawyer or to give him all of the relevant facts essential to the proper rendering of the requested legal service. This may be from shame, embarrassment, fear of disclosure, or ignorance of the attorney-client privilege. Other people, dissatisfied with the results of a case, may suspect the lawyer of collusion with the adversary. Another manifestation of the attitude toward

[13]*New York Times* (April 2, 1979).

lawyers are the frequent requests for the lawyer to assist the client in some clearly illegal scheme, such as preparation of a false document, a fraud on the Immigration Service, or a fraudulent business scheme. Thus, a lawyer's or accountant's advice, once sought and paid for, is often subsequently ignored. The professional's efforts are undermined by the *"kafenion* lawyer"—the friend or relative who is generous with gratuitous counsel on matters he knows little or nothing about. Much talent, money, and hard work are wasted by the failure to drop such self-destructive attitudes and habits. Those who are most successful in business are almost invariably the ones who quickly learn to conform to the new commercial norms.

The Greek is characterized by a strong sense of justice as it affects him and his loved ones and is outraged when he perceives injustice being wreaked on him by a lack of a legal remedy in our system. In the extreme case, this may involve the dismissal of a harassment charge brought in court for some real or imagined offense or the unavailability of a civil cause of action to enforce and protect his perceived rights. There is often a lack of comprehension that he cannot obtain a desired result in litigation because of the absence of adequate proof, and the restrictions imposed by the rules of evidence often mystify him. Far too often he may prove unwilling to enter into a reasonable settlement of a dispute.

The immigrant is understandably shocked when he encounters some of the glaring inadequacies in the law or in our judicial system. He is justifiably upset when he discovers that it may take six months to evict a destructive, noisy, and perhaps dangerous tenant from his own home. He finds it difficult to accept that a negligence case may take several years to adjudicate. Native Americans seem more likely to accept these failures in the legal system. In this respect, the immigrant's contrast with our system and that of Greece may be justified.

There is a general perception that in many areas justice is more swift and certain in Greece. Recently, the Athens Bar Association staged a boycott of the entire court system. One of the conditions they were protesting was that it may take from three to as much as six months from the time a civil case is filed to the time of a trial.[14] In the American system delay is the norm. A trial in six months, at least in New York or

[14]*Ta Nea* [Athens daily] (May 6, 1980); *Hoi Vradyni* [Athens daily] (May 6, 1980).

New Jersey, in most types of civil actions is unheard of.

These negative attitudes with respect to civil matters and business affairs are not unique to the new arrivals—they are deeply ingrained in the Greek character and probably stem from four centuries of oppression by a non-western culture. But the earlier immigrants, with fewer compatriots to reinforce the retention of the old ways and outlook, may have found themselves under greater pressure to adapt to the demands of a new environment. Now it seems there is a greater resistance to change.

This syndrome is not necessarily a function of education. Some people with little formal education manage to adjust quite quickly. Others, including graduates of universities in Greece with lucrative careers, fail to change and may suffer in their investments and legal relationships accordingly. In time most will learn by hard experience; those who fail to learn will fall by the wayside.

In conclusion, the overall experience of the Greek American community with the law has been a very positive one, and its contribution to American society has been extremely beneficial. Yet, in spite of my tendency to overemphasize the negative aspects of the Greek American experience with the law, the problem, in recent years, is sufficiently important to warrant community concern. A head-on confrontation through education and community action will greatly contribute to the adjustment process of the new wave of Greek immigrants.

CHAPTER 13

THE GREEK HERITAGE AND ITS IMPACT ON THE GREEK AMERICAN WRITER

BY

ATHENA G. DALLAS-DAMIS

Now that we have seen the progress of the Greek American community in population and religion, in politics and law, in education and social mobility, now that we have saluted those first immigrants who built new lives in America against barely surmountable odds, who gave us the Papanicholases, the Callases, the Pappases, the Sarbaneses, the Savalases—candles that glow vividly in what was once the darkness of ethnicity —we come to the last and perhaps most neglected child of the Greek American community: the writer, the professional whose work stems mainly from love and a burning desire to give a part of himself, his thoughts, his ideals, to those around him.

In the constant race for achievement, this runner appears last—not because he does not run as fast as the others, but because his road is more winding, more complex, less acceptable in the mainstream of vocations. He is last because as an artist he faces far greater obstacles that tax his patience and perseverance and sap his energies. It took many years for this runner to appear, and he did so only after the Greek American community finally set down its roots and attained economic security following the Second World War.

The breakthrough came in 1945 with Mary Vardoulakis' *Gold in the Streets*,[1] a novel of Greek immigrants in America

[1] *Gold in the Streets*, out of print; reviewed by A. G. Damis in the *National Herald*.

217

which appeared briefly and disappeared. Others followed
sporadically and so unobtrusively that we hardly noticed their
arrival and departure from the literary scene. In an article
appearing recently in *To Vima,* an Athens newspaper, George
Gianaris tells us that in the early forties there were three
novels by Paul Stefanellis and Michael Pezas, and that between 1945 and 1959 nearly ten other novels based on Greek
American life were published in the United States.[2] Yet we
heard little, if anything, about these. In view of the minority
prejudices of that period, the competition in trade books, and
the foothold of already established writers, it is little wonder
that these works by unknown Greek Americans passed us unheralded. Whoever they were, however, these pioneers surely
must have touched some readers in America. And though their
attempts to enter the field of American literature waned, they
are to be considered the forerunners.

Of all the fields of endeavor of the Greek Americans, writing was the last to be recognized, both by the Greek Americans
themselves and the American public. Indeed, it was the American reader who finally began to take our writers to his heart
with the advent of a new hero. This acceptance came about
with the appearance of Tom Chamales, whose novels headed
best-seller lists and appeared as important motion pictures.
His first novel, *Never So Few,* described the author's experiences as a soldier in World War II, but his second, *Go Naked
in the World* (1959) was an outpouring of his feelings and
frustrations as a member of a stringent, taut Greek American
family of the forties. Chamales' story deals with a young Greek
American returning from World War II. Anxious to devour
life's experiences and deeply needing love, he plunges into a
wealthy, turbulent Chicago world. The plot takes him into the
business enterprises of the "macho" father, carries him
through an intense love affair with a non-Greek mistress,
through many rebellions, and ultimately to emotional security.
A master of his craft, Chamales' words grip the reader with
an emotional intensity that is truly Greek. I recall the pride I
felt as I read him, pride that one of our own had finally been
accepted by the literary circles of America. But the joy was
short lived, and we were all saddened by the untimely death
of this restless young man who burned the candle at both ends

---

[2]George Gianaris, "The Greek Immigrant and Literature in America"
[in Greek], *To Vima* (June 15, 1980).

and accidentally put an end to his brilliant writing career. Soon others followed—Harry Mountzouris and Charles Jarvis, and George Christy, the noted Hollywood reporter whose *All I Could See from Where I Stood* was a sensitive story of childhood in Monessen, Pennsylvania's Greek community.[3] Here we saw the influence of Greek immigrant life again, and the author's social, religious and emotional worlds.

By the sixties the "writer-child" of the Greek immigrant had grown up and his heritage continued to guide his pen. In 1964 Thomas Doulis gave us *Paths for Our Valor*, the story of three paratroopers of the peacetime commando guerillas seeking their personal freedom. One of these is Sgt. Gus Damianos, a Greek American who finds his particular freedom in freefalling from airplanes. Elia Kazan, Oscar and Tony-winning director of the stage and films who for years underplayed his ethnicity, came onto the literary scene with a novel that surprised many by its ethnic pride. *America, America,* the story of Kazan's father and his family's trials in escaping Turkey for a life free from torment in America, was filmed in the early sixties and met with mixed reviews and feelings. This was mainly due to the fact that it was, in 1962, a work ahead of its time.

As a member of the press I attended the filming of various scenes in Athens and in the hills of Scaramanga outside Piraeus. I was greatly impressed by the Kazan mastery, by his careful, studied manipulation of the actors in bringing out the emotional "Greekness" of his characters. It was a film that contradicted Kazan's silence regarding his heritage; it was a film for which the American public was not prepared. The stark realism of *America, America*'s Greeks of Istanbul and their personal stories, their tragedies and triumphs, was hesitantly received by the American filmgoer. And yet today it is considered a film masterpiece.

Kazan evolved into full-time authorship in his maturity, as he was moving on, away from directing. In 1967 he gave us *The Arrangement,* the story of a Greek American and the arrangements by which he lived his life and his marriage. Here again, we see the strict, unbending Greek immigrant father, respected and feared and fought by the son who breaks away from the mold, resisting the pattern of life decreed by his culture. Here, as in *America, America,* we see a part of Kazan

[3]*All I Could See from Where I Stood,* out of print, unavailable.

that lay hidden the many years of his notability, when he withdrew into the nonethnic world of America. It seems that some part of him lay dormant, waiting for the time it could break its vise, as it finally did, proving again that the Greek heritage, so deep rooted and deeply instilled, cannot be taken lightly; it is too strong, too overpowering, and it fights the individual, resisting any forces that seek to crush it or keep it hidden.

The year 1965 brought us Stephen Linakis and his first novel, *In the Spring the War Ended*, the story of an AWOL soldier and his flight through Belgium which begins on V-E Day. It is the author's commentary on the nature of army justice and the fate of fugitives like his protagonist, Nick Leonidas. Linakis reappeared on the scene in 1976 when he co-authored *The Sixth Family*, with Peter Diapoulos, a member of the Gallo crew of the Mafia, or, as it is commonly known these days, organized crime.

The early sixties also brought us the giant in our midst, the man who gave the Greek American novel a permanent place in American literature. Critically lauded, nominated for the National Book Award, compared by his contemporaries to another giant, the Armenian, William Saroyan, Harry Mark Petrakis styled himself as a Greek American long before it was fashionable to do so. Here, at last, the Greek heritage found its apostle in the world of American literature. Petrakis, whose short stories based on the Chicago Greeks of his youth appeared in numerous magazines throughout the United States solely on their literary quality, exploded on the scene in 1959 with his *Lion at My Heart*, a story of emotional turmoil in a Greek American family of the forties. Here, we got a glimpse of the father in his disappointments and disillusionments, the patriarch fought by his sons. A second novel, *The Odyssey of Kostas Volakis* (1963), brought us a Greek who tears himself away from his roots to come to the land of good living only to find himself trapped, barely able to cling to his dignity. Here is a novel of such sensitivity, an embroidery of such delicate lines, hues, and shadows that America at last received a clear look into the world of the Greek immigrant. Seventeen years have gone by since I reviewed that novel, and I have never forgotten that one scene that tore at my heart. The newly arrived couple work as dishwashers in a restaurant from dawn to dusk, coming home to a windowless room for a few hours of tormented sleep. We see the wife, thin, pale, and crushed at what seems to be the end of a dream for them. The husband turns to her and says, "I am sick of this room . . . I am sick of never seeing the sun . . ." How many Greek immigrants must have uttered those words, one wonders. And then he adds, "I wish to go back where a man's life has some dignity even though he is poor. Do you understand?"[4] Dignity, here is the crux of the Odyssean Greek, of Petrakis' Greeks—dignity. Whether lost or lonely, sick or in despair, Petrakis' characters, good or bad, always survive in dignity. And as Petrakis labored, giving us book after book on the people of his heritage, the fashions changed: the advent of *Zorba the Greek* to American film made it fashionable to be Greek; the country opened its arms and its heart to its Greeks.

Petrakis followed his first success with *Pericles on 31st St.* (1965), *A Dream of Kings* (1966), *The Waves of Night* (1969), *Stelmark-Recollections* (1970), *In the Land of Morning* (1973), *The Hour of the Bell* (1976), and *Nick the Greek* in 1979. All the above, except for *Hour of the Bell*, deal with lives of Greeks in America. So powerful, so indelible are Petrakis' impressions of the world of his childhood, his young adulthood, all his life, which touched so piercingly on the Greek experience in Chicago, that he has built a monument to that immigrant through his writings.

There are many of his own ethnic background who resent Petrakis' delving into the psyche of what they call "untypical" Greeks in our establishment. His characters do not fit the mold, they say, of the quiet, peace-loving, issue-avoiding, church-attending, PTA-member Greeks and their families. And yet, were there not among us, the children of those first immigrants, such characters? Can we deny that there, among our groups, were the gamblers, the loud, ego-ridden males, crude, warm-hearted, life-loving individuals? Certainly they existed. Surely we can recall the Greek coffeehouses of the Greek communities in America, whether in a small town or city. And how many towns did contain the hip-swinging widow in black, or, too, the silent mistress of someone in the top echelon? It was those very people, not the masses, who left their impressions, who were taken by Petrakis and molded into his antiheroes and heroines. Perhaps he also took little, inconsequential people and made them ten feet tall. There is no doubt he can create giants who shout, curse, strike blows,

[4]Harry Mark Petrakis, *The Odyssey of Kostas Volakis* (New York: David McKay, 1963) 21.

who go against the grain, who satisfy their own egos. Remember Anthony Quinn personifying the antihero in *A Dream of Kings,* the film in which he starred with Irene Papas? Remember Theodore Bikel as he danced around the room waving his white handkerchief in the television version of *Pericles on 31st St.*? What memorable characters! It took me back to a small town in West Virginia, when we gathered at friends' homes to celebrate the saints' days—a fading scene of a handlebar moustache (there were only two in the whole community, but what moustaches!), wide, sagging trousers, bent old men who came alive with music and wine and the company of strapping, young Greeks.

Petrakis could weave any number of stories in his imagination, perhaps on more commercial themes. But it is his dedication, his devotion to that subject closest to his heart that, along with his talent, is the stuff great writers are made of. This is the difference between *For Whom the Bell Tolls* and *Scruples,* between Hemingway and Krantz. And when Petrakis decided to step out of the immigrant theme, he dealt with still another facet of his heritage: the Greek War of Independence of 1821. The author tells us that his research and writing of that period had a shattering impact on him. He speaks stirringly of an awakening to this other part of his life and past, which brought out a different facet of himself as a writer. He found a strange world, so new to him, in that neglected period in Greek history which he recorded in his novel, *The Hour of the Bell.*

I, too, felt this impact. Delving into the lives of my ancestors on the island of Chios during the Turkish massacre of 1822, I felt suddenly transported back into that time. I felt their terror and their frustrations. I walked the lonely hillsides up to the monasteries where the battles took place, looked at the hills once splattered with blood. And I could virtually smell the burning of flesh and hear the cries of women, the simpering of children, and the clashing of swords. My first novel, *Island of the Winds* (1976), was my own awakening to that period of the past. Until I began my research in 1972, exactly one hundred and fifty years after the massacre of Chios took place, I knew only of the lives of the ancient Greeks and the immigrants of the community of my childhood. I had heard of Kolokotronis and Diakos; certainly we knew of Turks and freedom and the raising of the banner at the Holy Laura that holy day of March 25 on the Greek mainland. But those were only faint wisps of history, fleeting stories related at Greek afternoon school or told by a mother who was determined her child should know the agonies of her ancestors, the building of a new nation. Yet I knew nothing . . . not until I walked those very paths my ancestors once trod, not until I read the twenty-one volumes of Greek lore and history from the Korais Library in Chios, not until I spoke with old men and women, descendants of those survivors of the massacre. Not until then did I really understand the meaning of that period of the Greek nation's history. Those ghosts who followed me in my journeys on the island were friendly ghosts who seemed to guide me, to want to make me truly see the part of their lives that lay hidden from the rest of the world. Many great writers have eulogized the Greek War of Independence; much poetry, many paintings span the globe. But the common people, the American masses, who know little of their own history, much less the Greek, can see glimpses of that past in these novels. From the beginning, this thought was my guide. And as I delved further into the Greek Revolution, it became a challenge, a desire to let the American reader see what transpired in the building of this new Greece, a nation born of manipulation and torn by injustice.

Island of the Winds covers the years 1805 through 1824, and the historical events are a background for the story of a woman whose twin sons are separated when one is abducted as a child and raised as an Ottoman Janissary. Her life in Turkish-occupied Chios climaxes with the Turkish massacre of the island and the fleeting reunion of the twin brothers. The novel portrays the struggle of a woman and a nation, the sacrifices each must make for freedom. The paperback version of the novel introduced it as the first of a trilogy, and its sequel *Windswept* (1981) picks up the story from 1824 until 1829, the end of the Greek Revolution. Here we see the Janissary son return to his Christian mother and his island home, resisting the heritage he was taught to hate, disillusioned by the people with which he is forced to associate. The story takes him on a journey back to the Sultan at Constantinople, to St. Petersburg as his emissary to the Tsar, and finally back to the Greek mainland, to the place of his birth, on those last days of the peace negotiations. The last book of the trilogy, *Follow the Winds,* will cover the period 1830 to 1860, the first Greek government, King Othon and the palace, and will take the Janissary-turned-Christian back to the island of Chios in a strange twist of fate that touches upon his family and loved ones.

My current project, a novel dealing with three American women trapped in Greece during the German occupation of that country, has a descendant of the island trilogy character as its heroine. Once again, in traveling through Greece for research purposes, I came in direct contact with my heritage and found that my feelings were stronger than ever, more alive than before. For now I faced the actual survivors of another period of history that brought glory to a long-ignored nation. I listened to vivid accounts of those dark days of 1941 and 1942. My journey took me to northwestern Greece, to the Albanian border, the very spot where the Italian armies crossed into Greece that fateful October 28, 1940. The authorities at Yiannina brought me in touch with one of the guards who was on duty that night, and his words, twenty years after the fact, made me a witness to that infamous scene. We drove past the Pindus Mountains, stopped at battle sites along the way, viewed caves and trenches, talked with old men who still tend sheep on the hillsides, inspected relics and mementos in the small museum of Delvinaki, and looked up sons and daughters of heroes who fought and died in battles. Let others write about today, I thought as I absorbed all these retrospects, let others write about the jet set and murders and the occult. Here is a land of unfathomable wealth, abounding stories, exciting history, and material for novels to serve me for years and years. I returned to New York rejuvenated, encouraged, bent on ignoring the obstacles I knew lay before me, those obstacles that say "who cares about the Greeks?" Petrakis made them care about his immigrants. I'd like to make them care about our history.

The writers discussed here are all Americans of Greek descent, and all have touched upon their heritage in one way or another in their writings. Now we have four native-born Greeks who have made important contributions to literature in America.

The first of these, Nicholas Gage, came to the United States as a child, graduated from the Columbia School of Journalism in the early sixties, and went on to become a well-known investigative reporter for the *New York Times*, specializing in organized crime. His work led to two acclaimed books on that subject—*The Mafia is Not an Equal Opportunity Employer*

(1971), and *Mafia* (1972), both of which made the best-seller lists and received critical acclaim (two factors which do not necessarily go hand in hand). He went on to write *Portrait of Greece,* a profile of his native country, and the novel *Bones of Contention.*[5] His next novel, *The Bourlotas Fortune* in 1975, was based on his knowledge of the life, customs, and moral code of the Greek villagers and shipowners he befriended through the years, who shaped his characters. His story begins with the Turkish massacre on Chios (1822) and follows the life of a Chiote youth to the present day. Less emotional a writer than Petrakis, Gage nonetheless has his own fervor in style, and tells a story that holds the reader's interest continuously. Now in Greece as the Athens Bureau Chief of the *New York Times,* Gage is working on a novel set in the time of the Greek Civil War (1946-1948), and his own shattering experiences as a child will doubtlessly play a major role in mirroring the mood of the period.

The second of the Greek-born writers, a man named Theodore Rubanis, brought us a little-publicized but highly explosive novel of the German occupation of his native land, *The Man with the Black Worry Beads.* This is the story of a Greek's personal vendetta against the German conquerors, and is an engrossing thriller. It followed its hardcover publication with a paperback edition in 1973, and has been or is being considered for possible filming as a motion picture on the order of *The Guns of Navarone.*

Theodore Vrettos, another native Greek author, teaches at the State College in Salem, Massachusetts and gave us *Hammer on the Sea, A Shadow of Magnitude,* and *Origen,* the last a study of one of the great mystics and renegades of the ancient world.[6] His latest novel, *Birds of Winter,*[7] is set in wartime Greece and has a Greek protagonist.

The last and most recent Greek-born author to appear on the scene is Stratis Haviaras, who has made his home in the United States since 1967 and who has had five poetry volumes published, four in the Greek language and one in English. Currently the curator of poetry collections at Harvard Uni-

[5] *Portrait of Greece* and *Bones of Contention,* out of print, unavailable.

[6] *Hammer on the Sea* and *A Shadow of Magnitude,* out of print, unavailable.

[7] Theodore Vrettos, *Birds of Winter* (New York: Houghton Mifflin, 1980).

versity Library, he is also the author of several unpublished novels in the Greek language, novels which he says he has simply filed away or lost. A pity, for one of these, *The Boy Who Could Not Smile*, which I read briefly years ago, was a beautiful, sensitive story reminiscent of the Myriviles style. Haviaras had his first novel published in the English language (written originally in English) in 1979. *When the Tree Sings* is a boy's picture of the German-occupied Greece of the forties. This small volume of a child's emergence into manhood in a period of tyranny won critical acclaim in America. Haviaras is currently working on his next novel, set in the period of the Greek Civil War. It is interesting indeed that so many of our writers are involved in that period of Greece's history (1940-1948).

What lies ahead for the Greek American writer? As is apparent from the number of names mentioned here, our authors are merely a handful. Will they be able to survive? Or, as most who have written one novel and disappeared, will they too, go the practical way of the nonartist? Each new writer that appears makes the way easier for the next one, prepares the public, makes them more receptive. Indirectly, our writers have been helped by the Greek American educators who have launched a tireless battle in universities throughout the country to gain acceptance of modern Greek courses within those institutions. Modern Greek studies programs and departments have been established in numerous colleges and universities through the efforts of American professors of Greek descent. Greek cultural and civic programs, though sparse, spring forth here and there, from time to time, and we find that the public has become somewhat more receptive and open to things Greek.

But we also find that in the publishing field it is not always the question of what the public wants, but what the publishers want to give that public. It is what the publishers wish to promote. America is a nation of "hard sell," of fast, forceful advertising that influences the people's tastes and desires. Americans usually want what they are told to want. It is a known fact that Madison Avenue has been able to package and sell anything and everything, from pet rocks to Presidents. Americans have learned to buy ouzo and moussaka, Zorba movies and feta cheese; why not books by Greek American authors? A long road lies ahead for these artists, for they know that, except for works of our established literary giants, the best-seller lists are filled with celebrities' autobiographies, "how to" books, novels on sex, sexuality, romance, the occult, and the Nazi holocaust. What is the answer, then? Should the Greek American writer give it up or cling hopefully with quixotic dreams of future success?

There *is* one solution, so simple that it is never considered, never implemented. The Greek Americans number nearly three million; they hold the power to keep any author on the best-seller lists if they so choose. (Until recently, a best-selling book constituted twenty thousand sales of the hardcover edition.) Harry Petrakis has attained positions on the best-seller lists several times, but this was not through the support of the Greek Americans. My own *Island of the Winds* went into five paperback printings, but that too, was not because of the Greek Americans. Why is this so? How can this be, when the enthusiasm of the Greek American for his hertitage is at its peak? It is true that our third and fourth generations are realizing that "Greekness" is more than feta cheese and bouzouki music. They have come forth, and brought their immigrant parents and grandparents forth, to form some political strength, to constitute a voice that can be heard. It has taken many years to accomplish this, and no doubt will take many more in the case of the arts.

Perhaps those who follow us in the coming years, our sons and daughters who have the stamina to take on artistic work, may carve their own niches in American literature. Yet will they have the same feeling, the same intensity of the author who was a child of the Greek immigrant? Can they possibly feel as deeply as we do? Perhaps their intensity, their "Greekness" will surface in other forms, other ways. Peter Dallas, a third-generation Greek American who, at twenty-nine, is perhaps the youngest Greek American author, looks upon the scene in a different light, with a view on practicality. Perhaps because he has witnessed the artistic struggles in his own family and among his friends, he has vowed to attain success without dependence on his heritage.

"Forget the Greeks," he has urged me through the years. "If you want to be a successful writer, take on a commercial theme. They don't care about us."

Nonetheless, when, at twenty-one, he produced his first writing effort, a short-subject film entitled *Broken Goddess*, which depicted "the universality of pain," his protagonist was a woman dressed in the black robes of the ancient Greek chorus, emoting in a silent film set to classical music.[8] He refutes this by categorizing that project as merely an experiment, an exercise in artistic endeavors. His first novel, *Blackbird*, commissioned by Bernard Geis Associates for publication in late 1981, is the story of a black singer who works her way from the ghetto to international acclaim, from Detroit to Paris and to Rome and Athens. Fighting insurmountable odds, manipulated and used, she fights to survive, to reach the top and to remain there. I searched for some influence of his Greek heritage upon Dallas' writing, and, reading a chapter of his manuscript, I found it. Here, in the pages of this script, lay the emotion and conviction of an American of Greek descent, one who tries to balk at the "pressure" of his heritage. The young author ponders my words, my searching, and finally says, "I want to show the universality of the human condition in this story, a human condition whatever the nationality or the background. My black heroine could have been an American Indian or a Greek woman under Turkish rule." And the final irony comes when the author's agent completes reading the final script and offers his comment: "My God . . . this is Greek tragedy!" It should be interesting to see the public's response.

[8]*Broken Goddess*, a short-subject film produced by Immortal Films, New York, N.Y., 1972.

SELECTED WORKS OF GREEK AMERICAN WRITERS

Chamales, Tom T. *Go Naked in the World.* New York: Charles Scribner's Sons, 1959.

_____. *Never So Few.* New York, 1953.

Christy, George. *All I Could See from Where I Stood.* 1959.

Dallas, Peter. *Blackbird.* To be published in 1981 or 1982.

_____. *Broken Goddess.* Filmscript. New York: Immortal Films, Inc., 1972.

Dallas-Damis, Athena G. *Island of the Winds.* New Rochelle: Caratzas Bros., 1976.

_____. *Windswept.* New York: NAL/Signet, 1981.

Doulis, Thomas. *Paths for our Valor.* New York: Simon & Schuster, 1963.

Gage, Nicholas. *The Bourlotas Fortune.* New York: Holt, Rinehart and Winston, 1975.

_____. *The Mafia Is Not an Equal Opportunity Employer.* New York: McGraw-Hill, 1971.

Haviaris, Stratis. *When the Tree Sings.* New York: Simon & Schuster, 1979.

Kazan, Elia. *America, America.* New York: Stein & Day, 1963.

_____. *The Arrangement.* New York: Stein & Day, 1967.

Linakis, Stephen. *In the Spring the War Ended.* New York: G. P. Putnam's Sons, 1965.

_____, with Peter Diapoulos. *The Sixth Family.* New York: E. P. Dutton, 1976.

Petrakis, Harry Mark. *A Dream of Kings.* New York: David McKay, 1966.

_____. *The Hour of the Bell.* New York: Doubleday, 1976.

_____. *In the Land of Morning.* New York: David McKay, 1973.

_____. *Lion at My Heart.* New York: David McKay, 1960.

_____. *Nick the Greek.* New York: Doubleday, 1979.

_____. *The Odyssey of Kostas Volakis.* New York: David McKay, 1963.

_____. *Pericles on 31st St.* Chicago: Quadrangle Books, 1965.

_____. *Stelmark-Recollections.* New York: David McKay, 1970.

_____. *The Waves of Night.* New York: David McKay, 1970.

Rubanis, Theodore. *The Man with the Black Worry Beads.* California, 1973.

Vardoulakis, Mary. *Gold in the Streets,* 1945.

CHAPTER 14

A BIBLIOGRAPHIC GUIDE ON GREEK AMERICANS

BY

JOHN G. ZENELIS

The first notable bibliography on the Greeks in America was compiled by Theodore Saloutos, appearing in his *The Greeks in the United States* (Cambridge, Mass.: Harvard University Press, 1964) 389-400. Two years later appeared Evangelos C. Vlachos' *An Annotated Bibliography on Greek Migration*, Research Monographs on Migration, no. 1 (Athens: Social Science Centre, 1966), which included a section on the Greeks in the United States. It was not until the 1970s, however, that the subject of bibliography on the Greek experience in America first started to receive systematic treatment.

The first such work was Michael N. Cutsumbis' *A Bibliographic Guide to Materials on Greeks in the United States, 1890-1968* (Staten Island, N.Y.: Center for Migration Studies, 1970). A most useful bibliographic compilation, it contains sections on books and articles by and about Greeks in the United States; Greek Americans in fiction; publications dealing with the Greek Orthodox Church in the United States; unpublished works; almanacs, guides, and directories; Greek American serials currently published; Greek American serials suspended; fraternal publications; parish and Archdiocesan materials; manuscript collections; and research in progress. Including works in both English and Greek, this bibliography is generally accurate and contains an index. One of its most useful features is that it provides references to libraries holding the materials listed.

In 1976 appeared *A Comprehensive Bibliography for the Study of American Minorities,* by Wayne Charles Miller with Faye Nell Vowell and others (New York: New York University Press, 1976). The first volume of this work includes a section on Greek Americans entitled "Greek Americans: A Guide to the Greek-American Experience" (531-49). A good and very useful bibliography on the Greeks in the United States classified by subject, it lists works, for the most part published, on general history; immigration and economic problems; local and regional studies; education and language; religion; politics; biography and autobiography; literature; and folklore. It also includes a listing of directories of organizations and groups; periodicals; and some bibliographies and guides to collections. Many entries contain brief but useful annotations.

It is hoped that the present bibliography will complement and update the aforementioned compilations. The compiler's methodology varied: "hidden" references and bibliographies contained in published works dealing with Greeks in the United States were examined; library catalogues were searched; indexes and abstracts to published and unpublished literature were checked; and, of course, published bibliographies such as those mentioned above were consulted. Most of the entries have been bibliographically verified.

Although not always easily accomplished, I have attempted to organize this bibliography by subject matter and, in some cases, by format or purpose of the publication. The arrangement, which is somewhat arbitrary, is as follows:

1. Bibliographies and Guides to Archives and Collections (p. 233)
2. Almanacs, Directories, Yearbooks, etc. (p. 234)
3. General and Historical Works (p. 235)
4. Local and Regional Works (p. 239)
5. Sociology; Social Life and Customs (p. 245)
6. Immigration and Economic Conditions (p. 250)
7. Population (p. 252)
8. Organizations (p. 253)
9. Politics (p. 254)
10. Education, Intellectual Life, the Professions (p. 256)
11. Language (p. 257)
12. Folklore (p. 258)

Those works that deal with several subjects will be found under more than one heading. A limitation of topics covered by this bibliography is that it does not include fiction and works on literature.

The bibliography is comprised almost exclusively of works in English and Greek. Greek-language entries have been romanized following the Library of Congress system of transliteration and an English translation of the title has been provided.

1. *Bibliographies and Guides to Archives and Collections*

Binsfield, Edmund L. "Church Archives in the United States and Canada: A Bibliography." *American Archivist* 21 (July 1958) 311-32. Eastern Orthodox Church, 322.

Culolias, Nicholas. "Papers and Manuscripts on Greeks in Boston and Elsewhere." In Houghton Library, Harvard University.

Cutsumbis, Michael N. *A Bibliographic Guide to Materials on Greeks in the United States, 1890-1968.* Staten Island, N.Y.: Center for Migration Studies, 1970.

_____. *Selective Bibliography for the Sociological Study of Greek-Americans.* Lancaster, Pa.: Franklin and Marshall College, Department of Sociology, 1967.

Federal Works Agency, Works Project Administration. *Bibliography of Foreign Language Newspapers and Periodicals Published in Chicago.* Chicago, 1942. Greek language, 61-7.

"Greek Americans: A Guide to the Greek-American Exeprience." In Miller, Wayne Charles, et al., *A Comprehensive Bibliography for the Study of American Minorities,* vol. 1, 531-49. New York: New York University Press, 1976.

Historical Records Survey, Inventory of the Church Archives in New York City. *Eastern Orthodox Churches.* New York: Works Progress Administration, 1940. Mimeographed.

Molek, Mary. *Bibliographic Data [Greek] in Immigrant Archives, 1965.* Minneapolis, Minn., 1967.

University of Utah, Marriott Library. *[Greek Archives]*. In initial stages of organization.

Vlachos, Evangelos C. *An Annotated Bibliography on Greek Migration.* Research Monographs on Migration, no. 1. Athens: Social Science Centre, 1966. Includes a section on the Greeks in the United States.

Wasserman, Paul, and Jean Morgan, eds. *Ethnic Information Sources of the United States.* Detroit, Mich.: Gale Research Co., 1976. Information on the Embassy and consulates, various organizations, libraries and research centers, newspapers and newsletters, magazines, radio programs, festivals, fairs, and other topics relevant to Greek Americans is included on pp. 214-30.

Wayne State University, Department of English. "Folklore Archives." Includes about fifty pieces of material on Greek American folklore.

2. *Almanacs, Directories, Yearbooks, etc.*

Canoutas, Seraphim G., comp. and ed. *Helleno-amerikanikos hodegos. Greek-American Guide and Business Directory.* New York, 1907 (Greek Commercial and Information Bureau, Inc.); 1909 (Phoenix Printers); 1910, 1912 (Helmis Press); 1913, 1915. Greek and English text. Advertising material included.

_____. *Hellenikos emporikos hodegos. United States and Canada Greek Business Directory.* New York: Commercial and Information Bureau, Inc., 1921/1922. Text in English and Greek.

_____. *Ho symvoulos kai procheiros dikegoros tou Hellenos en Amerike* (The adviser and handy lawyer of the Greek in America). 3d ed. New York: Cosmos, 1917. Greek and English text. Includes advertising material.

_____. *Ho symvoulos tou Hellenos en Amerike* (The adviser for the Greek in America). New York: Cosmos, 1915.

_____, and M.A. Savvaides. *Greek Immigrant's Guide. Hodegos tou metanastou en Amerike.* New York: Typographeion Chelme, 1909. English and Greek text. Pictorial and advertising material included.

Desfis, Angelos. *Hellenic Americans of Arizona and Los Angeles and Vicinity: Directory.* Hollywood, Calif., 1947.

Gkines, Michael. *American Cookery for Non-English Speaking Cooks.* New York: The "Atlantis," 1917. Text in Greek. Includes menus with suggested prices. Advertising material also included.

The Greek Blue Book: A Purchasing Guide for 50,000 Greek-American Business Establishments. New York: Greek Blue Book, Inc., 1939.

Greek Business Guide and Directory of the Western States. San Francisco: Associated Greek Press of America, 1925.

Greek Directory of Chicago and Vicinity. Chicago: Nicholson Brothers, 1921.

Greek Directory of 1923. Chicago: Greek Directory Publishing Co., 1923.

Greek Orthodox Archdiocese of North and South America. *Yearbook.* 195?-. New York.

Helmis, George N. *Greek-American Guide and Business Directory.* New York: Helmis Press, 1915. Text in English and Greek. Advertising material included.

Hellenic-Americans of Los Angeles and Vicinity: Directory. Hollywood, Calif., 1946.

Hemerologion "Thermopylon" kai Hellenikos hodegos tes Amerikes. Almanac and Greek Guide of America. New York: Typographeion Thermopylon, 1904. Text in Greek and English.

Iliopoulos, Nicholas D., comp. and ed. *Who's Who of Greek Origin in Institutions of Higher Learning in United States and Canada.* New York: Greek Orthodox Archdiocese of North and South America, Office of Education, 1974.

Nickolson, Nick, George Nickolson, and Sam Nickolson. *Greek Directory of 1923: Covering Illinois, Indiana, Iowa, Michigan, Minnesota, Wisconsin.* Chicago: Greek Directory Publishing Co., 1923. Includes advertising material.

Rossides, Eugene T., ed. *American Hellenic Who's Who in Business and the Professions.* Washington, D.C.: American Hellenic Institute, 1979.

Who's Who ton Apodemon Hellenon. Who's Who of Greeks Living Abroad. Athens: Interpress, 1973. In English and Greek. Includes Greek Americans.

Xanthaky, Sokrates A. *"The Greeks' Companion": A General Guide for Greeks in the United States and Canada.* New York: The "Atlantis," 1903. Text in English and Greek. Includes advertising material.

3. *General and Historical Works*

Adamic, Louis. "Americans from Greece." In Louis Adamic, ed., *Nation of Nations,* 266-86. New York: Harper & Row, 1944.

_____. "Americans from Greece." *Woman's Day* 7:10 (July 1944) 22ff.

Alexopoulos, Angelos N. (Angel Alex). *Dyo kosmoi: dokimia. Two Worlds: Essays.* Athens, 1966. Forty essays, including several touching Greek American themes, in Greek and English.

"America." *Look* 19 (May 31, 1955) 34-9.

Androutsopoulos, Gregorios D. *Skepseis tines peri diatereseos tou Hellenismou tes Amerikes* (Some thoughts on the preservation of Hellenism in America). Athens, 1955. Includes summary in English.

Anton, John P. "The Greek Heritage and the American Republic." Paper presented at the Bicentennial Symposium on the Greek Experience in America. University of Chicago, 1976.

Binsee, H. L. "Mr. Phasoulias: Eating in a Greek Restaurant." *Commonweal* 33 (January 31, 1941) 372-3.

Booras, John A. *Hai ethnikai Thermopylai. The National Thermopylae.* New York, 1910.

Burgess, Thomas. *Greeks in America: An Account of their Coming, Progress, Customs, Living and Aspirations; with an Introduction and the Stories of Some Famous American-Greeks.* Boston: Sherman, French & Co., 1913. Reprinted in San Francisco by R and E Research Associates, 1970; and in New York by Arno Press, 1970 (in the American Immigration Collection, series 2).

Calodikes, C. S. *The Golden Book, or the Greek and American Spirit.* New York, 1917 and 1923.

Canoutas, Seraphim G. *Christopher Columbus: A Greek Nobleman.* New York: St. Mark's Printing Corp., 1943.

_____. *Ho Hellenismos en Amerike* (Hellenism in America). New York: Cosmos, 1918. Text in Greek, but with two chapters, "Hellenism in America" and "Present Greek Contribution," in English. Strong coverage of the very early immigration period.

Cassavetis, N. J. "L'avenir de l'hellénisme d'Amérique." *Études franco-grècques* [Paris] 3 (1920) 86-100.

Cateras, Spyros. *Christopher Columbus Was a Greek Prince and His Real Name was Nicolaos Ypsilantis from the Greek Island of Chios.* Manchester, N.H., 1937.

Choukas, Michael. "Greek Americans." In Francis J. Brown and Joseph Salabey Roucek, eds., *Our Racial and National Minorities: Their History, Contributions and Present Problems*, 339-57. New York: Prentice-Hall, 1937.

Christowe, Stoyan. "Kyotchek." *Outlook and Independent* 155 (May 14, 1930) 48-9, 74-5.

Chryssikis, George John. *The Heritage of Lacedemonians and the American Opportunities.* New York, 1938.

Cooke, S. T. "The Greeks in the United States." *Eastern and Western Review* 3:6 (November 1910) 1-5.

Dendias, Michael A. *Hellenikai parikoiai ana ton kosmon* (Greek colonies around the world). Athens, 1919. Concerned with immigration to Russia, Rumania, Egypt, the United States, and elsewhere.

Doxas, Takes. *Anamesa sten homogeneia tes Amerikes* (Among the Greek community of America). New York: Greek Orthodox Archdiocese of North and South America, 1972.

Economidou (Oikonomidou), Maria Sarantopoulou. *Hoi Hellenes tes Amerikes hopos tous eida* (The Greeks of America as I saw them). New York: D. C. Divry, 1916.

Ephthimiou, V. *Skiagraphia ton apodemon Hellenon tes Amerikes kai historia tou Kathedrikou Neas Hyorkes* (A sketch of the immigrant Greeks in America and history of the Cathedral in New York). New York: Cosmos, 1949.

Fairchild, Henry Pratt. *Greek Immigration to the United States.* New Haven: Yale University Press, 1911.

_____. "The Greeks." In Henry Pratt Fairchild, ed., *Immigrant Backgrounds*, 58-70. New York: J. Wiley and Sons, 1927.

Giannakoules, Theodoros. "Eisagoge sten historia ton Hellenoamerikanon" (Introduction to the history of Greek Americans). *Argonautes* [New York] 1 (1959) 165-77.

"Greeks in the United States." *Literary Digest* 49 (December 7, 1918) 37.

Hecker, Melvin, and Heike Fenton, comps. and eds. *The Greeks in America, 1528-1977: A Chronology and Fact Book.* Ethnic Chronology Series, no. 30. Dobbs Ferry, N.Y.: Oceana Publications, 1978.

Jones, Jayne Clark. *The Greeks in America.* The In America Series. Minneapolis: Lerner Publications, 1969. Juvenile literature.

Karpathian Heritage. New York: Federation of Karpathian Societies of America, 1978.

Kollias, Sephes G., ed. *Hellenikoi palmoi ton apodemon tes Amerikes: ta penentachrona tou D. Kallimachou* (Greek vibrations of the immigrants in America: The fifty years of D. Callimachos). New York, 1954. Chiefly a collection of speeches delivered at a dinner in honor of Callimachos in New York on April 16, 1953.

Kontargyres, Theodoros N. *Ho apodemos Hellenismos tes Amerikes* (The overseas Hellenism of America). 2d ed. Athens, 1964.
Kordopates, Antreas, ed. *Synaxari: Amerike* (Collection: America). Athens: Kedros, 1972. A collection of essays written by Thanasis Valtinos.
Kotsiphos, Antones. *To parapono henos nekrou metanaste* (The complaint of a dead immigrant). 1st ed. London, Ontario, 1960.
Lacey, Thomas J. *Our Greek Immigrants.* New York 1918.
Lykoudes, Emmanouel S. *Hoi metanastai* (The immigrants). Syllogos Pros Diadosin Ophelimon Vivlion, ar. 43. Athens: Vasilike Typographia Raphtane-Papageorgiou, 1903; New York: Ekdotikos Oikos "Proskopos," 1919. One of the first general accounts of Greeks in America in the Greek language.
Maisel, Albert Q. "The Greeks among Us." *Reader's Digest* 67 (July 1955) 113-8. Greek translation in: *Argonautes* [New York] 1 (1959) 61-6.
Malafouris, Bobby. *Hellenes tes Amerikes, 1528-1948* (Greeks in America, 1528-1948). New York: Isaac Goldman, printer, 1948. One of the most useful books on Greeks in America in the Greek language.
Manganara, Ioanna, Eustathios Sorokos, and Xene Argyropoulou, eds. *Apodemoi Hellenes. Greeks Abroad.* Athens: National Centre of Social Research, 1972. Text in Greek and English.
Maniakes, C. N. *America and Greece: A Treatise.* Athens: A. Constantinidis, 1899.
Manos, K. S. *He zoe henos metanaste* (The life of an immigrant). Athens, 1964.
Marinos, G. M. *To Kratos tou ploutou* (The country of wealth). Seira ophelimon vivlion. Athens: Syllogos pros Diadosin Ophelimon Vivlion, 1904. Along with Lykoudes' book, among the first books published in Greece which give a general account of the early Greeks in America.
Mazacoufa, Demetrius. *The Story of the Greeks in America.* 1st ed. Atlanta: Argonne Press, 1977.
Metropoulos, D. A. *Hellas kai ho exo Hellenismos* (Greece and the Greeks abroad). Athens, 1951.
Moskos, Charles C., Jr. *Greek Americans: Struggle and Success.* Ethnic Groups in American Life Series. Englewood Cliffs, N.J.: Prentice-Hall, 1980. The most recent general work on Greek Americans. Many aspects of Greek life in America are examined, including the community's institutions, population, ideology and gaps between generations. Topics such as Greek Americans in politics, Greek Americans in fiction, and Greeks and restaurants are also surveyed.
"My Heritage." *Atlantic Monthly* 162 (December 1938) 846-7.
Palaiologos, Paulos. *Hoi Hellenes exo apo ten Hellada: Orthodoxia kai genos, Athenagoras, Makarios, Iakovos, Phanari, Kypros, Amerike, Europe* (Greeks outside of Greece: Orthodoxy and Race, Athenagoras, Makarios, Iakovos, the Phanar, Cyprus, America, Europe). Athens: Bires, 1972. With a preface by Patriarch Athenagoras.
Pampoukes, Panos Chr. *Apodemos hellenismos* (Migrant Hellenism). 3d ed. "epeuxemene." Athens, 1961. Makes numerous references to the Greeks in America as well.

Pettas, Soterios de. *He charauge tes thrylikes historias ton protoporon Hellenon tes Amerikes* (The dawn of the legendary history of the Greek pioneers in America). Athens, 1971.

Politis, M. J. "Greek Americans." In Francis J. Brown and Joseph S. Roucek, eds., *One America*, rev. ed., 242-57. New York: Prentice-Hall, 1945.

Polyzoides, Adamantios Th. "What the Greeks Think of America." *Travel* 47 (October 1926) 20-3.

Roumanes, Georgios I. *Provlemata tou Hellenismou tes Amerikes* (Problems of Hellenism in America). Athens: Ekdosis Hellenoamerikanikou Epimorphotikou Institoutou, 1957.

Rozakos, N. "Ho apodemos hellenismos, hoi protoi Lakedaimonioi metanastai sten Amerike" (Migrant Hellenism, the first Lacedamonian migrants in America). *Nea Hestia* [Athens] 48 (1950) 1080-4.

Saloutos, Theodore. "Hai entiposeis mou peri Helleno-Amerikanon" (My impressions of Greek Americans). *Argonautes* [New York] 1 (1959) 120-7.

_____. "Greeks." In Stephan Thernstrom, ed., *Harvard Encyclopedia of American Ethnic Groups*, 430-40. Cambridge, Mass. and London, England: The Belknap Press of Harvard University, 1980.

_____. "The Greeks in America: The New and the Old." Paper presented at the Bicentennial Symposium on the Greek Experience in America. University of Chicago, 1976.

_____. *The Greeks in America: A Student's Guide to Localized History*. Localized History Series. New York: Teachers College Press, 1967.

_____. *The Greeks in the United States*. Cambridge, Mass.: Harvard University Press, 1964. One of the most complete and authoritative works on Greeks in the United States. Surveys the Greek American experience from the early immigration to the period right after World War II, with particular emphasis on the political and religious controversies affecting the community during this period. Includes extensive bibliography and notes.

_____. "The Greeks in the United States." *South Atlantic Quarterly* 44 (January 1944) 69-81. Reprinted in William Hamilton, ed., *Fifty Years of the South Atlantic Quarterly*, 396-418. Durham, N.C.: Duke University Press, 1952.

_____. *They Remember America: The Story of Repatriated Greek-Americans*. Berkeley and Los Angeles: University of California Press, 1956.

Sikelianos, Demetrios. *He Hellenike katagoge tou Christophorou Kolomvou* (The Greek background of Christopher Columbus). Athens, 1950.

Sills, K. C. M. "Greek-Americans." *Nation* 97 (October 2, 1913) 309.

Stauropoulos, Charalampos P. *He zoe tou Hellenos sten Amerike* (The life of the Greek in America). 2d ed. Athens, 1956.

Syriotes, Georgios. *He Amerike choris phantasia* (America without illusions). Athens: Aetos, 1954.

Theodorides, Demetrios E. "The Greek People in America." Master's thesis. Boston University, 1933.

Triantaphyllides, Manoles A. *Hellenes tes Amerikes: mia homilia* (Greeks in America: A talk). Athens, 1952.

Tsakonas, Aristotle S. *Learning the United States through Printed Word in the Principal Foreign Languages.* Philadelphia, 1920. English and Greek text.

Valaoras, Vasileios G. *Ho Hellenismos ton Henomenon Politeion. Hellenism in the United States, with an English Summary.* Foreword by M. C. Balfour. Athens: Typois P. Leone, 1937.

Vlachos, Andreas. "Ho en Amerike Hellenismos" (Hellenism in America). *Hellenismos* [Athens] 33 (February 1930) 90-106.

_____. "Peri tou en Amerike Hellenismou apo emporikes, koinonikes kai ethnikes apopseos" (About Hellenism in America from a commercial, social, and national viewpoint). *Hellenismos* [Athens] 12 (May 1909) 271-83.

Vlavianos, B. J. "Greek Americans." In Francis J. Brown and Joseph S. Roucek, eds., *One America*, 3d ed., 239-44. New York: Prentice-Hall, 1952.

Vournas, George C. "Greeks in America." *Congressional Record.* 86th Congress, 2d session, 1960. A137-A142.

Wells, R. R. "American Hellenes." *Nation* 99 (July 23, 1914) 102.

Xenides, J. P. *The Greeks in America.* New York: George H. Doran, 1922. Issued as part of the New American Series under the auspices of the Interchurch World Movement. Reprinted in San Francisco by R and E Research Associates, 1972.

Ziogas, Elias K. *Hoi Hellenes tes Amerikes: Hena megalo all' atragoudisto epos* (The Greeks of America: A great but unsung epic). Athens: Iolkos, 1977.

_____. *Ho Hellenismos tes Amerikes, autos ho agnostos* (Hellenism in America, that unknown quantity). Athens: Hellenic American Publication Agency, 1958.

Zotos, Stephanos. *Hellenic Presence in America.* Wheaton, Ill.: Pilgrimage Press, 1976.

Zoustis, Basil Th. *Ho en Amerike Hellenismos kai he drasis tou: Historia tes Hellenikes Archiepiskopes Amerikes Voreiou kai Notiou* (Hellenism in America and its activities: A history of the Greek Archdiocese of North and South America). New York: D. C. Divry, 1954.

4. Local and Regional Works

Abbott, Grace. "A Study of the Greeks in Chicago." *American Journal of Sociology* 15:3 (November 1909) 379-93.

Adallis, D. *Fiftieth Anniversary Historical Sketch: Nashville, Tennessee, Greek Community, 1884-1934.* Nashville, Tenn., 1934.

_____. *Thirtieth Anniversary Historical Brochure of Asheville Greek-American Community.* Asheville, N.C., 1935.

_____. *Fiftieth Anniversary: History of Columbia, South Carolina, Greek-American Colony, 1884-1934.* Columbia, S.C., 1934.

_____. *Historical Sketch: Lexington, Kentucky, Greek Colony, 1909-1935.* Lexington, Ky. 1935.

_____. *Thirtieth Anniversary: History of Knoxville, Tennessee, Greek-American Colony, 1904-1934.* Knoxville, Tenn., 1934.

_____. *Thirtieth Memorial Anniversary Historical and Business Brochure, Greek, Syrian, Armenian Colonies of Williamson, West Virginia.* Williamson, W.Va., 1937.

_____. *Thirtieth Memorial Anniversary Historical and Business Brochure, Greek and Syrian Colonies, Logan, West Virginia.* Logan, W.Va., 1937.

_____. *Thirtieth Memorial Anniversary Historical and Business Brochure, Syrian, Greek, American Albanian Colonies of Pikeville, Kentucky, 1937.* Williamson, W.Va., 1937.

_____. *Thirty-fifth Anniversary: Altoona, Pennsylvania Greek-American Colony, 1898-1933.* Altoona, Pa., 1933.

_____. *Twenty-fifth Anniversary: Cumberland, Maryland, Greek-American Colony, 1908-1933.* Cumberland, Md., 1933.

_____. *Twenty-fifth Anniversary: Frederick, Maryland, Greek-American Colony, 1908-1933.* Frederick, Md., 1933.

_____. *Twenty-fifth Anniversary: Fredericksburg, Virginia, Greek-American Colony, 1908-1933.* Fredericksburg, Va., 1933.

_____. *Twenty-fifth Anniversary Historical Sketch and Business Guide of Middlesboro and Pineville (Kentucky) Greek-American Colonies, 1910-1935.* [n.p., 1935?].

_____. *Twenty-fifth Anniversary: Winchester Greek-American Colony, 1908-1933.* Winchester, Va., 1933. All of the above works by Adallis were published with the cooperation of the leading members of each of the communities mentioned and their friends.

Adamic, Louis. "Greeks Came to Tarpon Springs." In Louis Adamic, ed., *From Many Lands*, 1st ed., 116-31. New York: Harper and Brothers, 1940.

Alex, Angel (Angelos Nikolaou Alexopoulos). *The Greek Story of Canton, Ohio, 1898-1973.* n.p., 1974. Published by the author. Cover title: *Greek Pioneers of America.*

"America's Vest-pocket Athens." *Literary Digest* 54 (March 17, 1917) 743-4. A description of the Greek American community of Lowell, Massachusetts.

Anamnestikon leukoma ekdothen ep' eukairia ton heorton tes tessarakontaeteridos tes Hagias Triados, 1897-1937 (Commemorative album published on the occasion of the celebration of the forty years of the Holy Trinity Church, 1897-1937). Chicago, 1937. Cover title: *Forty Years of Greek Life in Chicago.* Text in Greek.

Antoniou, Mary. *Welfare Activities among the Greek People in Los Angeles.* San Francisco: R and E Research Associates, 1974. Originally written as a master's thesis at the University of Southern California, 1939.

Arnakes, Giorgos G. *Hellenika dokimia apo to Texas* (Greek essays from Texas) Austin, Texas: Center for Neo-Hellenic Studies, 1978.

Barnard, H. Russell. "Greek Sponge Boats in Florida." *Anthropological Quarterly* 38:2 (April 1965) 41-55.

Bicos, Constance. "Greek Institutions in Chicago." Master's thesis. Roosevelt University, 1966.

Bitzes, J. G. "The Anti-Greek Riot of 1909—South Omaha." *Nebraska History* 51 (1970) 199-224.

Boyd, Rosamonde Ramsay. *The Social Adjustment of the Greeks in Spartanburg, South Carolina.* Spartanburg, S.C.: Williams Printing Co., 1949.

Bruce, Karen S. "The Social Organization of the Greek Community in Minneapolis." Manuscript in the Center for Immigration Studies, University of Minnesota, n.d.

Buxbaum, Edwin Clarence. *The Greek-American Group of Tarpon Springs, Florida: A Study of Ethnic Identification and Acculturation.* American Ethnic Groups Series. New York: Arno Press, 1980. Reprint of the author's doctoral thesis, University of Pennsylvania, 1967.

_____. "World View and Attitude in a Greek-American Ethnic Group." Master's thesis. University of Pennsylvania, 1965. A study of the Greek Americans in Tarpon Springs, Florida.

Cassidy, Ina Sizer. "Christmas in New Mexico." *El Palacio* 57 (1950) 402-6. Describes the Christmas customs of Greek miners.

Chapin, Helen G. "The Queen's 'Greek Artillery Fire': Greek Royalists in the Hawaiian Revolution and Counterrevolution." *The Hawaiian Journal of History* 15 (1981) 1-23.

Coburn, Frederick W. *History of Lowell and its People.* New York: Lewis Historical Publishing Co., 1920. Vol. 2 includes an account of the coming and assimilation of the Greeks.

Cole, William I. *Immigrant Races in Massachusetts: The Greeks.* Boston: Massachusetts Bureau of Immigration [1919?].

Collins, Donna Misner. "Ethnic Identification: The Greek Americans of Houston, Texas." Doctoral thesis. Rice University, 1976.

Cononelos, L. J. "Greek Immigrant Laborers in the Intermountain West: 1900-1920." Master's thesis. University of Utah, 1978.

Constant, Theodore N. "Greek-American Colonies, Churches and Schools in the United States." *Athene* 11 (Autumn 1950) 26-7; 11 (Winter 1951) 22-3, 54; 12 (Spring 1951) 34-5, 50.

Corse, Carita, and the Florida Writers Project. "Greek-Americans of Florida." *Athene* 3:5 (1942) 17-21; 3:6, 22-5, 29; 3:7, 22-6; 3:8, 10-2, 15; 3:9, 10-2; 3:10, 14-5; 4:2 (1943) 12-3; 4:3, 10-1, 13.

Desfis, Angelos. *Hellenic Americans of Arizona and Los Angeles and Vicinity: Directory.* Hollywood, Calif., 1947.

Doggett, Carita, Dr. *Andrew Turnbull and the New Smyrna Colony of Florida.* n.p., 1919. An account of the first Greek colony in the United States, written by a descendant of Dr. Turnbull.

Doulis, Thomas. *A Surge to the Sea: The Greeks in Oregon; A Photographic History of the Holy Trinity Greek Orthodox Community of Oregon and Southern Washington.* Portland, Ore.: J. Lockie, 1977.

Ellis, Ann W. "The Greek Community in Atlanta during the Era of World War II, 1939-1947." *Atlanta Historical Bulletin* 20:1 (1976) 33-42.

Ellis, Leonora B. "Harvest of the Sea Floor: Sponge Gathering by the Largest Unmixed Greek Community in America." *Natural History* 41 (January 1938) 62-6. An account of the Greek spongers of Tarpon Springs, Florida.

Fordyce, Wellington G. "Immigrant Colonies in Cleveland." *Ohio State Archaeological and Historical Quarterly* 45 (1936) 320-40. Includes Greeks.

_____. "Immigrant Institutions in Cleveland." *Ohio State Archaeological and Historical Quarterly* 47 (April 1938) 87-103. Includes Greek organizations.

_____. "Nationality Groups in Cleveland Politics." *Ohio State Archaeological and Historical Quarterly* 46 (April 1937) 109-27. Includes an account of the Greek presence.

Frantzis, George T. *Strangers at Ithaca: The Story of the Spongers of Tarpon Springs.* St. Petersburg, Fla.: Great Outdoors Publishing Co., 1962.

Georgas, Demitra. *Greek Settlement of the San Francisco Bay Area.* San Francisco: R and E Research Associates, 1974. Originally written as a master's thesis at the University of California at Berkeley, 1951.

Glaser, Richard. "Greek Jews in Baltimore." *Jewish Social Studies* 38 (1976) 321-36.

Greek Business Guide and Directory of the Western States. San Francisco: Associated Greek Press of America, 1925.

Greek Directory of Chicago and Vicinity. Chicago: Nicholson Brothers, 1921.

Greek Directory of 1923. Chicago: Greek Directory Publishing Co., 1923.

The Greeks in California: Their History and Achievements. San Francisco: Prometheus Publishing Co., 1918. Cover title: *Hai Hellenikai paroikiai ton dytikon politeion tes Voreiou Amerikes* (The Greek colonies in the western states of North America). Text in Greek.

Grey, Sara A. *The Greeks in Memphis: An Early History.* Memphis, Tenn. [1968?]. Mimeographed.

Halley, Helen. "An Historical Functional Approach to the Study of the Greek Community of Tarpon Springs." Doctoral thesis. Columbia University, 1952.

Harris, Jennie E. "Sponge Fishermen of Tarpon Springs." *National Geographic Magazine* 91 (January 1947) 119-36.

Hartley, H. "Greek Way: Sponge Divers of Tarpon Springs." *Colliers* 107 (May 17, 1941) 18-9.

Hauser, Philip Morris. *Local Community Fact Book: Chicago Metropolitan Area.* Chicago, 1938. Includes information on the Greek community of the area.

Hellenic American Neighborhood Action Committee. *The Needs of the Growing Greek-American Community in the City of New York.* New York: HANAC, 1973.

Hellenic-Americans of Los Angeles and Vicinity: Directory. Hollywood, Calif., 1946.

Holbrook, Agnes Sinclair. "Map, Notes and Comments." In Jane Addams, ed., *Hull House Maps and Papers: A Presentation of Nationalities and Wages in a Congested District of Chicago*, 3-23. Boston: Crowell and Co., 1895. Greeks are included among the nationalities in this study. Also includes 1893 Department of Labor Tenement and Family Schedules and Nationality and Wage Maps.

Hole, Jonathan A. "Greek Community in Reading [Pennsylvania], Berks County." *Historical Review of Berks County* 24:1 (Winter 1958-1959) 17-30.

Hunt, Milton B. "The Housing of Non-family Groups of Men in Chicago." *American Journal of Sociology* 16 (1910) 145-71. The fourth section (155ff) is concerned with Greek immigrant men and their non-family living arrangements in the neighborhood of Hull House.

Institute of Texan Cultures. *The Greek Texans.* The Texians and the Texans Series. San Antonio: Institute of Texan Cultures and the University of Texas at San Antonio, 1974.

International Institute of Metropolitan Detroit. *Peoples of Detroit: Project.* Detroit: Survey of Ethnic and Parish Organizations in Detroit, Michigan, 1968.

Jackson, Maria. "The American Greek Community of Bridgeport, Connecticut, 1955." University of Bridgeport Community Area Study, student monograph no. 7. [Bridgeport, Conn. 1955?].

"Joys of Anxiety: P. Kogiones' Dianna's Opaa Restaurant in Greektown [Chicago]." *Forbes* 124 (September 17, 1979) 197.

Key, A. "Treasure on the Ocean Floor: Greek Divers Make Tarpon Springs the Sponge Port of the Earth." *Saturday Evening Post* 214 (June 20, 1942) 12-3ff.

Koenig, Samuel. *Immigrant Settlements in Connecticut: Their Growth and Characteristics.* Hartford: Connecticut State Department of Education/Works Progress Administration, Federal Writers Project for the State of Connecticut, 1938. Includes Greeks.

Kopan, Andrew T. "Education and Greek Immigrants in Chicago, 1892-1973: A Study in Ethnic Survival." Doctoral thesis. University of Chicago, 1974.

Lagoudakis, Charilaos. "Greece and Michigan." *Colonial Review* (March 31, 1930).

_____. "Greeks and Michigan." *Michigan History Magazine* 14 (1930) 15-27.

Lawren, J. "The Sponge Capital of America." *Travel* 91:1 (May 1948) 23-5, 34. An account of Tarpon Springs, Florida.

Lovejoy, Gordon W. "The Greeks of Tarpon Springs." Master's thesis. University of Florida at Gainesville, 1938.

Markides, Kyriakos. "Assimilation of Greeks in Youngstown." Master's thesis. Bowling Green State University, 1966.

"Marrying the Adriatic in Florida." *Golden Book* 16 (November 1932) suppl. 16a. An account of the Tarpon Springs Greek community.

Mayer, Albert. *Ethnic Groups in Detroit.* Detroit: Wayne State University, Department of Sociology and Anthropology, 1951. Includes Greeks.

_____. *A Study of the Foreign-born Population of Detroit: 1870-1950.* Detroit: Wayne State University, 1951. Mimeographed. Includes Greeks.

Monos, Dimitrios Ioannis. "Upward Mobility, Assimilation and the Achievements of the Greeks in the United States, with Special Emphasis on Boston and Philadelphia." Doctoral thesis. University of Pennsylvania, 1976.

Montgomery, Margaret. "A Macedonian Wedding in Indianapolis." *Hoosier Folklore* 7 (1948) 101-4.

Nickolson, Nick, George Nickolson, and Sam Nickolson. *Greek Directory of 1923: Covering Illinois, Indiana, Iowa, Michigan, Minnesota, Wisconsin.* Chicago: Greek Directory Publishing Co., 1923. Includes advertising material.

Panagopoulos, E. P. *New Smyrna: An Eighteenth Century Greek Odyssey.* Gainesville, Fla.: University of Florida Press, 1966. Also published under the same title by the Holy Cross Orthodox Press in Brookline, Mass., 1978.

Papanikolas, Helen Z. "The Exiled Greeks." In Helen Z. Papanikolas, ed., *The Peoples of Utah*, 1st ed. Salt Lake City: Utah State Historical Society, 1976.

_____. "Greek Workers in the Intermountain West: The Early Twentieth Century." *Byzantine and Modern Greek Studies* 5 (1979) 187-215. An earlier version under the same title appeared in the *Journal of the Hellenic Diaspora* 4:3 (1977) 4-13.

_____. "The Greeks of Carbon County." *Utah Historical Quarterly* 22:2 (April 1954) 143-64.

_____. *Toil and Rage in a New Land: The Greek Immigrants in Utah.* 2d rev. ed. Salt Lake City: Utah State Historical Society, 1974. Reprinted from the *Utah Historical Quarterly* 38:2 (Spring 1970) 97-203.

Papazoglou, Orania. "Greek Town Detroit: Fortress Under Siege." *Greek Accent* 1:8 (March 1981) 12-5.

Patterson, James. "The Unassimilated Greeks of Denver." Doctoral thesis. University of Colorado, 1969. An abstracted version of this work appeared under the same title in *Anthropological Quarterly* 43:4 (1970) 243-53.

Rankin, Lois. "Detroit Nationality Groups." *Michigan Historical Magazine* 23:2 (Spring 1939) 140-6. Includes references to Greeks.

Rozakos, Nikos I. *Neoellenike anagennese ste Vostone* (Modern Greek renaissance in Boston). San Francisco: Wire Press, 1975.

Saloutos, Theodore. *The Greeks in America: A Student's Guide to Localized History.* Localized History Series. New York: Teachers College Press, 1967.

_____. "The Greeks of Milwaukee." *Wisconsin Magazine of History* 53 (Spring 1970) 175-93.

_____. "Growing up in the Greek Community of Milwaukee." *Historical Messenger* 29:2 (1973) 46-60.

Stellos, Marie Helen. "The Greek Community in St. Louis (1900-1967): Its Agencies for Value Transmission." Doctoral thesis. St. Louis University, 1968.

Stephanides, Marios. "Detroit's Greek Community." In Conference on Ethnic Communities of Greater Detroit (Detroit 1970), *Ethnic Groups in the City: Culture, Institutions, and Power*, ed. Otto Feinstein, 115-28. Lexington, Mass.: Heath Lexington Books, 1971.

_____. "Greeks and Cypriots of Detroit." *Michigan History Magazine* 56:2 (1972) 131-50.

_____. *The Greeks in Detroit: Authoritarianism—A Critical Analysis of Greek Culture, Personality, Attitudes, and Behavior.* San Francisco: R and E Research Associates, 1975. Based on the author's doctoral thesis, "Educational Background, Personality Characteristics, and Value Attitudes towards Education and Other Ethnic

Groups among the Greeks in Detroit," Wayne State University, 1972.

Stycos, Mayone J. "The Spartan Greeks of Bridgetown." *Common Ground* 8 (Winter 1948) 61-70.

_____. "The Spartan Greeks of Bridgetown: Community Cohesion." *Common Ground* 8 (Spring 1948) 24-34.

_____. "The Spartan Greeks of Bridgetown: The Second Generation." *Common Ground* 8 (Summer 1948) 72-86.

Talagan, Dean P. "Faith, Hard Work and Family: The Story of the Wyoming Hellenes." In Gordon Olaf Hendrickson, ed., *Peopling the High Plains: Wyoming's European Heritage*, 149-68. Cheyenne: Wyoming State Archives and Historical Department, 1977.

Theodoratus, Robert James. *A Greek Community in America: Tacoma, Washington*. Sacramento Anthropological Society Papers, no. 10. Sacramento, Calif.: Sacramento Anthropological Society, Sacramento State College, 1971. Based on the author's doctoral thesis, "The Influence of the Homeland on the Social Organization of a Greek Community in America," University of Washington, 1961.

Turnbull, Andrew. "Narrative of Dr. Andrew Turnbull." British Museum Landsdowne Manuscripts, vol. 88, p. 133. Turnbull's own account of the Greek colony he founded at New Smyrna, Florida, in 1767.

Vlachos, Evangelos C. *The Assimilation of Greeks in the United States, with Special Reference to the Greek Community of Anderson, Indiana*. Publications, no. 2. Athens: National Centre of Social Research, 1968. Based on the author's doctoral thesis under the same title, Indiana University, 1964.

Walker, Natalie. "Chicago Housing Conditions: Greeks and Italians in the Neighborhood of Hull House." *American Journal of Sociology* 21:3 (November 1915) 285-316.

Wessel, Bessie B. "The Ethnic Survey of New London, Connecticut, 1938-1944." *American Journal of Sociology* 50 (1944) 85-98. Includes Greeks, among other groups.

Weinberger, Helen. "A Study of the Assimilation of Foreign Born Greeks in Cincinnati, Ohio." Master's thesis. University of Cincinnati, 1942.

Yeracaris, Constantine A. "A Study of the Voluntary Associations of the Greek Immigrants of Chicago from 1890 to 1948, with Special Emphasis on World War II and Post War Period." Master's thesis. University of Chicago, 1950.

5. *Sociology; Social Life and Customs*

Abbott, Grace. "A Study of the Greeks in Chicago." *American Journal of Sociology* 15:3 (November 1909) 379-93.

Antoniou, Mary. *Welfare Activities among the Greek People in Los Angeles*. San Francisco: R and E Research Associates, 1974. Originally written as a master's thesis at the University of Southern California, 1939.

Bardis, Panos. "Main Features of the Greek Family during the Early Twentieth Century." *Alpha Kappa Deltan* 26 (1956) 17-21. Contrasts family structures of immigrants with traditional structures of the family in Greece.

Buxbaum, Edwin Clarence. *The Greek-American Group of Tarpon Springs, Florida: A Study of Ethnic Identification and Acculturation.* American Ethnic Groups Series. New York: Arno Press, 1980. Reprint of the author's doctoral thesis, University of Pennsylvania, 1967.

Chock, Phyllis Pease. "Greek-American Ethnicity." Doctoral thesis. University of Chicago, 1969.

Collins, Donna Misner. "Ethnic Identification: The Greek Americans of Houston, Texas." Doctoral thesis. Rice University, 1976.

Constant, Theodore N. "Problems of Greek-Americans." *Athene* 12:3 (1951) 29-30, 60-4; 12:4, 22-34; 13:1 (1952) 28-9, 56-8. This study grew out of the Chicago Symposium of the Hellenic Bar Association.

_____. "Racial Prejudice and the Greek Stock in the United States." *Athene* 5 (Autumn 1944) 8-11. Studies the discrimination against the Greeks in the US and considers its effect on their adaptation to life here.

Costantakos, Chrysie Mamalakis. *The American-Greek Subculture: Processes of Continuity.* American Ethnic Groups Series. New York: Arno Press, 1980. Based on the author's doctoral thesis for Teachers College, Columbia University, 1971.

Covert, Alice Lent. "Chronicle of Americanization." *Reader's Digest* 50 (February 1947) 51-4.

Cutsumbis, M. N. "Greek-Americans: A Study of *Anomie*." Typescript. Columbus, Ohio, 1957.

Dunkas, Nicholas, and Arthur G. Nikelly. "Group Psychotherapy with Greek Immigrants." *International Journal of Group Psychotherapy* 25:4 (October 1975) 402-9.

_____. "The Persephone Syndrome." *Social Psychiatry* 7 (1972) 211-6.

"The Forgotten Generation." *Athene* 10:4 (Winter 1950) 22-3, 41-2. Notes problems encountered by second-generation Greek Americans in reconciling both cultures.

Green, Arnold W. "A Re-examination of the Marginal Man Concept." *Social Forces* 26:2 (December 1947) 167-71. Several paragraphs are devoted to large numbers of Greek Americans entering New England universities and their problems in reconciling home and campus values.

Hellenic American Neighborhood Action Committee. *The Needs of the Growing Greek-American Community in the City of New York.* New York: HANAC, 1973.

Holbrook, Agnes Sinclair. "Map, Notes and Comments." In Jane Addams, ed., *Hull House Maps and Papers: A Presentation of Nationalities and Wages in a Congested District of Chicago,* 3-23. Boston: Crowell and Co., 1895. Greeks are included among the nationalities in this study. Also includes 1893 Department of Labor Tenement and Family Schedules and Nationality and Wage Maps.

Hunt, Milton B. "The Housing of Non-family Groups of Men in Chicago." *American Journal of Sociology* 16 (1910) 145-71. The fourth section

(155ff) is concerned with Greek immigrant men and their non-family living arrangements in the neighborhood of Hull House.

Ioakeim (Bishop of Boston). *He kindynoi tou en Amerike Hellenismou kai ta mesa tes diasoseos autou* (The dangers facing the Greeks of America and the means for their salvation). Boston, 1926. Two studies reprinted from the *Ethnikos Keryx (National Herald)*.

Katsoulis, Nicholas G. "Greek Mixed Marriages." Master's thesis. Columbia University, 1968.

Kiriazis, James W. "A Study of Change in Two Rhodian Immigrant Communities." Doctoral thesis. University of Pittsburgh, 1967.

Kourvetaris, George A. *First and Second Generation Greeks in Chicago: An Inquiry into Their Stratification and Mobility Patterns.* Athens: National Centre of Social Research, 1971. Originally written in 1965 as a master's thesis at Roosevelt University in Chicago.

_____. "First and Second Generation Greeks in Chicago: An Inquiry into their Stratification and Mobility Patterns." *International Review of [Modern] Sociology* 1:1 (March 1971) 37-47.

_____. "The Greek American Family." In Charles H. Mindel and Robert W. Habenstein, eds., *Ethnic Families in America*, 168-91. New York: Elsevier, 1976.

_____. "Patterns of Generational Subculture and Intermarriage of the Greeks in the United States." *International Journal of Sociology of the Family* 1 (May 1971) 34-48.

Krikos, Alexandros. *He thesis tou Hellenismou en Amerike* (The status of Hellenism in America). Athens: Blazoudake Brothers, 1915.

Lacey, Thomas James. *A Study of Social Heredity as Illustrated in the Greek People.* New York: E. S. Gorham, 1916.

Lagos, Mary. "A Greek Family in American Society." Typescript. Lima, Ohio, 1962.

Lauquier, Helen Capanidou. "Cultural Change among Three Generations of Greeks." *American Catholic Sociological Review* 22 (1961) 223-32. Examines the nature and degree of cultural change among three generations of Greeks in San Antonio, Texas.

Loukas, Christ. "Status of Greek Population in the United States." *Hellenic Spectator* 1:1 (February 1940) 3-9.

Lovell-Troy, L. A. "Ethnic Occupational Structures: Greeks in the Pizza Business." *Ethnicity* 8 (March 1981) 82-95.

Mistaras, Evangeline. "A Study of First and Second Generation Greek Outmarriages in Chicago." Master's thesis. University of Chicago, 1950.

Monos, Dimitrios Ioannis. "Upward Mobility, Assimilation and the Achievements of the Greeks in the United States, with Special Emphasis on Boston and Philadelphia." Doctoral thesis. University of Pennsylvania, 1976.

Montgomery, Margaret. "A Macedonian Wedding in Indianapolis." *Hoosier Folklore* 7 (1948) 101-4.

Moskos, Charles C., Jr. *Greek Americans: Struggle and Success.* Ethnic Groups in American Life Series. Englewood Cliffs, N.J.: Prentice-Hall, 1980. The most recent general work on Greek Americans. Many aspects of Greek life in America are examined, including the community's institutions, population, ideology and gaps between generations. Topics such as Greek Americans in politics, Greek

Americans in fiction, and Greeks and restaurants are also surveyed.

_____. "Growing Up Greek American." *Society* 14 (January 1977) 64-71.

Markides, Kyriakos. "Assimilation of Greeks in Youngstown." Master's thesis. Bowling Green State University, 1966.

Papajohn, John. "The Relations of Intergenerational Value Orientation Change and Mental Health in an American Ethnic Group [Greeks]." Unpublished paper. Brandeis University, 1977.

Papas, Ares. "He prosopikotes tou Helleno-amerikanou" (The personality of the Greek American). Doctoral thesis. University of Athens, 1964.

Patterson, James. "The Unassimilated Greeks of Denver." Doctoral thesis. University of Colorado, 1969. An abstracted version of this work appeared under the same title in *Anthropological Quarterly* 43:4 (1970) 243-53.

Petrakis, Harry Mark. "Great American Melting Pot." *Holiday* 58 (April 1977) 24-5.

Petropoulos, Nicholas P. "Social Mobility, Status Inconsistency, Ethnic Marginality, and the Attitudes of Greek-Americans toward Jews and Blacks." Doctoral thesis. University of Kentucky, 1973.

Rosen, Bernard C. "Race, Ethnicity, and the Achievement Syndrome." *American Sociological Review* 24:1 (February 1959) 47-60. Study found that Greek Americans had the highest achievement motivation compared to white Protestant Americans and other ethnic groups sampled.

Safilios-Rothschild, Constantina. *Survey of Sociologists Who Have Completed or Are Working on Greek-Americans, 1968.* Detroit: Merrill-Palmer Institute [1968?]. Continuing research.

_____, Chrysie Costantakos, and Basil B. Kardaras. "The Greek-American Woman." Paper presented at the Bicentennial Symposium on the Greek Experience in America. University of Chicago, 1976.

Saloutos, Theodore. "The Greek Orthodox Church in the United States and Assimilation." *International Migration Review* 7:4 (Winter 1973) 395-408.

Schultz, Sandra Lee. "Intermarriage in a Greek-American Community: An Analysis of Ethnic Boundaries." Doctoral thesis. University of Arizona, 1977.

Scourby, Alice. *Third Generation Greek Americans: A Study of Religious Attitudes.* American Ethnic Groups Series. New York: Arno Press, 1980. Based on the author's doctoral thesis for the New School of Social Research (New York), 1967.

_____. "Three Generations of Greek Americans: A Study in Ethnicity." Included as chapter 5 of the present volume, above, 111-21. Originally printed in the *International Migration Review* 14:1 (Spring 1980) 43-52. Study measures ethnic identity among three generations of Greek Americans living in the New York metropolitan area.

Seder, Doris L. "The Influence of Cultural Identification on Family Behavior." Doctoral thesis. Brandeis University, 1966. Includes a section on "The Greeks in the U.S.A.—Religion."

Simon, Andrea Judith. "Ethnicity as a Cognitive Model: Identity

A Bibliographic Guide on Greek Americans

Variations in a Greek Immigrant Community." *Ethnic Groups* 2:2 (1979) 133-53.

_____. "The Sacred Sect and the Secular Church: Symbols of Ethnicity in Astoria's Greek Community." Doctoral thesis. City University of New York, 1977.

Smith, Mapheus. "National Origins of Prominent Immigrants." *Sociology and Social Research* 20 (May-June 1936) 422-32. Makes references to Greeks, among others.

Stellos, Marie Helen. "The Greek Community in St. Louis (1900-1967): Its Agencies for Value Transmission." Doctoral thesis. St. Louis University, 1968.

Stephanides, Marios. *The Greeks in Detroit: Authoritarianism—A Critical Analysis of Greek Culture, Personality, Attitudes, and Behavior.* San Francisco: R and E Research Associates, 1975. Based on the author's doctoral thesis, "Educational Background, Personality Characteristics, and Value Attitudes towards Education and Other Ethnic Groups among the Greeks in Detroit," Wayne State University, 1972.

Tavuchis, Nicholas. *Family and Mobility among Greek-Americans.* Athens: National Centre of Social Research, 1972. Based on the author's doctoral thesis, "An Exploratory Study of Kinship and Mobility among Second Generation Greek-Americans," Columbia University, 1968.

_____. "Naming Patterns and Kinship among Greeks." *Ethnos* 36:1-4 (1971) 152-62

Terhune, Leoloa Benedict. "Greek Bootblack." *Survey* 26 (September 16, 1911) 852-4. Reports and provides commentary on the exploitation and abuse of recently arrived Greek children by some of the older and more established Greek immigrants.

Theodoratus, Robert James. *A Greek Community in America: Tacoma, Washington.* Sacramento Anthropological Society Papers, no. 10. Sacramento, Calif.: Sacramento Anthropological Society, Sacramento State College, 1971. Based on the author's doctoral thesis, "The Influence of the Homeland on the Social Organization of a Greek Community in America," University of Washington, 1961.

Treudley, Mary B. "Formal Organization and the Americanization Process, with Special Reference to the Greeks of Boston." *American Sociological Review* 14 (February 1949) 44-53. Examines the role of fraternal organizations, the Church, and business in the Americanization process.

Triandis, Harry C., and Vasso Vassiliou. "A Comparative Analysis of Subjective Culture." In Harry C. Triandis, ed., *The Analysis of Subjective Culture,* 299-335. New York: Wiley-Interscience, 1972. Includes a good summary of Greek character development and value orientations.

Vassiliou, Vasso, Harry C. Triandis, George Vassiliou, and Howard McGuire. "Interpersonal Contact and Stereotyping." In Harry C. Triandis, ed., *The Analysis of Subjective Culture,* 89-115. New York: Wiley-Interscience, 1972. Includes a good summary of Greek character development and value orientations.

Vlachos, Evangelos C. *The Assimilation of Greeks in the United States, with Special Reference to the Greek Community of Anderson, In-*

diana. Publications, no. 2. Athens: National Centre of Social Research, 1968. Based on the author's doctoral thesis under the same title, Indiana University, 1964.

Walker, Natalie. "Chicago Housing Conditions: Greeks and Italians in the Neighborhood of Hull House." *American Journal of Sociology* 21:3 (November 1915) 285-316.

Warner, W. Lloyd, and Leo Srole. *The Social Systems of American Ethnic Groups*. Yankee City Series, no. 3. New Haven: Yale University Press, 1945. Published simultaneously in London, England by H. Milford and Oxford University Press. Makes frequent mention of Greeks in a New England mill town.

Weinberger, Helen. "A Study of the Assimilation of Foreign Born Greeks in Cincinnati, Ohio." Master's thesis. University of Cincinnati, 1942.

Wessel, Bessie B. "The Ethnic Survey of New London, Connecticut, 1938-1944." *American Journal of Sociology* 50 (1944) 85-98. Includes Greeks, among other groups.

6. *Immigration and Economic Conditions*

Adamic, Louis. "Greek Immigration to the United States: What They Do, What They Contribute, What They Think." *Commonweal* 33 (January 31, 1941) 366-8.

Agapitidis, Sotirios. "Emigration from Greece." *Migration* 1 (January-March 1961) 53-61.

Balk, Helen H. "Economic Contributions of the Greeks to the United States." *Economic Geography* 19 (1943) 270-5.

Burgess, Thomas. *Greeks in America: An Account of their Coming, Progress, Customs, Living and Aspirations; with an Introduction and the Stories of Some Famous American-Greeks*. Boston: Sherman, French & Co., 1913. Reprinted in San Francisco by R and E Research Associates, 1970; and in New York by Arno Press, 1970 (in the American Immigration Collection, series 2).

Canoutas, Seraphim G. *Ho Hellenismos en Amerike* (Hellenism in America). New York: Cosmos, 1918. Text in Greek, but with two chapters, "Hellenism in America" and "Present Greek Contribution," in English. Strong coverage of the very early immigration period.

Cononelos, L. J. "Greek Immigrant Laborers in the Intermountain West: 1900-1920." Master's thesis. University of Utah, 1978.

Constant, Theodore N. "Employment and Business of the Greeks in the United States." *Athene* 6 (Winter 1945) 37-9; 7 (Summer 1946) 40-1; 7 (Autumn 1946) 28-9; 7 (Winter 1947) 37-41, 46.

_____. "Greek Immigration and Its Causes." *Athene* 8 (Spring 1947) 21-4.

_____. "Life of the Earlier Greek Immigrants in the United States." *Athene* 8 (Winter 1948) 26-9.

Davidson, Thomas. "The Present Condition of Greece." *International Review* 6 (June 1879) 597-615.

Dimitras, Elie. *Enquêtes sociologiques sur les émigrants grecs.* 3 vols. Athens: National Centre of Social Research, 1971. Vol. 1: *Première enquête: avant le départ de Grèce.* Vol. 2: *Deuxième enquête: lors du séjour en Europe occidentale.* Vol. 3: *Third Survey: Upon the Return to Greece,* by E. Dimitras in collaboration with E. Vlachos. Volume 3, in English, has the general title *Sociological Surveys on Greek Emigrants.*

Doukopoulos, K. "He katastasis tou Hellenikou plethysmou tes Amerikes" (The condition of the Greek population in the United States). *Archeion Oikonomikon kai Koinonikon Epistemon* [Athens] 15 (1935).

Ethnikon Kentron Koinonikon Ereunon. *Apodemoi Hellenes* (Greeks abroad). Athens, 1972.

Fairchild, Henry Pratt. "Causes of Emigration from Greece." *Yale Review* 18 (August 1909) 176-96.

——————. *Greek Immigration to the United States.* New Haven: Yale University Press, 1911.

Greece, Voule (Parliament). *He ex Hellados metanasteusis: He ekthesis tes Epitropes tes Voules* (Immigration from Greece: The report of the committee of Parliament). Athens, 1916.

Hamilton, A. "Family Reunion, U.S.A." *Reader's Digest* 68 (March 1956) 189-90ff. The struggle of Mike Katsanevas to bring his family to Salt Lake City.

Handlin, O. "Immigrants Who Go Back." *Atlantic Monthly* 198 (July 1956) 70-4.

"Happiness as an Import." *Life* 38 (January 10, 1955) 26-7. Describes the struggle of Mike Katsanevas with the help of friends and neighbors in Salt Lake City to bring his family to America.

Hellenike metanasteusis (Greek immigration). Introduction by Andreas M. Adreades. Athens, 1917.

International Labor Office. "Remittances of Greek Immigrants." *Monthly Record of Immigration,* no. 50 (November 1926) 426.

Krikos, Alex. *He metanasteusis: pleonektemata, meionektemata, synepeiai* (Immigration: Advantages, disadvantages, consequences). Athens, 1950. Summary in English.

Loures, N. "He metanasteusis sten Amerike kai ta apotelesmata tes gia ten Hellada" (Immigration to America and its results for Greece). *Argonautes* [New York] 1 (1959) 178-85.

Lovell-Troy, L. A. "Ethnic Occupational Structures: Greeks in the Pizza Business." *Ethnicity* 8 (March 1981) 82-95.

Lykoudes, Emmanouel S. *Hoi metanastai* (The immigrants). Syllogos Pros Diadosin Ophelimon Vivlion, ar. 43. Athens: Vasilike Typographia Raphtane-Papageorgiou, 1903; New York: Ekdotikos Oikos "Proskopos," 1919. One of the first general accounts of Greeks in America in the Greek language.

Marshall, Grace E. *Eternal Greece.* Rochester, N.Y.: Dubois Press, 1938. Concerned with the motivations that led Greeks to immigrate to the United States and Canada.

Mears, E. G. "Unique Position in Greek Trade of Emigrant Remittances." *Quarterly Journal of Economics* 37 (May 1923) 535-40.

Papanikolas, Helen Z. "Greek Workers in the Intermountain West: The Early Twentieth Century." *Byzantine and Modern Greek Studies* 5

(1979) 187-215. An earlier version under the same title appeared in the *Journal of the Hellenic Diaspora* 4:3 (1977) 4-13.

_____. *Toil and Rage in a New Land: The Greek Immigrants in Utah.* 2d rev. ed. Salt Lake City: Utah State Historical Society, 1974. Reprinted from the *Utah Historical Quarterly* 38:2 (Spring 1970) 97-203).

Polenes, Em. *Enkolpion metanastou* (The immigrant's manual). Athens, 1945.

Roberts, Peter. *The New Immigration.* New York: Macmillan, 1912.

Rozakos, N. "Hoi protoi Lakedaimonioi metanastes sten Amerike" (The first Lacedaemonian immigrants in America). *Nea Hestia* [Athens] 48 (August 15, 1950) 1080-4.

Repoules, Emmanuel. *Melete meta schediou nomou peri metanasteuseos* (A study on immigration with suggested legislation). Athens, 1912.

Saloutos, Theodore. "Causes and Patterns of Greek Emigration to the United States." *Perspectives in American History* 7 (1973) 381-437.

_____. "Greece and Recovery." *Yale Review* 43 (June 1954) 535-47. Portrays general conditions in Greece after World War II.

_____. *They Remember America: The Story of Repatriated Greek-Americans.* Berkeley and Los Angeles: University of California Press, 1956.

Steger, Frank D. "Emigration and Immigration Laws Affecting Greek, Armenian and Turkish Immigrants to the United States." Master's thesis. Columbia University, 1924.

Steiner, Edward A. *On the Trail of the Immigrant.* New York: Fleming H. Revell Co., 1906.

"Tax Law Sparks a Modern Odyssey: Greek Shipowners Leaving U.S." *Business Week* (April 6, 1963) 43-4.

Terhune, Leoloa Benedict. "Greek Bootblack." *Survey* 26 (September 16, 1911) 852-4. Reports and provides commentary on the exploitation and abuse of recently arrived Greek children by some of the older and more established Greek immigrants.

To vivlion tou metanastou: Chresimon eis kathe Hellena metanasten apo ten hora pou tha skephthe to taxidi dia ten Ameriken heos ten hora pou tha ten gnorise (The Immigrant's Book: Of use to every Greek immigrant from the time that he thinks of the trip to America until the time of arrival). New York, 1916.

Vlachos, Evan C. "Historical Trends in Greek Migration to the United States." Paper presented at the Bicentennial Symposium on the Greek Experience in America. University of Chicago, 1976.

7. *Population*

Doukopoulos, K. "He katastasis tou Hellenikou plethysmou tes Amerikes" (The condition of the Greek population in the United States). *Archeion Oikonomikon kai Koinonikon Epistemon* [Athens] 15 (1935).

Loukas, Christ. "Status of Greek Population in the United States." *Hellenic Spectator* 1:1 (February 1940) 3-9.

_____. *United States Population of Greek Origin, First and Second Generation. United States Census 1930.* New York: Columbia University, Department of Sociology, n.d.
Reimer, Toni Tripp. "Genetic Demography of an Urban Greek Immigrant Community." Doctoral thesis. Ohio State University, 1977.
United States, Bureau of the Census. *Census of the Population: 1970.* Washington, D.C.: US Government Printing Office, 1972. Vol. 1: *Characteristics of the Population.* Vol. 2: *Subject Reports.*

8. Organizations (Fraternal, Political, Social)

The AHEPA Hospitals for Greece Program. Washington, D.C.: AHEPA, 1956.
Bicos, Constance. "Greek Institutions in Chicago." Master's thesis. Roosevelt University, 1966.
Canoutas, Seraphim G. *To provlema tou Hellenismou tes Amerikes: AHEPA, he paradoxotera Hellenike organosis en Amerike* (The problem of Hellenism in America: AHEPA, the most paradoxical Greek organization in America). New York: Herald Printing Syndicate, 1927.
Chebithes, Vasilios I. *AHEPA and the Progress of Hellenism in America.* New York, 1935. Report by a former president of AHEPA.
Chyz, Yaroslav, and Read Lewis. "Agencies Organized by Nationality Groups in the United States." *Annals of the American Academy of Political and Social Science* 262 (March 1949) 148-58. Includes the Greeks.
Demeter, George C. *AHEPA Manual: Official Guide of the Order of AHEPA; Containing Early History and Miscellaneous Fundamentals of the Order.* Boston: Athens Printing Co., 1926. Adopted by the 4th Annual Convocation, Philadelphia, Pa., August 30-September 3, 1926.
Doukas, Kimon. "The Story of AHEPA." *Athene* 11 (Summer 1950) 39-43.
The 50th Anniversary of the Daughters of Penelope, 1929-1979. [Washington, D.C.?]: AHEPA, Daughters of Penelope [1979?].
Fordyce, Wellington G. "Immigrant Institutions in Cleveland." *Ohio State Archaeological and Historical Quarterly* 47 (April 1938) 87-103. Includes Greek organizations.
Greek American Progressive Association (GAPA). *Fifteenth Annual Convention.* Miami, 1950.
Greek Orthodox Archdiocese of North and South America. *Yearbook.* 195?-. New York. A section on "Federations & Organizations" is featured regularly.
Hellenic Association of Boston. *Katastatikon, 1920-1922* (Bylaws, 1920-1922). Boston [1922?]. Includes names of officers and members.
Kyrisis, Photius P. *Report of Photius P. Kyrisis, Supreme President, to the Fifth Annual Panepirotic Convention, July 2, 1947.* Mimeographed.

Leber, George J. *The History of the Order of AHEPA (The American Hellenic Educational Progressive Association) 1922-1972, Including the Greeks in the New World, and Immigrants to the United States.* Washington, D.C.: AHEPA, 1972. Primary source of information on the leading Greek American voluntary organization.

Panhellenic Union. *Katastatikon tes Panelladikes Henoseos. By-laws of the Panhellenic Union.* New York: Cosmos, 1910; and New York: Helmis Press, 1914. Text in Greek and English.

Vournas, George C. *A Message from the Supreme President [of AHEPA].* Washington, D.C.: AHEPA, 1944.

Wynar, Lubomyr R., et al., comps. and eds. *Encyclopedic Directory of Ethnic Organizations in the United States.* Littleton, Colo.: Libraries Unlimited, Inc., 1975. Greek American organizations are listed on pp. 157-66.

Yeracaris, Constantine A. "A Study of the Voluntary Associations of the Greek Immigrants of Chicago from 1890 to 1948, with Special Emphasis on World War II and Post War Period." Master's thesis. University of Chicago, 1950.

9. *Politics*

Adamic, Louis. "Greece and Greek Americans." In Louis Adamic, ed., *Two Way Passage,* 144-8. New York: Harper and Brothers, 1941. Describes the national pride of Greeks at the beginning of World War II and their abuse of Italian Americans during the Italian-Greek War. Author pleads against old world enmities, lest they cause division and strife in America.

Calogeropoulos, N., and G. Stratos. *Notes on the Greek Question: Addresses to President Wilson.* n.p., 1920.

Chamberlain, Nicholas (Nikolaos Chamates). *A Citizen in the Making.* Akron, Ohio, 1941.

Cohen, Richard M., and Jules Whitcover. *A Heartbeat Away.* New York: Viking Press, 1974. About Spiro T. Agnew.

Couloumbis, Theodore A., John A. Nicolopoulos, and Vassilis Pantazoglou. "Impact of the Agnew Resignation on the Greek-American Community." *Athens News* (November 7, 1973) 5.

Fatouros, A. A. "The Turkish Aid Ban: Review and Assessment." *Journal of the Hellenic Diaspora* 3:2 (April 1976) 5-25.

Fordyce, Wellington G. "Nationality Groups in Cleveland Politics." *Ohio State Archaeological and Historical Quarterly* 46 (April 1937) 109-27. Includes an account of the Greek presence.

Greek-American Committee for National Unity. *Greek Liberation.* New York, 1944.

Greek-American Labor Committee. *Greece Fights for Freedom.* New York, 1944.

Greek-American Union for Democracy. *New American Problem in the Light of Nazi Aggression.* New York, 1939.

Greek Republican Club, Boston. *Greek Republican Members of Massachusetts.* [Boston?], 1920.

Greek War Relief Association. *Annual Meeting of Members*. New York, 1945.

_____. *Ho hyper patridos eranos ton topikon epitropon Neas Anglias kai [B']: Logodosia tes periphereiakes epitropes N. Anglias* (Funds collected for the fatherland by the New England Committees and [B]: An accounting of the Regional Committee of New England). Boston: Greek War Relief Association, Regional Committee of New England, 1941.

_____. *News-letter* 1-6 (December 1941-September 1946). New York.

_____. *Press Releases* (November 20, 1940-1943). New York.

_____. *$12,000,000*. New York, 1946.

Greek White Book: Supplementary Documents, 1913-1917. New York, 1919.

Hicks, Sallie M. "Ethnic Impact on United States Foreign Policy: Greek-Americans and the Cyprus Crisis." Doctoral thesis. American University (Washington, D.C.), 1979.

Howe, Russell Warren, and Sarah Hays Trott. *The Power Peddlers: How Lobbyists Mold America's Foreign Policy*. Garden City, N.Y.: Doubleday, 1977. A hostile view of Greek American influence in the US Congress is found in the chapter entitled "Greeks Bearing Grievances," 406-68.

Humphrey, Craig R., and Helen Brock Louis. "Assimilation and Voting Behavior: A Study of Greek Americans." *International Migration Review* 7:1 (Spring 1973) 34-45.

Kondracke, M. "Greek Lobby." *New Republic* 178 (April 29, 1978) 14-7.

Kyriakides, N.G. *Ethnike hodeporia eis ten Ameriken, 1918-1919* (Patriotic mission to America, 1918-1919). Athens: Ekdotikos Oikos "Eleutheroudakes," 1924.

Mathias, Charles McC., Jr. "Ethnic Groups and Foreign Policy." *Foreign Affairs* 59:5 (Summer 1981) 975-98. An account of the lobbying efforts of Greek Americans towards the imposition of a Turkish arms embargo by the U.S. Congress in the aftermath of Turkey's invasion of Cyprus in 1974 is found on pp. 987-90.

"New Lobby in Town: The Greeks." *Time* (July 17, 1975) 31-2.

Panhellenic Committee for the Defense of Greek Rights. Mimeographed, released April 7, 1946.

Petropoulos, Nikos. "Greek-American Attitudes toward Agnew." *Journal of the Hellenic Diaspora* 2:3 (July 1975) 5-25.

Pinchot, Ann, et al. *Where He Stands: The Life and Convictions of Spiro T. Agnew*. New York: Hawthorn, 1968.

Skouras, Spyros P. *Address to the Fourth Annual Meeting of the G.W.R.A. by the President, Spyros P. Skouras, October 21, 1944*. n.p.: Greek War Relief Association, 1944.

Vlaton, Elias. "Documents." *Journal of the Hellenic Diaspora* 9 (Spring-Winter 1982). In four installments. United States Government files on the Greek American community during World War II obtained through the Freedom of Information Act.

Whitcover, Jules. *White Knight: The Rise of Spiro T. Agnew*. New York: Random House, 1972.

Zigdes, Ioannes G. *Gia te demokratia kai ten Kypro: Tessereis menes agona stis E.P.A.* (For democracy and Cyprus: Four months of struggle in the USA). Athens: Ekdoseis Papazese, 1975.

10. *Education, Intellectual Life, the Professions*

Alessios, Alison B. *The Greek Immigrant and His Reading.* Chicago: American Library Association, 1926.
_____. "Selection and Purchase of Modern Greek Books." *Library Journal* 47:18 (1922) 866.
Archiepiskope Voreiou kai Notiou Amerikes, Anotaton Ekpaideutikon Symvoulion (Greek Orthodox Archdiocese of North and South America, Supreme Educational Council). *Analytikon programma ton hellenikon scholeion* (Analytical program of the Greek schools). New York, 1935.
_____. *Analytikon programma meth' hodegion dia ta hellenika scholeia tes Amerikes* (Analytical program with instructions for the Greek schools in America). New York, 1950.
Asteriou, Asterios. *Ta Hellenika scholeia en Amerike* (The Greek schools in America). New York, 1931.
Bones, Konst. "To neon 'Athenaion' etoi to Hellenikon Orthodoxon Panepistemion en Brookline, Mass." (The new 'Athenian' or the Greek Orthodox university in Brookline, Mass.). *Argonautes* [New York] 2 (1960-1962) 24-41.
Constant, Theodore N. "Greek-American Colonies, Churches and Schools in the United States." *Athene* 11 (Autumn 1950) 26-7; 11 (Winter 1951) 22-3, 54; 12 (Spring 1951) 34-5, 50.
Corovilles-Isaakidiou, Theodora. "Greek Church Schools in America." Master's thesis. Presbyterian College of Christian Education, 1933.
Donahue, Francis M. "Greek Fulbright Research Project: A Study in Cross-cultural Education, Summary Report." Submitted to the US Department of State, Board of International Education, 1956.
Eaton, Allen H. *Immigrant Gifts to American Life: Some Appreciation of the Contribution of Our Foreign-born Citizens to American Culture.* New York: Russell Sage Foundation, 1932.
Flouris, George. "The Self-concept and Cross-cultural Awareness of Greek-American Students Enrolled in the Monolingual and Bilingual Schools." Doctoral thesis. Florida State University, 1978.
Grame, T. C. "Hellenic Arts Program." *Design (United States)* 81 (October 1979) 37-9.
"Greek Schools." *Hellenic Spectator* 1:2 (March 1940) 5-6. "By the Editor."
"Greek Tradition Lives at the Greek-American Institute in New York." *Christian Science Monitor Magazine Section* (February 7, 1948) 8-9.
Hellenic Professional Society of Illinois. *Fifty Years of Reflection, 1925-1975: A Past to Honor, A Future to Mold.* Chicago, 1975.
Iliopoulos, Nicholas D., comp. and ed. *Who's Who of Greek Origin in Institutions of Higher Learning in United States and Canada.* New

York: Greek Orthodox Archdiocese of North and South America, Office of Education, 1974.

Kallimachos, Demetrios. "Helleniko panepistemio sten Amerike" (Greek university in America) *Argonautes* [New York] 1 (1959) 43-8.

Karanikas, Alexander. *Hellenes and Hellions: Modern Greek Characters in American Fiction, 1825-1975.* Urbana: University of Illinois Press, 1980.

Klement, Andrew. "The History and Development of Plato School of the Greek Orthodox Church 'Assumption.'" Master's thesis. DePaul University, 1961.

Kopan, Andrew T. "Education and Greek Immigrants in Chicago, 1892-1973: A Study in Ethnic Survival." Doctoral thesis. University of Chicago, 1974.

Kourvetaris, George A. "Greek-American Professionals: 1820's-1970's." *Balkan Studies* 18:2 (1977) 285-323.

Lagios, George Arthur. "The Development of Greek American Education in the United States, 1908-1973: Its Theory, Curriculum, and Practice." Doctoral thesis. University of Connecticut, 1977.

Loles, Soph. *To ekpaideutikon provlema ton Hellenon tes Amerikes* (The educational problem of the Greeks in America). Athens, 1952.

Loukas, Christ. "Effective Greek Schools: A Program." *Hellenic Spectator* 1:5 (July 1940) 3-4.

Quigley, Margery. "The Greek Immigrant and the Library." *Library Journal* 47:18 (1922) 863-5.

Raizis, M. Byron. "Suspended Souls: The Immigrant Experience in Greek-American Literature." Paper presented at the Bicentennial Symposium on the Greek Experience in America. University of Chicago, 1976.

Rossides, Eugene T., ed. *American Hellenic Who's Who in Business and the Professions.* Washington, D.C.: American Hellenic Institute, 1979.

Rozakos, Nikos I. *Neoellenike anagennese ste Vostone* (Modern Greek renaissance in Boston). San Francisco: Wire Press, 1975.

Selz, Thalia Cheronis. "Greek-Americans in the Visual Arts." Unpublished paper. New York, 1976.

11. *Language*

Alatis, James E. "The American English Pronunciation of Greek Immigrants: A Study in Language Contact with Pedagogical Implications." Doctoral thesis. Ohio State University, 1966.

_____. "The Americanization of Greek Names." Master's thesis. Ohio State University, 1952.

_____. "The Americanization of Greek Names." *Names* (September 1955) 137-56.

Bardis, Panos D. *The Future of the Greek Language in the United States.* San Francisco: R and E Research Associates, 1976.

Brown, Carroll N. "Shall the Children of Greek Americans Learn Greek?" *Hellenic Spectator* 1:3 (May 1940) 3-4.

Doxas, Takes. *Anamesa sten homogeneia tes Amerikes* (Among the Greek community of America). New York: Greek Orthodox Archdiocese of North and South America, 1972.

Laimos, G. Ch., and Dem. Kallimachos. *Dia ten epiviosin tou apodemou Hellenismou: he Hellenike glossa* (For the survival of the overseas Hellenism: The Greek language). London: Ekdosis Krikou tou Apodemou Hellenismou [196?].

Lontos, S. S. "American Greek." *American Speech* 1 (1926) 307-10.

Macris, James A. "An Analysis of English Loanwords in New York City Greek." Doctoral thesis. Columbia University, 1955.

_____. "Changes in Lexicon of New York City Greek." *American Speech* 32:2 (May 1957) 102-9.

Markakis, John D. "The Influence of English upon Modern Greek as Spoken in America." Master's thesis. Ohio State University, 1952.

Nelson, Lowry, "Speaking of Tongues." *American Journal of Sociology* 54 (November 1948) 202-10. Study shows that the rate of persistence of the Greek language beyond the first generation is low, suggesting that Greeks are highly assimilable.

Seaman, P. David. *Modern Greek and American English in Contact.* Janua Linguarium. Series Practica, no. 132. The Hague: Mouton, 1972. Based on the author's doctoral thesis, "Modern Greek and American English in Contact: A Sociolinguistic Investigation of Greek-American Bilingualism in Chicago," Indiana University, 1965.

Triantaphyllides, Manoles. *Ta Hellenika ton Hellenon tes Amerikes* (The Greek of Greeks in America). Thessaloniki: Hetaireia Makedonikon Spoudon, 1953. Reprinted from *Hellenika*, vol. 12, 302-31.

12. *Folklore*

Doering, Eileen Elita. "A Charm of the Gulf of Mexico Sponge Fishers." *Journal of American Folklore* 52 (1939) 123.

Doering, J. Frederick. "Folk Customs and Beliefs of Greek Sponge Fishers of Florida." *Southern Folklore Quarterly* 7 (June 1943) 105-7.

Dorson, Richard M. "Tales of a Greek-American Family on Tape." *Fabula* 1 (1957) 114-43; 2 (1958) 202-3 (errata).

Georges, Robert A. *Greek-American Folk Beliefs and Narratives.* Folklore of the World Series. New York: Arno Press, 1980. Originally presented as the author's doctoral thesis at Indiana University, 1963.

_____. "Greek Folk Remedy in America." *Southern Folklore Quarterly* 26 (1962) 122-6. An account of the "venduza" as described by Greek Americans of Savannah, Georgia and Tarpon Springs, Florida.

_____. "The Greeks of Tarpon Springs: An American Folk Group." *Southern Folklore Quarterly* 29 (1965) 129-41.

_____. "Matiasma: Living Folk Belief." *Midwest Folklore* 3 (1962) 69-74. Folk beliefs centering around the *matiasma*, or "evil eye."

Gizelis, Gregory. "Foodways Acculturation in the Greek Community of Philadelphia." *Pennsylvania Folklife* 20:1 (1970) 9-15.

_____. "The Function of the Vision in Greek-American Culture." *Western Folklore* 33 (1974) 65-76. Religious revelations usually associated with icons and sacred objects.

_____. *Narrative Rhetorical Devices of Persuasion: Folklore Communication in a Greek-American Community*. Athens: National Centre of Social Research, 1974. Also published in New York in the Folklore of the World Series of Arno Press, 1980, under the title *Narrative Rhetorical Devices of Persuasion in the Greek Community of Philadelphia*. Originally presented as the author's doctoral thesis at the University of Pennsylvania, 1972.

_____. "The Use of Amulets among Greek Philadelphians." *Pennsylvania Folklife* 20:3 (1971) 30-7.

Hionis, Peri. "Greek Folk Tales." *New Jersey Folklore* 1:2 (1977) 8-11.

Jaffe, Grace M. "Folkways and Mores in a Greek-American Community." *Transactions of the Illinois State Academy of Science* 45 (1957) 148-54.

Jones, Louis C. "The Evil-Eye among European-Americans." *Western Folklore* 10 (1951) 11-25. Discussion includes beliefs of Greek Americans.

Kiriazis, James W. "Folklore and Cultural Character." *Bulletin of the Pennsylvania State Modern Language Association* 49:1-2 (1971) 8-16.

Lee, Dorothy Demetracopoulou. "Folklore of the Greeks in America." *Folklore* 47 (1936) 294-310.

_____. "Greece." In *Cultural Patterns and Technical Change*. Ed. Margaret Mead. New York: New American Library, 1955.

_____. "Greek Accounts of the Vrykolakas." *Journal of American Folklore* 55 (1942) 126-32.

_____. "Greek Personal Anecdotes of the Supernatural." *Journal of American Folklore* 64 (1951) 307-12.

_____. "Greek Tales of Nastradi Hodjas." *Folklore* 57 (1946) 188-95.

_____. "Greek Tales of Priest and Priest-wife." *Journal of American Folklore* 60 (1947) 163-7.

_____. "Three Romances from Pontos." *Folklore* 62 (1951) 388-97, 449-53.

Matthews, Ernest S. "Merry Greek Tales from Buffalo." *New York Folklore Quarterly* 5 (1949) 268-75.

Nichols, Priscilla M. "Greek Lore from Syracuse, New York." *New York Folklore Quarterly* 9 (1953) 109-17.

Notopoulos, Demetrios A. "Tragoudia Dodekanesion tes Amerikes" (Songs of the Dodecanesians in America). *Laographia* [Athens] 17 (1957) 22-9.

Papanikolas, Helen Z. "Greek Folklore of Carbon County." In T. E. Cheney, ed., *Lore of Faith and Folly*, 61-77. Salt Lake City: University of Utah Press, 1971.

_____. "Greek Immigrant Folklore in Utah." *Greek World*. Special issue [1978?] 23-5.

_____. "Magerou: The Greek Midwife," *Utah Historical Quarterly* 38 (1970) 50-60.

Teske, Robert Thomas. "The Eikonostasi among Greek Philadelphians." *Pennsylvania Folklife* 23:1 (1973) 20-30.

_____. "On the Making of Bobonieres and Martyria in Greek-Philadelphia: Commercialism and Folk Religion." *Journal of the Folklore Institute* 14 (1977) 151-8.

_____. "Rules Governing Votive Offerings among Greek Philadelphians." *Keystone Folklore* 18 (1973) 181-95.

_____. *Votive Offerings among Greek-Philadelphians: A Ritual Perspective.* Folklore of the World Series. New York: Arno Press, 1980. Originally written as the author's doctoral thesis at the University of Pennsylvania, 1974.

Theophano, Janet. "Feast, Fast and Time." *Pennsylvania Folklore* 27:3 (1978) 25-32.

Wayne State University, Department of English. "Folklore Archives." Includes about fifty pieces of material on Greek American folklore.

13. The Church and Religious Publications

Anamnestikon leukoma ekdothen ep' eukairia ton heorton tes tessarakontaeteridos tes Hagias Triados, 1897-1937 (Commemorative album published on the occasion of the celebration of the forty years of the Holy Trinity Church, 1897-1937). Chicago, 1937. Cover title: *Forty Years of Greek Life in Chicago.* Text in Greek.

Anderson, Paul B. "Eastern Orthodox Churches in the United States." *Information Service* 34:43 (December 24, 1955).

Anglican and Eastern Orthodox Churches Union. *Second Annual Report.* London, 1908. The American branch is covered on pp. 37-8.

The Assumption Church in History, 1939-1979. Seattle, Wash.: Greek Orthodox Church of the Assumption [1979?].

Athenagoras (Bishop). "Holy Cross Greek Orthodox Theological School: Twenty Years of Progress, 1937-1957." *Greek Orthodox Theological Review* 3:1 (Summer 1957) 15-22.

_____. "Will the Greeks in America Lose Their Racial Identity?" *Hellenic Spectator* 1:5 (July 1940) 5.

Azkoul, Michael. *An Open Letter to the Orthodox Hierarchy.* Saint Nectarios Education Series, no. 10. Seattle [1968?]. Mimeographed. Appeared also in the *Russian Orthodox Journal* (June 1968).

Binsfield, Edmund L. "Church Archives in the United States and Canada: A Bibliography." *American Archivist* 21 (July 1958) 311-32. Eastern Orthodox Church, 322.

Bird, Thomas E. "Eastern Orthodox." In Stephan Thernstrom, ed., *Harvard Encyclopedia of American Ethnic Groups,* 302-3. Cambridge, Mass. and London, England: The Belknap Press of Harvard University, 1980.

Bogolepov, A. A. *Toward an American Orthodox Church: The Establishment of an Autocephalous Orthodox Church.* New York: Morehouse-Barlow Co., 1963.

Bones, Konst. "To neon 'Athenaion' etoi to Hellenikon Orthodoxon Panepistemion en Brookline, Mass." (The new 'Athenian' or the Greek Orthodox university in Brookline, Mass.). *Argonautes* [New York] 2 (1960-1962) 24-41.

Concern. 1968-. New York. Quarterly. Greek Orthodox Religious publication in English.

Constant, Theodore N. "Greek-American Colonies, Churches and Schools in the United States." *Athene* 11 (Autumn 1950) 26-7; 11 (Winter 1951) 22-3, 54; 12 (Spring 1951) 34-5, 50.

Constantelos, Demetrios J., ed. *Encyclicals and Documents of the Greek Orthodox Archdiocese of North and South America: The First Fifty Years, 1922-1972.* Thessaloniki: Patriarchal Institute for Patristic Studies, 1976.

_____. "The Greek Orthodox Church in the United States." Unpublished paper. Stockton State College (New Jersey), 1976.

Contos, Leonidas. *Guidelines for the Orthodox in Ecumenical Relations.* Standing Conference of Canonical Orthodox Bishops in America, 1966. "Commended to the clergy for guidance."

Corovilles-Isaakidiou, Theodora. "Greek Schools in America." Master's thesis. Presbyterian College of Christian Education, 1933.

Counelis, James Steve. "A New Church: The Americanization of the Greek Orthodox Church." Paper presented at the Bicentennial Symposium on the Greek Experience in America. University of Chicago, 1976.

Douglas, J. A. *The Relation of the Anglican Churches with the Eastern-Orthodox, Especially in Regard to Anglican Order.* London: Faith Press, 1921.

Doulis, Thomas. *A Surge to the Sea: The Greeks in Oregon; A Photographic History of the Holy Trinity Greek Orthodox Community of Oregon and Southern Washington.* Portland, Ore.: J. Lockie, 1977.

Doumouras, Alexander. "Greek Orthodox Communities in America before World War I." *St. Vladimir's Seminary Quarterly* 11:4 (1967) 172-92.

_____. "The Origins of the Greek Orthodox Church in America." B. Div. thesis. St. Vladimir's Orthodox Theological Seminary, 1964.

Doxas, Takes. *Anamesa sten homogeneia tes Amerikes* (Among the Greek community of America). New York: Greek Orthodox Archdiocese of North and South America, 1972.

Dukakis, Constantine S. *Betrayal of a Sacred Trust.* Arlington, Mass., 1958.

_____. *The Eastern Orthodox Church in Grave Danger.* Philaletheia, no. 4. Arlington, Mass., 1966.

_____. *The Fate of the Greek Orthodox Church in America.* Philaletheia, no. 2. Arlington, Mass., 1960. New ed., 1963.

_____. *The Proposed Hellenic University.* Philaletheia, no. 3. Arlington, Mass., 1961.

_____. *Tragic Situation at the Greek Theological School.* Philaletheia, no. 5. Arlington, Mass., 1967. The above works of Dukakis are pamphlets concerned primarily with the Holy Cross Seminary in Brookline, Mass.

Eggebroten, A. "Americanizing Greek Orthodoxy." *Christianity Today* 14 (July 31, 1970) 30-1.

Emhardt, William. *The Episcopal and Greek Churches: Report of an Unofficial Conference on Unity.* New York: Department of Missions and Church Extension of the Episcopal Church, 1920.

_____. *Historical Contact of the Eastern Orthodox Church and the*

Anglican Churches: A Review of the Relations between the Ortho-dox Church of the East and the Anglican Church since the Time of Theodore of Tarsus. New York: Department of Missions and Church Extension of the Episcopal Church, 1920.

_____. *Recent Contact with Eastern Orthodox Churches: Advance Copy for General Convention.* New York: Christian Americanization Department, Board of Missions, 1919.

_____. *An Unofficial Anglican Programme for Reunion as Con-tained in a Letter to His Grace, the Metropolitan of Athens, October 26, 1918.* New York: Department of Missions and Church Extension of the Episcopal Church, 1920. Approved by the presidents of the Anglican and Eastern Association and the Christian Unity Founda-tion and used as the basis for a conference on unity, October 26, 1918.

_____, Thomas Burgess, and Robert Frederick Lau. *Eastern Church in the Western World.* Milwaukee: Morehouse, 1928; London: Mow-bray, 1928.

Ephthimiou, V. *Skiagraphia ton apodemon Hellenon tes Amerikes kai historia tou Kathedrikou Neas Hyorkes* (A sketch of the immigrant Greeks in America and history of the Cathedral in New York). New York: Cosmos, 1949.

The Episcopal and Greek Churches: Report of an Unofficial Conference between Members of the Episcopal Church in America and His Grace, Meletios Metaxakis, Metropolitan of Athens and His Ad-visors. New York: Department of Missions and Church Extension of the Episcopal Church, 1920. Conference held on October 26, 1918.

Gabriel, George. *Letter to Archbishop Iakovos for not Accepting Ordina-tion, December 24, 1965.* St. Nectarios Education Series, no. 9. Seattle, n.d. Mimeographed.

Galanos, Michael I. *To ekklesiastikon zetema tou Hellenismou tes Amerikes: Melete. Meros proton* (The church issue among Greeks in America: A study. Part one). 2d ed. Chicago: Ekdosis Henoseos Episkopes Sikagou, 1924.

Genet, H. "Westernizing the Eastern Church: Two Models." *Christianity Today* 25 (April 10, 1981) 54-5ff.

Goyan. 1953-. Chicago: Greek Orthodox Youth of America. Bimonthly. Text in English.

Gray, L. M. "Eastern Orthodoxy in America." *Commonweal* 15 (April 13, 1932) 656-8.

"Greek Church Charges State Persecution." *Christian Century* 69 (February 13, 1952) 180; Reply. P. H. W. Olander. 69 (April 23, 1952) 498.

Greek Orthodox Archdiocese of North and South America. *The Historic Decision of the 10th Biennial Ecclesiastical Congress at St. Louis.* New York, 1950.

_____. *Twelfth Biennial Ecclesiastical Congress of the Greek Ortho-dox Church of North and South America, Savannah, Georgia.* New York, 1954.

_____. *Yearbook.* 195?-. New York.

"Greek Orthodox Comment on the Evanston Assembly." *Christian Century* 72 (January 19, 1955) 68.

Greek Orthodox Theological Review. 1964-. Brookline, Mass.: Holy Cross Greek Orthodox Theological Seminary. Semi-annual. Text in English.

Greek Orthodox Youth Association. *Bulletin.* 1958-. New York: GOYA. Bimonthly. Text in English.

Greek Orthodox Youth of America. *Six District Conference, Diocese IX, District 1, Watertown, New York, June 2-4, 1967.* Watertown, N.Y., 1967. Brochure.

_____. *Sixth Annual Districts 1-2, Diocese V, G.O.Y.A. Conference, June 15-17, 1962.* Charleston, South Carolina, 1962. Brochure.

"Greek Tragedy: Archdiocese of North and South America Congress in Greece." *Time* 92 (August 16, 1968) 57.

Grigorieff, D. "Historical Background of Orthodoxy in America." *St. Vladimir's Seminary Quarterly* 5:1-2 (1961) 3-53.

Hellenic College, Alumni Association. *Alumni Lectures.* 1972?-. Brookline, Mass.

Historical Records Survey, Inventory of the Church Archives in New York City. *Eastern Orthodox Churches.* New York: Works Progress Administration, 1940. Mimeographed.

Holy Transfiguration Monastery. *Concerning Father Neketas Palassis and the Parish of St. Nectarios in Seattle, 1968.* Saint Nectarios Education Series, no. 5. Seattle, 1968. Mimeographed.

_____. *An Open Letter to the Logos, 1968.* Saint Nectarios Education Series, no. 1. Seattle [1968?]. Mimeographed.

_____. *Second Open Letter of the Holy Transfiguration Monastery to the Logos, 1968.* Saint Nectarios Education Series, no. 3. Seattle, 1968. Mimeographed.

Ioakeim (Bishop of Boston). *He kindynoi tou en Amerike Hellenismou kai ta mesa tes diasoseos autou* (The dangers facing the Greeks of America and the means for their salvation). Boston, 1926. Two studies reprinted from the *Ethnikos Keryx (National Herald).*

Ioannidis, B. "Orthodox Church at Evanston." *Christian Century* 70 (November 18, 1953) 1321-3.

Istavridis, V. T. (Vasileios T. Staurides). *Orthodoxy & Anglicanism.* Tr. from Greek by Colin Davey. London: SPCK, 1966.

Johnstone, John. *The Victory for Unity.* Saint Nectarios Education Series, no. 12. Seattle, 1968. Mimeographed.

Kavarnos, Konstantinos. *He orthodoxia en Amerike* (The Orthodox faith in America). Athens, 1958.

Klement, Andrew. "The History and Development of Plato School of the Greek Orthodox Church 'Assumption.' " Master's thesis. DePaul University, 1961.

Kourides, Peter T. *The Evolution of the Greek Orthodox Church in America and Its Present Problems.* New York: Cosmos, 1959.

Lacey, Thomas James. *A Study of the Eastern Orthodox Church.* 2d ed. New York: E.S. Gorham, 1912. Includes a consideration of Orthodoxy in America.

Landis, Benson Y. "A Guide to the Literature in Statistics of Religious Affiliation with Reference to Related Social Sciences." *Journal of the American Statistical Association* 54 (1959) 335-57. Includes statistics and bibliography on members of the Greek Orthodox Church, among others.

O Logos, 1950-. St. Louis: Orthodox Lore of the Gospel of Our Saviour. Bimonthly. Greek Orthodox religious publication, in English.

The Logos. 1968-. Fort Wayne, Ind. Monthly. Greek Orthodox religious publication in English.

Michelis, Dennis. *In the Realm of Grace.* Warren, Ohio [1956?]. A series of lectures delivered by the author, the pastor of St. Demetrios Church in Warren, Ohio, from 1955 to 1956.

Miller, William. "Changing Role of the Orthodox Church." *Foreign Affairs* 8 (January 1930) 274-81. Provides good background—in the light of the changing leadership and role of the Orthodox Church due to the political upheavals in Greece, Bulgaria, and Turkey—on the American controversy over support of either the Ecumenical Patriarch or the Autocephalous Church of Greece. Includes a short section on the Church in the United States.

"Moustakis v. Hellenic Orthodox Society." *New England Reporter* 159, 453. Important court opinion on the struggle for supreme ecclesiastical authority in the United States.

National Youth Conference of the Greek Orthodox Church in America. *Official Minutes and Proceedings.* Chicago, 1951.

Orthodox Life. 1950-?. Jordanville, N.Y.: Holy Trinity Monastery. Bimonthly.

The Orthodox Church. 1965-. New York: Metropolitan Council of the Orthodox Church in America. Monthly.

Ho Orthodoxos Parateretes. The Orthodox Observer. 1934-. New York: Greek Orthodox Archdiocese of North and South America. Monthly, later biweekly. In English and Greek.

Palaiologos, Paulos. *Hoi Hellenes exo apo ten Hellada: Orthodoxia kai genos, Athenagoras, Makarios, Iakovos, Phanari, Kypros, Amerike, Europe* (Greeks outside of Greece: Orthodoxy and Race, Athenagoras, Makarios, Iakovos, the Phanar, Cyprus, America, Europe). Athens: Bires, 1972. With a preface by Patriarch Athenagoras.

Palassis, Neketas (Rev.). "The Greek Ecumenical Ideal." *Orthodox Christian Witness* (Sept. 30/Oct. 13, Oct. 7/20, Oct. 14/27, Oct. 28/Nov. 10, 1968). Also in Saint Nectarios Education Series, no. 13. Seattle.

Papaioannou, George. *From Mars Hill to Manhattan: The Greek Orthodox in America under Athenagoras I.* Minneapolis: Light and Life Publishing Co., 1976. Based on the thesis written by the author for Boston University under the title "Patriarch Athenagoras I and the Greek Orthodox Church of America."

Papas, John. *The Greek Church in the Courts.* Sanford, Maine, 1945.
_____. *The Scandals of the Greek Church.* Sanford, Maine, 1945.

"Patriarchate to Permit Independent Orthodox Church of America." *Christianity Today* 87 (February 18, 1970) 199.

Patrinacos, Nicon. *The Orthodox Liturgy.* Garwood, N.J.: Graphic Arts Press, 1974.

He Phone tou Euangeliou (The voice of the Gospel). 1941-. Ridgefield, N.J.: American Mission to Greeks. Monthly. Edited by Spyros Zotiades.

Piepkorn, Arthur Carl. *Profiles in Belief: The Religious Bodies of the United States and Canada.* 3 vols. New York: Harper & Row, 1977-1979. Greek Orthodox Americans are covered in volume 1, *Roman Catholic, Old Catholic, Eastern Orthodox.*

Polyzoides, Germanos. *He katechesis tou hellenopaidos dia tous mathetas ton scholeion tes diasporas* (The catechism of Greek children for pupils of schools of the diaspora). New York: D.C. Divry, 1934.

Protestant Episcopal Church in the USA, Domestic and Foreign Missionary Society, Department of New England. *A Report of the Commission Appointed . . . to Consider Cooperating with the Eastern Orthodox Churches, the Separated Churches of the East, and Other Slavs.* Springfield, Mass., 1913.

Rife, J. Merle. "Do Greeks Worship?" *Christian Century* 58 (October 8, 1941) 1244-5. A letter to the editor describing the Greek Orthodox liturgy and sacraments in various American cities.

Romanides, J. S. "Orthodox: Arrival and Dialogue." *Christian Century* 80 (November 13, 1963) 1399-1403.

"Russians and Greeks: The Cost of Unilateral Ecumenism." *Christian Century* 87 (March 11, 1970) 284-5.

St. Constantine Church and Koraes School. *Yearbook . . . 1936.* Chicago, 1937.

St. Vladimir's Theological Quarterly, 1967-. Crestwood, N.Y.: St. Vladimir's Orthodox Theological Seminary. Continuation of *St. Vladimir's Seminary Quarterly,* 1953-1967.

Saloutos, Theodore. "The Greek Orthodox Church in the United States and Assimilation." *International Migration Review* 7:4 (Winter 1973) 395-408.

Scourby, Alice. *Third Generation Greek Americans: A Study of Religious Attitudes.* American Ethnic Groups Series. New York: Arno Press, 1981. Based on the author's doctoral thesis for the New School of Social Research (New York), 1967.

Seder, Doris L. "The Influence of Cultural Identification on Family Behavior." Doctoral thesis. Brandeis University, 1966. Includes a section on "The Greeks in the U.S.A.—Religion."

Sharpe, A. R. (Rev.). *Constantinople First: A Plea for a Sound Reunion.* Bournemouth, England: Sydenham & Co., 1923.

Simon, Andrea Judith. "The Sacred Sect and the Secular Church: Symbols of Ethnicity in Astoria's Greek Community." Doctoral thesis. City University of New York, 1977.

Stylianopoulos, T. G. "Orthodox Church in America." *Annals of the American Academy of Political and Social Science* 387 (January 1970) 41-8.

Tarasar, Constance J., gen. ed. *Orthodox America, 1794-1976: Development of the Orthodox Church in America.* Syosset, N.Y.: Orthodox Church in America, Department of History, 1975.

Tinckon-Fernandez, W. G. "Eastern Orthodox Peoples and Churches in the United States." *Christendom* 4 (Summer 1939) 423-36.

Tsoumas, George J. "Founding Years of Holy Cross Greek Orthodox Theological School (1937-1942)." *Greek Orthodox Theological Review* 12:3 (1967) 241-82.

Turkevich, Leonid. "Problems of the Eastern Orthodox Church in America." *Constructive Quarterly* 3 (June 1915) 311-27.

United States, Bureau of the Census. *Religious Bodies: 1936.* Washington, D.C.: US Government Printing Office, 1941. Vol. 2, part 1, 572-3, covers the Greek Orthodox denomination.

Verkhovskoy, S. S. "Unity of the Orthodox Church in America." *St. Vladimir's Seminary Quarterly* 5:1-2 (1961) 101-13.

The Vineyard. 1968-? Brooklyn, N.Y.: Brotherhood of St. Mark of Ephesus. Monthly.
Voice of Orthodoxy. 1925-1927? Chicago.
Volaitis, Constantine. "Orthodox Church in the United States as Viewed from the Social Sciences." *St. Vladimir's Seminary Quarterly* 5:1-2 (1961) 63-87.
Wiest, Walter E. "The Centenary of the Greek Orthodox Archdiocese of North and South America." In A. J. Philippou, ed., *The Orthodox Church Ethos: Studies in Orthodoxy*, vol. 1, 3-20. Oxford: Holywell, 1964.
Zoustis, Basil Th. *Ho en Amerike Hellenismos kai he drasis tou: Historia tes Hellenikes Archiepiskopes Amerikes Voreiou kai Notiou* (Hellenism in America and its activities: A history of the Greek Archdiocese of North and South America). New York: D. C. Divry, 1954.

14. The Press

Giannakoulis, T. "The Greek Press in America." *Athene* (August 1941) 16-9, 30, 32.
_____. "Ho Hellenoamerikanikos typos" (The Greek American press). *Argonautes* [New York] 2 (1960-2) 416-28.
_____, and E. Ziogas. "To chroniko tou Hellenikou typou tes Amerikes" (Chronicle of the Greek press in America). *Krikos* [London] (July-August, 1960) 47-50.
"He Hellenike demosiographia tes Amerikes" (Greek journalism in America). *Meniaios Eikonographemenos Ethnikos Keryx* [New York] 11 (April 1925) 59-63.
Papacosma, S. Victor. "The Greek Press in America." *Journal of the Hellenic Diaspora* 5:4 (Winter 1979) 45-61.

15. Newspapers, Periodicals, and Other Serial Publications

The AHEPA Messenger. 1931-. New York: Metropolitan Chapter of AHEPA. Monthly.
The AHEPAN. 1923-. Washington, D.C.: Order of AHEPA. Bimonthly. Text in English.
American and Greek Commerce and Industries Monthly. New York. In English and Greek. "Printed 20,000 copies for its first issue in 1921, but few numbers followed." See S. Victor Papacosma (in section 14), p. 57.
American Greek. January 1920-January 1921. New York. Monthly. "Official organ of the Greek-American Merchants Protective Association of America." English and Greek text.
American Greek Review. 1923-1928. Chicago. Monthly. From June 1923 to December 1924 published under the title *Greek Review.* Edited

by Demetrios A. Michalaros. A good example of early Greek American journalism in the English language, providing a broad range of cultural and news coverage.

American Hellenic World. 1925-1931. Chicago. Weekly (1925-1927), monthly (1927-1931). Founded and edited by Demetrios A. Michalaros. Another outstanding example of the quality of early Greek American journalism in the English language.

Argonautes: Etesia Hellenoamerikanike ekdosis philologias kai draseos. Argonaut: An Annual Hellenic-American Review of Life and Thought. 1 (1959), 2 (1960-1962), 3 (1967). New York. Mostly in Greek.

Archon Magazine. 1 (July 1927), 2 (August 1927). Philadelphia: Order of AHEPA.

Athena (Athens). 1905-1913. Chicago. Semiweekly. In Greek.

Athenai (Athens). 1928-. Detroit. Weekly. In Greek.

Athene: American Magazine of Hellenic Thought. 1940-1967. Chicago. Monthly, later quarterly. Edited by Demetrios A. Michalaros.

Atlantis. 1894-October 1973. New York. Daily since 1905. In Greek. Along with *Ethnikos Keryx (The National Herald)*, one of the premier Greek American newspapers in the Greek language. Conservative and pro-royalist in Greek politics.

Challenge. February 1963-? Washington, D.C.: St. Sophia Greek Orthodox Cathedral. Irregular.

The Charioteer: A Review of Modern Greek Culture. 1960-. New York: Parnassos Greek Cultural Society of New York. Annual. Includes translations of modern Greek literary texts, book reviews, and articles on Greek art, literature, and culture.

Chicago Greek Daily. 1921-1935. Chicago. Daily.

The Chicago Pnyx. 1939-. Glenview, Ill. Semimonthly. English text, newspaper.

Commercial Review. New York. Published before and during World War I (see Papacosma, 57).

Ho Daimonios (The demon-like). 1908-1923? Lynn, Mass. Satirical journal.

The Democrat. 1923-1931. Chicago. Weekly (1923-1925), monthly (1925-1931). Billed itself as "The first Greek newspaper published in English" and as a "Political and social newspaper."

Demokrates (Democrat). 1924-1930. Chicago. Monthly. In Greek.

Dodekanesios (Dodecanesian). 1969-. New York. Provides news and informative articles on the Dodecanese. Mostly in Greek.

Eastern and Western Review. 1909-1916. Boston: Greek American Publishing Co. Monthly. T. T. Timayenis, editor. Continuation of the *National Greek-American Newspaper.* The first significant effort in English-language Greek American journalism (Papacosma, 57-8).

Eirenikos (Pacific). San Francisco. Appeared before World War I. In Greek. Superseded by *Prometheus.*

Eleutheria (Freedom). October 1938-1941? New York. "Greek-American Front of Democracy." Supersedes *Empros* (Forward).

Eleutheros Typos (Free press). 1944-1946. New York. Edited for a period by Demetrios Callimachos.

Emporion (Commerce). New York. In Greek. Published before and during World War I (Papacosma, 57).

Empros (Forward). July 1923-1938. New York. Daily? since July 1927. Official organ of the "Greek Section of the Communist Party of the United States." Superseded by *Eleutheria*.

Ergates (The worker). Manchester, N.H. In Greek. Appeared before World War I.

Estiator (Restaurant keeper). 1938-1940. New York. Trade publication.

Ethnikos Hellenikos Keryx (National Greek tribune). 1920-? Detroit. Weekly. In Greek.

Ethnikos Keryx. National Herald. 1915-. New York. Daily. Edited by Demetrios Callimachos from 1915 to 1942. Along with the *Atlantis*, one of the premier Greek American newspapers. More liberal and pro-republican in Greek politics.

Greek Accent. 1980-. New York: Greek Accent Publishing Corp. Monthly.

Greek-American. December 1927-May 1928. New York.

Greek American Council. *Bulletin.* October 1944-1947. New York. Title varied. From October 1944 to February 1945 issued by the Greek American Committee for National Unity; from October 1946 to February 1947 issued by the American Council for a Democratic Greece.

Greek American News. 1936-? Chicago. Semimonthly.

Greek-American Review. March 1917-April 1918. Boston.

Greek Confectioner. 1922-1926. Chicago. Trade publication.

Greek Heritage. 1963-. Chicago.

Greek News. 1935-? Chicago. Weekly.

Greek News. Los Angeles. Weekly.

Greek World. 1976-1978? New York. Bimonthly. Edited by Emmanuel Plaitakis.

Hellas (Greece). 1963-. Monthly. Chicago. In Greek.

The Hellenic American National Picture Magazine. September 1965-? Detroit. Monthly.

The Hellenic Chronicle. 1950-. Boston. Weekly. English-language newspaper.

Hellenic Free Press. 1957-. Chicago. Semimonthly. Text in English and Greek.

The Hellenic Journal. 1975-. San Francisco. Biweekly. English-language newspaper.

Hellenic National Newspaper. Rockville, Md. Monthly. Cf. the 1980 *Yearbook* of the Greek Orthodox Archdiocese of North and South America.

Hellenic News. Chicago. Monthly. See Wasserman and Morgan, *Ethnic Information Sources of the United States,* listed in section 1 of this bibliography (p. 233).

Hellenic News. Philadelphia. Monthly. Cf. the 1980 *Yearbook* of the Greek Orthodox Archdiocese of North and South America.

Hellenic Renaissance. May-July 1919. Chicago. Monthly.

Hellenic Review and International Report. 1959-? New York. Monthly. Title varied, issued from November 1959 to October 1960 as the *Hellenic Review and Economics, Trade, Shipping, Travel.* Trade publication.

Hellenic Spectator. February 1940-February 1941. Washington, D.C. Monthly. Edited by Constantine Poulos.

Hellenic Times. 1973-. New York. Weekly. Newspaper in English.

Hellenicana: Bulletin of Information. December 1947-Spring 1961. New York: Anglo-American-Hellenic Bureau of Education Scholars. Irregular. Primarily carried news items rather than scholarly studies.
Hellenika Nea. Hellenic News. 1963-. New York. Weekly. General newspaper in Greek and English.
Hellenike Zoe (Hellenic life). 196?-? San Francisco. Semimonthly. Text in Greek.
Hellenikos-Aster (Greek star). 1903-. Chicago. Weekly. Newspaper, issued originally in Greek, now in a bilingual format.
Hellenikos Kosmos—To Periodiko tou Apodemou Hellenismou ("Ellinikos Kosmos—The Magazine of the Greeks Overseas"). 1980-. Long Island City, N.Y. Monthly. Greek language text.
Hellenikos Typos (Greek press). 1911-. Chicago. Monthly. Originally in Greek, now in a bilingual format.
Helleno-Amerikaniko Vema (Greek American tribune). 1941-post-World War II. New York. Espoused the Greek labor point of view. Supported primarily by Greek maritime and fur workers unions along with the Greek branch of the International Workers Order.
Hellenoamerikanos (The Greek American). 1969-? New York: Grekam Publications, Inc. Semimonthly. General and local news coverage in Greek and English.
Henosis (Union). Pittsburgh, Penn. In Greek. Appeared before World War I.
Journal of the Hellenic American Society. Fall 1973-1974. Indianapolis, Three numbers of the first volume were issued. Continued by the *Journal of the Hellenic Diaspora.*
Journal of the Hellenic Diaspora. 1974-. New York: Pella Publishing Co. Quarterly. Continuation of the *Journal of the Hellenic American Society.*
Kampana. Cambana. (The bell). 1919-. New York. Semimonthly.
Krete (Crete). 1927-. New York. Monthly. Provides news and informative articles on Crete, in Greek and English.
Ho Krikos: Meniaia Ekdose tou Apodemou Hellenismou (The link: Monthly publication of Greeks abroad). 1950-? London. Includes articles and other information on the Greeks in America.
Kyriakatika Nea. The Sunday News. 1944-. Boston. Weekly. Greek and English text.
Kypros (Cyprus). 196?-. New York. Official publication of the Cyprian Federation. Primarily in Greek.
Loxias (The blade). 1908-1919. Chicago. Weekly. Text in Greek.
Makedonia (Macedonia). 1948-. New York. Monthly. Official publication of the Macedonian Federation. Provides news and informative articles on Macedonia, mostly in Greek.
Meniaia Eikonographemene Atlantis. Monthly Illustrated Atlantis. 1910-196? New York.
Meniaios Eikonographemenos Ethnikos Keryx. Monthly Illustrated National Herald. July 1915-1923? New York.
National Union. April 1928-November 1930. Springfield, Mass.: The American-Hellenic Union. Irregular. "An educational progressive magazine for the advancement of new Americans." English text.
Nea Kalifornia. New California. 1907-. San Francisco: Acropolis Pub-

lishing Corp. Weekly. Greek and English newspaper, previously published under the title *Kalifornia. California.*

Neo-Hellenika; Annual Publication of the Center for Neo-Hellenic Studies. 197?-. Austin, Texas.

Neos Kosmos (New world). 1892. Boston. The first Greek American newspaper. Circulated only for several months.

New York. 1948-. Passaic Park, N.J. Monthly. Text in English and Greek.

Nomotages (The loyal one). April 5, 1919-? Weekly. Founded by the Greek-American Loyalists' League to further King Constantine's cause (see Papacosma, 53).

Organosis (Organization). 191?-192? [New York?] "Greek Official Organ of the Socialist Labor Party."

Panellenios (The panhellenic). 1908-1913. New York. Triweekly. Edited and published by Sokrates A. Xanthaky. Served as the mouthpiece of the Panhellenic Union, the first national organization seeking to coordinate Greek interests in America.

Panhellenic Union. 1914-1915. New York.

Patris (The fatherland). Lowell, Mass. In Greek. Appeared before World War I.

Philhellene: Bulletin of the American Friends of Greece. 1942-1950. New York. Irregular.

Phone tou Ergatou (The voice of the worker). July 1918-1923. New York. [Weekly?] Continued from July 1923 as *Empros* (Forward).

Phos (The light). Long Island City, N.Y. Monthly. See the 1980 *Yearbook* of the Greek Orthodox Archdiocese of North and South America.

Phos (The light). Salt Lake City, Utah. Appeared before World War I.

Pilgrimage: Monthly Magazine for Greeks Everywhere. 1975-1976. Wheaton, Ill. Text in English and Greek.

Proine. Proini (Morning). 1977-. New York. Daily. One of the latest newspapers primarily in Greek.

Prometheus (Prometheus). San Francisco. In Greek. Appeared before World War I. Superseded *Eirenikos* (Pacific).

Proodos (Progress). 1918-1937. Detroit (1918-1931), Chicago (1931?-1937). Irregular.

Protoporos (Pioneer). March 1935-June 1937. New York. Monthly. Organ of the Greek Workers' Educational Federation of America.

Restaurant Keepers Guide. 1925-1928. Chicago. Trade publication, by Greeks and for Greeks.

Romios Metanastes (The Greek immigrant). 1908-? New York. Satirical journal.

Roumeli Press: Antilaloi tes Roumeles—Anexartetos ephemeris ton apodemon Roulelioton. 1964-. Long Island City, N.Y. Monthly.

Sanida (The plank). 1905. Chicago. Satirical journal.

Satyros (The satyr). 1917-193? New York. Satirical and literary journal.

Thessalonike (Thessaloniki). 1912?-1934. Chicago. Weekly. In Greek. Title varied. Merged with *Hellenikos Typos* (Greek press) on March 29, 1934.

To Vema tes GAPAS. The Tribune of GAPA. 1924-. Pittsburgh, Pa.: Greek American Progressive Association. Issued five times a year. In Greek and English.

The Voice. Cleveland. Biweekly. See the 1980 *Yearbook* of the Greek Orthodox Archdiocese of North and South America.

Western Hellenic Journal. 1975-. San Francisco. Bimonthly. In English and Greek.

16. *Autobiographies, Biographies, Personal Narratives, and Reminiscences*

Anagnostopoulos, Demetrios Ch., and Georgios P. Anagnostopoulos. *Ho Michael Anagnostopoulos (he Anagnos), etoi syntomos viographia autou* (Michael Anagnostopoulos [or Anagnos], a short biography). Athens: Typois Sakellariou, 1923.

Chamberlain, Nicholas (Nikolaos Chamates). *A Citizen in the Making.* Akron, Ohio, 1941.

Christowe, Stoyan. *My American Pilgrimage.* Boston. Little, Brown and Co., 1947. Autobiographical.

Cohen, Richard M., and Jules Whitcover. *A Heartbeat Away.* New York: Viking Press, 1974. About Spiro T. Agnew.

Geannopoulos, James Nicholas. *Mother's Wish: My Life in Greece and My Life in America.* St. Louis: Smith, 1936.

Goulas, Demosthenes Georgiou. *Rovolaei henas leventes* (A brave man hastens). Athens, 1959.

Howard, Jane. *Families.* New York: Simon and Schuster, 1978. The chapter entitled "I'm Afraid He'll Squeeze His Brains" (110-25) portrays Greek American journalist Nicholas Gage and the Gage clan of Worcester, Mass., many of whose members own pizza parlors there.

Kollias, Sephes G. *Ho Archiepiskopos Amerikes Michael ho apo Korinthias* (The Archbishop of America Michael from Corinthia). Athens, 1964. Includes a list of works of Archbishop Michael, 76-8.

_____. *Dem. Kallimachos: mia artia agonistike syneidese* (Dem. Callimachos: An entire fighting conscience). Athens, 1963. A list of works of Callimachos is provided, 27-30.

_____, ed. *Hellenikoi palmoi ton apodemon tes Amerikes: ta penentachrona tou D. Kallimachou* (Greek vibrations of the immigrants in America: The fifty years of D. Callimachos). New York, 1954. Chiefly a collection of speeches delivered at a dinner in honor of Callimachos in New York on April 16, 1953.

Ladogianne, Nina. *Henas Hellenas sten Amerike* (One Greek in America). Volos, 1954.

"Life Story of a Pushcart Peddler." *Independent* 60 (February 1, 1906) 274-9.

Malafouris, Bobby. *Hellenes tes Amerikes, 1528-1948* (Greeks in America, 1528-1948). New York: Isaac Goldman, printer, 1948. The second part of the book consists of a large collection of biographical sketches of prominent Greek Americans who contributed personally to its publication.

Metaxas, John. "The Story of John Phocas: Explorer of America." *Athene* 9 (1949) 3-8, 44.

Michalaros, Demetrios A. *Demetrios P. Kallimachos.* Chicago, 1953. Callimachos was editor of New York's *Ethnikos Keryx (National Herald)* daily newspaper from 1915 to 1942.

Miller, E. "One Chance in a Million: Story of S. Giallelis; From Greek Village to Stardom." *Seventeen* 22 (September 1963) 124-5ff.

Paleologas, Emmaline Amelia Milburn. *I Married a Greek.* Mansfield, Ohio: Stirling Press, 1941.

Papoulias, Angelos. *Anamneseis: apo te zoe tou Hellenismou tes Kalifornias* (Reminiscences: From Greek life in California). San Francisco, 1960.

Perros, George P. *Officers of Greek Descent in the Union Navy, 1861-1865.* Washington, D.C.: National Paragon Press, 1964.

Petrakis, Harry Mark. *Nick the Greek.* Garden City, N.Y.: Doubleday, 1979. Fictionalized account of Nick Dandolos.

_____. *Stelmark: A Family Recollection.* New York: McKay, 1970.

Pinchot, Ann, et al. *Where He Stands: The Life and Convictions of Spiro T. Agnew.* New York: Hawthorn, 1968.

Rice, Cy. *Nick the Greek.* New York: Funk and Wagnalls, 1969. The story of Nick Dandolos.

Sanborn, Franklin B. *Michael Anagnos, 1837-1906.* Boston: Wright and Potter, 1907.

Steffanides, George F. *America, the Land of My Dreams: The Odyssey of a Greek Immigrant.* Fitchburg, Mass., 1974. Published by the author. Autobiographical.

Thompson, Ariadne. *The Octagonal Heart.* Indianapolis: Bobbs-Merrill, 1956. Condensed with new material by the author in "Our Octagonal World." *Reader's Digest* 82 (May 1963) 279-99. Author's autobiographical tribute to her Greek American childhood in St. Louis, Missouri.

Topping, Eva Catafygiotou. "John Zachos: American Educator." *Greek Orthodox Theological Review* 21:4 (Winter 1976) 351-66.

Tzanetes, Elias I. *He autou megaliotes ho metanastes* (His highness the immigrant). New York: Anatolia Press, 1946. A collection of short humorous articles based on actual experiences in America. The articles have also appeared in several periodicals in the United States under the pseudonym Phil Nax.

Tzatzanes, Georgios A. *Ho exo Hellenismos: entyposeis apo hena taxidi eis Europen kai Ameriken* (Greeks abroad: Impressions from a trip to Europe and America). Piraeus, 1954.

Weyl, Walter E. "Pericles of Smyrna and New York." *Outlook* 94 (February 26, 1910) 463-72. About Pericles Anagnostopoulos.

Whitcover, Jules. *White Knight: The Rise of Spiro T. Agnew.* New York: Random House, 1972.

INDEX

Abbott, Grace 22, 23, 25
acculturation 11, 59, 75, 196, 199, 202
Adamic, Louis 24n, 34n
adaptation 123, 216
Addams, Jane 22
Aegean Islands 144
Aetoloakarnanian Mutual Society 86
Africa 11, 61, 137, 195
Aghios Philippos of Andros Society 86
Agnew, Spiro T. 100-1, 102, 103-4, 105, 107, 108
Agnos, Art 103
AHEPA (American Hellenic Educational Progressive Association) 28n, 45, 48, 88, 96, 106, 203
Alaska 35, 174, 195
Albania 224
Albany, New York 9, 66
Alexander, Archbishop 43, 44, 67, 68
Alexander, Lee 101
Alexiades, Anastasia 9
Alfange, Dean 97
Allilovoithitikos Syllogos Cyprion "Zenon" 86
American Council on Education 19n, 53n
American Hellenic Institute 106
American Labor Party 97
Amira, A. 201
Anagnos, Michael 36
Andersson, T. 171n
Anker, Irving 176
Annapolis, Maryland 102
Annunciation Church, New York City 67

anti-Church attitudes 56, 118, 132, 134
Antoniou, Mary 23n
Apostol, John 102
Arabs 108
Arcadia, Greece 94, 99
Arcadian Association of America "O Geros tou Morea" 86
Archbishop Iakovos Athletic Center, St. Basil's Academy 196
Archdiocese—Greek Orthodox, of North and South America 51, 62n, 70, 71, 74, 81, 83, 87n, 120, 183, 186, 193, 194, 195, 204, 206; Cyprus Relief Fund 195; Department of Education 186, 188; history of 29, 43-4, 48, 68, 82, 127, 181; Mission Project 195; school system 85, 184-6, 188; Social Health and Welfare Center (Astoria) 194
Armenians 108, 220
Asia 137, 195
Asia Minor 23, 35, 70, 144, 191
ASPIRA Consent Decree 175, 176
ASPIRA of New York Inc. v. the Board of Education of the City of New York 175, 176
assimilation 11, 14-5, 17, 22, 32, 44, 45, 48, 49, 52, 59, 60, 63, 76, 77, 80, 84, 92, 115, 116, 172, 181, 191, 202
Association of Hellenes of Egypt in America 86
Astoria, Queens 49, 70, 72, 76, 83, 89, 107, 177, 194
Athanson, George 101
Athenagoras, Archbishop, later Ecumenical Patriarch 29, 44, 48, 126, 181, 182, 193

NOTES ON CONTRIBUTORS

VIVIAN ANEMOYANIS received her B.S. in education and her M.A. in Spanish from the City University of New York. She received a professional diploma and a Ph.D. from Fordham University, in educational administration and supervision. She has been involved in the development, administration, and supervision of bilingual programs since 1971. She is currently the Director of Bilingual Education in Community School District 30, Queens, and is also an adjunct assistant professor at St. John's University. She has worked for the Board of Education of the City of New York since 1961, and has extensive experience in teaching, curriculum development, and administration and supervision. She has published several articles dealing with bilingual education.

CHRYSIE M. COSTANTAKOS is Professor of Family Relationships and Child Development and Chairperson of the Department of Home Economics and Consumer Studies at Brooklyn College of the City University of New York. She received a B.A. in chemistry from Barnard College and had her graduate training at Teachers College, Columbia University. She holds an M.S. in nutrition and an Ed.D. in marriage and family studies. She is the author of *The American-Greek Subculture: Processes of Continuity* (1981) and of numerous articles on nutrition, the family, consumer affairs, and aging. Her articles on the Greek American community include "Preventing Psycho-social Malfunctioning Among Mediterranean Immigrant Families in the United States," "The Greek-American Community: Diverse Constituency, Varied Needs," and "The Greek-American Community in the Context of the Larger Society." She is now conducting research on Greek American men: role expectations and ethnicity.

STELLA (PILARINOS) COUMANTAROS is the director and administrator of the national office of the Greek Orthodox Ladies Philoptochos Society, representing some 500 chapters in North and South America. She previously served as director of the Archdiocese's Social Health and Welfare Center. She was educated in the New York public school system, Douglas College, and the New School for Social Research. She has an extensive background in business and social work.

ATHENA G. DALLAS-DAMIS is the author of *Island of the Winds* (1976), its sequel *Windswept* (1981), *Religious Poems for Children* (1959), and co-author of *Once Upon a Bus*, a bilingual screenplay filmed in Greece in 1961. She is the translator of Nikos Kazantzakis' last novel *The Fratricides* (1964), *Three Plays by N. Kazantzakis—*

Melissa, Kouros, Christopher Columbus (1969), and *Buddha*, a play by Kazantzakis, this last with Kimon Friar. Her other translations include *Greek Dances for Americans* by Rozanna Mouzaki (1981), and various religious books and pamphlets for the Greek Archdiocese of North and South America (1956-1958). She has also had a fruitful career in journalism and the theater. She is currently working on a novel set in the German occupation of Greece which will be followed by the last of her Island Trilogy.

EMMANUEL HATZIEMMANUEL has been director of the Department of Education of the Greek Orthodox Archdiocese of North and South America since 1969. He studied theology at the University of Athens, and education at Selly Oak College, Birmingham, England. He has taught history and religion at the Teachers Training Department of St. Basil's Academy, Garrison, New York from 1952 to 1968. He has served as editor of *The Orthodox Observer*, the official publication of the Greek Archdiocese of North and South America (1954-1957); as associate director of the Greek Archdiocese's Research and Publications Department (1966-1972); and as editor of the Greek Archdiocese's Yearbook (1967-1972, 1974, and 1975). His publications include *The Church and the Child* (1947), *Men of Faith* (1950), *I am Learning Greek the Play Way* (1958), *Modern Greek for Secondary Schools* (1973), and *The Golden Age of Athens* (1979).

MANOS M. LAMPIDIS is an attorney, practicing in Queens, New York. He is a member of the New York and New Jersey Bars. He received a B.A. degree from Ohio State University and his J.D. from the University of Cincinnati Law School. In 1979, he received an LL.M. degree from New York University with a concentration in international commercial and trade regulation law. He is a contributor to von Kalinowski's *Legal Treatises, Antitrust Laws and Trade Regulation* (1973–). He is a past president of the Hellenic University Club of New York and has been active with many Greek American organizations.

PETER N. MARUDAS is administrative assistant to US Senator Paul S. Sarbanes of Maryland. He also served as chief administrative assistant to former Baltimore mayors Theodore R. McKeldin and Thomas J. D'Alesandro, III. In 1963-1967, he worked for the *Baltimore Evening Sun* covering city government and politics. A graduate of the University of Michigan with an M.A. in journalism, he also studied political science and economics at the University of Athens School of Law.

CHARLES C. MOSKOS is Professor of Sociology at Northwestern University. He received his B.A. from Princeton University and his Ph.D. from the University of California, Los Angeles. He is the author of several books and numerous articles on armed forces and society. His most recent book is *Greek Americans: Struggle and Success* (1980). In 1980-1981 he was a fellow at the Woodrow Wilson International Center for Scholars at the Smithsonian Institute in Washington, D.C.

NICON D. PATRINACOS, an Archimandrite of the Greek Orthodox Church, studied theology and education in Greece and philosophy and psychology in Australia (University of Queensland). He received his Ph.D. in the philosophy and psychology of religion from Oxford University. He taught psychology of religion at Washington University in St. Louis, served as Dean of the Greek Orthodox School of Theology in Brookline, Massachusetts, and taught philosophy at St. Basil's Institute, Garrison, New York. He served as chairman of the Department of Education of the Greek Archdiocese for many years and edited the official organ of the Church, the *Orthodox Observer*. For the last five years before his retirement from the active service of the Church in 1978, he was the permanent representative of the Greek Orthodox Church in the National Council of Churches and in the US Conference of the World Council of Churches. He has published extensively on ecumenical affairs, on the cultural identity of Eastern Orthodoy, and on ecclesiastical reform. His books include *The Individual and His Orthodox Church* (1970), *The Orthodox Liturgy* (1973), and *The Orthodox Church and Birth Control* (1976).

HARRY J. PSOMIADES received his early education at the Boston Public Latin School. He received his B.A. from Boston University and graduate training at Columbia University (M.I.A., Ph.D.). Before joining the faculty at Queens College of the City University of New York in 1965, he was Associate Dean of Columbia University's Graduate School of International Affairs. Currently he is Professor of Political Science and Director of the Center for Byzantine and Modern Greek Studies at Queens College. He has written extensively on the politics of the eastern Mediterranean, contributing over fifty articles in various books and professional journals. He is the author of *The Eastern Question: The Last Phase, A Study in Greek-Turkish Diplomacy* (1968) and co-author of *Foreign Interference in Greek Politics: An Historical Perspective* (1976). He has also been very active in Greek American community affairs.

EVA E. SANDIS is Professor of Sociology at Fordham University. She received her B.A. from Oberlin College and her M.A. and Ph.D. from Columbia University. Her area of specialization is the sociology of migration. She has published numerous books and articles dealing with migration trends and policies, and has served as research consultant on a variety of migration-related projects. She has been a visiting scholar at the Greek National Centre of Social Research, and has taught at Pierce College in Athens. Her current activities include membership on the editorial board of the *International Migration Review* and co-chair of the Columbia University seminar on cultural pluralism. She is also a charter member of the CUNY seminar on the modern Greek state.

ALICE SCOURBY received her Ph.D. from the Graduate Faculty of the New School for Social Research. She is Professor of Sociology and Coordinator of Women's Studies at C.W. Post Center of Long Island University. She has been a consultant to various projects relating to the Greek American community, and is currently a consultant to the Anti-Defamation League of B'nai B'rith. Among her publications are *Third Generation Greek Americans: A Study of Religious Attitudes* (Arno Press), and *Marriage and the Family: A Comparative Analysis of Contemporary Problems* (Random House). Professor Scourby is a member of the Advisory Council of the Center for Byzantine and Modern Greek Studies, Queens College.

THEONI VELLI-SPYROPOULOS received her graduate training in psychology at Rutgers University, receiving her Ph.D. in 1977, and has since been the Director of the Child and Family Counseling Service of the Hellenic American Neighborhood Action Committee in New York City. Among other appointments, she has served on President Carter's Commission on Mental Health, the White House Conference on the Elderly, and was formerly an adviser to the National Center for Urban Ethnic Affairs in Washington, D.C. She is currently an Associate of Rutgers University Graduate School of Public Administration and an adjunct associate professor at Queens College.

JOHN G. ZENELIS is a librarian at Columbia University Law Library where he heads the Bibliographic Control Department. Formerly, he was a librarian with the Research Libraries of the New York Public Library where his responsibilities included selection, cataloguing and reference service for the Modern Greek collection. He received B.A. and M.A. degrees in Political Science from Temple University and the Graduate School of the City University of New York, respectively, and an M.L.S. from the University of Pittsburgh. His publications include "United States Policy Toward Greece and Cyprus Since the Second World War: A Bibliography," in *Greek-American Relations: A Critical Review* (edited by T. A. Couloumbis and J. O. Iatrides, 1980) and "Bibliographie" (with Esche and Henrich), in *Südosteuropa-Handbuch, Band III: Griechenland* (edited by K.-D. Grothusen, 1980). He is a member of several academic and library professional associations.